100 COUNTRYSIDE WALKS
AROUND EDINBURGH

100 Countryside Walks around

Edinburgh

Derek Storey

MAINSTREAM
PUBLISHING

EDINBURGH AND LONDON

First published in Great Britain in 2000 by
MAINSTREAM PUBLISHING COMPANY (EDINBURGH) LTD
7 Albany Street
Edinburgh EH1 3UG

ISBN 1 84018 182 6

A catalogue record for this book is available from the British Library

Typeset in Futurist and Janson Text
Printed and bound in Great Britain by Creative Print Design Wales

CONTENTS

SOUTHERN REGION

EASTERN REGION

WESTERN REGION

Arthur's Seat and Salisbury Crags

INTRODUCTION

Welcome to *100 Countryside Walks around Edinburgh*: the comprehensive guide to countryside walks in southeast Scotland. Inside you will find 'easy-to-follow' directions to one hundred walking routes in some of the most scenic parts of Fife and the Lothians. There are energetic walks over hills and heather-clad moorland, bracing coastal walks along cliff tops and across sandy bays, mysterious walks through deep, wooded glens and fascinating rambles through woodlands, along rivers, over undulating agricultural land and along disused railway tracks. There is even a walk around an island that requires a boat trip to reach it and another on a cliff face where one has to dangle out over the sea while holding on to a length of chain. There are walks for everyone, from the beginner to the enthusiast. Most will take about half a day to complete, are suitable for the whole family and lie within a 30-mile drive of central Edinburgh. There are some walks of longer duration for the enthusiast, but those more interested in serious hill walking are referred to the companion to this book, *100 Hill Walks around Edinburgh*.

Many of the walks described within this guidebook pass through areas of great historical interest and there is often much to see and find that reminds us of our heritage. What must have it been like to take these same steps in days gone by? Imagine the raiding party stealthily climbing Dollar Glen towards Castle Campbell; the twin steam locomotives straining to haul the London Express up the long incline out of Gorebridge; or the cries and agony in Roslin Glen in 1303 when the Scots suddenly emerged from the early morning mist and dispatched 30,000 English soldiers to their Maker.

Wherever possible, the walks described follow a circular route. That is, they start and finish at the same point without passing over more than a little of the same ground twice. When this is not feasible, linear walks (those that commence at one point and finish at another) have been included, but only when there is a frequent public transport service linking each end. If you are using your own transport to reach such walks, the end at which your vehicle is left is merely a matter of personal preference or convenience. If it is left at the finish, it will serve as a goal and avoid a bus journey when tired. However, the party is then committed to complete the entire route. Of course, only the drivers amongst the walking party need take the short bus or train journey.

In this guidebook, road walking is avoided wherever possible. When a route does necessitate a short section along a road, it is generally along a quiet country lane. Remember, even when on quiet country roads, to take care and keep close to the edge.

All the walks follow established tracks and paths frequently used by walkers. However, the inclusion of a route in this book does not imply a right of way unless specifically stated. Nor does it guarantee that access will always be available. The responsible countryside walker is generally well accepted in Scotland and access is almost always granted. However, some areas may become temporarily closed due to ploughing, spraying, lambing, nesting of game birds, etc. If you are ever asked to leave an area – a very rare occurrence – then there is sure to be a very good reason, so please do so gracefully and without question.

The routes described herein were accurate and feasible at the time of writing but conditions in the countryside continuously change; new forests are planted, fences erected, new roads laid. Most obstructions can be circumnavigated but, sometimes, one has to turn back. Should you discover that a route has become impassable or requires a major detour, please advise the author, care of Mainstream Publishing, so that a revision may be included in future editions.

Most importantly, enjoy your excursion into the countryside. Dress sensibly, so as to keep warm and dry, and do not be put off by the weather. A friend once said to me, 'In Scotland there is no such thing as bad weather; only inappropriate clothing.' Walk at the pace that best suits yourself and the members of your party and stop whenever you wish. You do not have to complete the walk within the time suggested in the description; nor, in most cases, is it necessary to complete the entire route. Take time to enjoy the views, historic sites, wild flowers, insects and birds. You may even wish to stop for a swim or a picnic.

Regular countryside walking is not only a pleasure but also a very effective form of exercise. It does not require sweat and tears to maintain the heart in good condition. A couple of hours' regular walking will keep the body trim, reduce stress and blood pressure and reduce the risk of stroke and heart disease. What more pleasant way can there be to stay fit and healthy?

NOTES ON THE WALK DESCRIPTIONS

AREAS COVERED

For ease of location, the walks are presented in the following broad groups:

CENTRAL	Within ten miles of the centre of Edinburgh
NORTH	North of the Forth
SOUTH	South of Edinburgh between the Pentland Hills and the A68
EAST	East of Edinburgh and as far south as the A68
WEST	West of Edinburgh and as far south as the Pentland Hills

Most walks are close to Edinburgh. Those further afield generally have features that make them especially appealing and worth the extra travelling.

MAPS

A sketch map and references to the relevant Landranger and Pathfinder Ordnance Survey maps accompany each walk. The sketch maps are designed to illustrate the description given in the text and not to be a substitute for an Ordnance Survey map. Although many of the shorter, low-level routes may be completed using only the description and sketch map provided, it will be found that an Ordnance Survey map provides far greater detail and accuracy than is possible in any guidebook. For the hill walks an Ordnance Survey map and compass, plus the ability to use both, are essential in case one becomes enveloped in mist, becomes lost or desires a quicker way down.

DISTANCE, AMOUNT OF CLIMBING AND TIME

DISTANCE FROM EDINBURGH The distance to the start of each walk is measured from Registry House at the east end of Princes Street in the centre of Edinburgh using the route described in 'How to get there'.

WALKING DISTANCE This is an estimate acquired by using the traditional 'map and length-of-thread' method. Remember to allow extra for zigzags when climbing and for detours around boggy areas, fallen trees and other obstructions.

AMOUNT OF CLIMBING The sum of all the uphill sections of the route.

ESTIMATED TIME This is very difficult to estimate as people walk at their own pace and will spend differing amounts of time on stops. The figure given is based on an average walking speed of four kilometres per hour (2½ mph) plus one minute for each ten metres of ascent, plus five minutes per hour for rests, and rounded up to the nearest quarter of an hour. Please note that it does not include time for deviations, getting lost, waiting for the kids to catch up, eating lunch, having a swim, taking photographs, admiring the views or smelling the flowers.

DESCRIPTION
This section gives a brief description of the type of terrain to be covered, outstanding features of the route and any special items that might be useful to wear or to take along.

START AND FINISH
Most routes start and finish at the same point. When a linear walk is described (one that starts and finishes at different points) the company and route number of the bus service that links each end of the route is given. Ordnance Survey grid references for the start and, where appropriate, the finish, are also given in this section.

HOW TO GET THERE

Recommendations are given on how to reach each walking area by car and, where practical, by public transport. Although it is assumed that the journey will begin in Edinburgh, it is not difficult to devise a means of joining the recommended route from other places within the area covered by this book. Please note that the directions given are for the easiest route to follow and not necessarily the shortest. Abbreviations used for public transport companies and their addresses and telephone numbers (so you can check times before setting out) are given in Appendix 2.

PARKING

In most cases, the recommended parking place is a designated car park or a quiet residential street. In a few instances, parking space may be limited to only one or two vehicles. However, additional parking space can usually be found nearby. Remember always to park with due consideration for other road users and local residents. Do not obstruct entrances to property or fields and always leave plenty of space for large cattle and timber lorries. If parking somewhere other than in a car park, it is often a good idea to inform a local householder or farmer or to leave a note in your car window to allay possible anxieties of local residents. Wherever you park, never leave anything visible inside the vehicle. Leave valuables at home or carry them with you rather than leave them in the boot.

DISTANCES WITHIN THE TEXT

These are approximations meant for guidance only. Metres (m) and kilometres (km) are used within the walking route directions because modern maps, footpath signposts and most walkers have now been converted to the metric system. Distances for motorists are given in miles (ml) because the odometers of most cars use this unit.

PATHS AND TRACKS

Within the text a 'track' refers to a passage wide enough to accommodate a four-wheeled vehicle, whereas a 'path' is suitable only for walking in single file.

MAP OF AREA COVERED

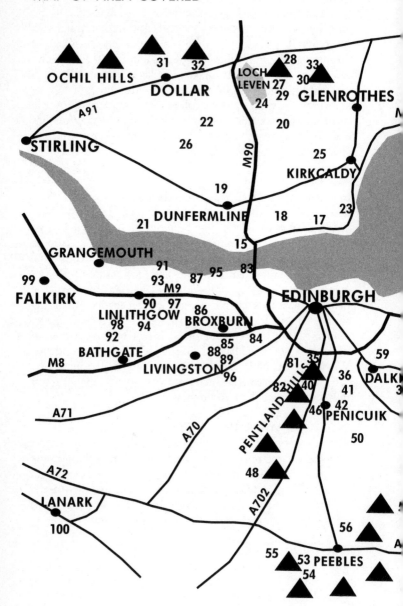

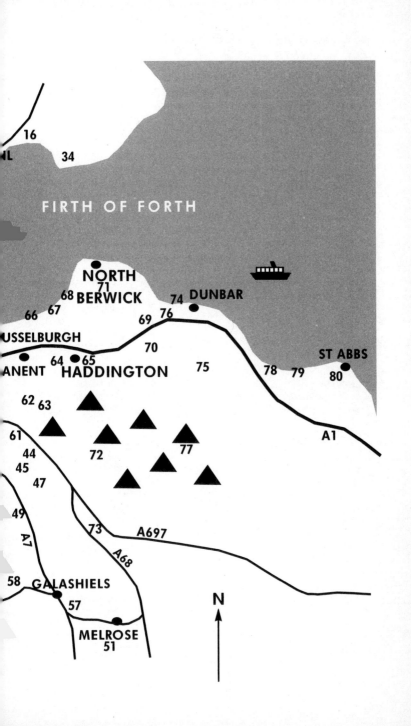

KEY OF SYMBOLS USED

═══ ROAD   ···· FOOTPATH   –·– TRACK

RAILWAY STATION   ▲ HILL   ROCKY AREA

BUILDINGS   BRIDGE   CHURCH

HISTORICAL BUILDING   TOWER   INDUSTRIAL BUILDING

MILL   HISTORICAL SITE   AREA WITH BOATS OR SHIPPING

OBSERVATORY   RADIO MAST   BEACON

SEALS   CONIFEROUS WOODLAND   DECIDUOUS WOODLAND

MARSHLAND   P CAR PARK   GATE

PICNIC AREA   CARAVAN PARK   VIEWPOINT

GOLF COURSE   HIDE   ELECTRICITY LINES

TENNIS COURT   TUNNEL   AIRPORT

AIRFIELD   SITE OF BATTLE   STILE

CENTRAL REGION

WALK 1: ARTHUR'S SEAT & HOLYROOD PARK

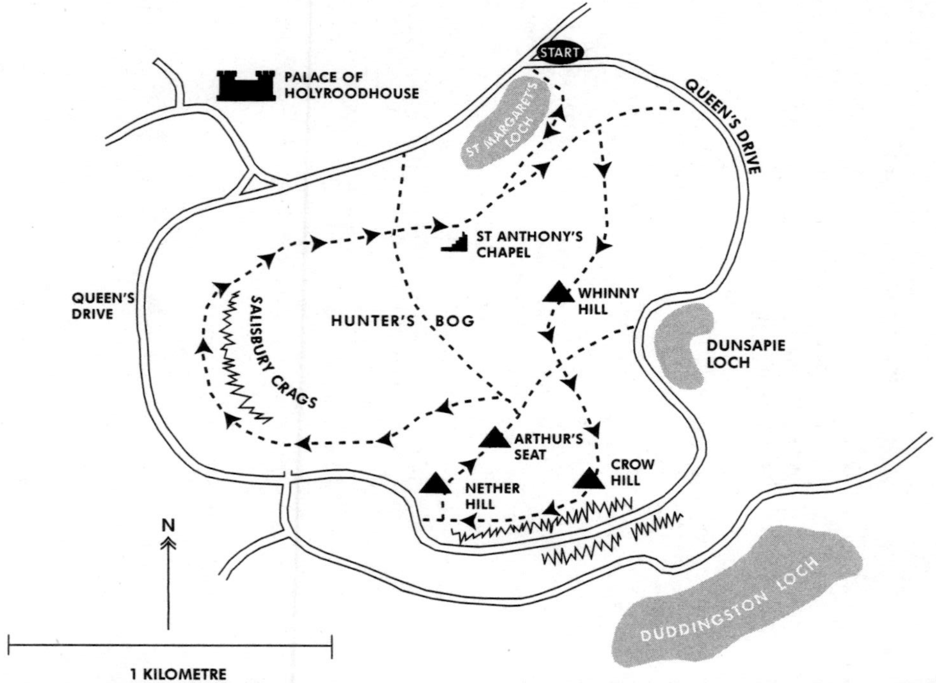

QUEEN'S DRIVE

DUNSAPIE LOCH

DUDDINGSTON LOCH

START

ST MARGARET'S LOCH

PALACE OF HOLYROODHOUSE

ST ANTHONY'S CHAPEL

WHINNY HILL

CROW HILL

ARTHUR'S SEAT

NETHER HILL

HUNTER'S BOG

SALISBURY CRAGS

QUEEN'S DRIVE

N

1 KILOMETRE

1. ARTHUR'S SEAT & HOLYROOD PARK

ORDNANCE SURVEY MAP NO	LANDRANGER 66
	PATHFINDER 407
DISTANCE FROM EDINBURGH	2 KM (1 ML)
WALKING DISTANCE	5½ KM (3½ ML)
AMOUNT OF CLIMBING	370 M (1,214 FT)
ESTIMATED TIME	2½ HR

DESCRIPTION This is a must for all Edinburgh residents and visitors. Within ten minutes' walk of the bustling city centre, one can be in this wilderness area and be totally unaware of the urban surroundings until the hill summits are reached. One might even be fortunate enough to catch a glimpse of a deer, badger, fox or bird of prey. There are many good paths within this area and an endless variety of routes. The route described below includes most of the main features of the park but may easily be modified.

START AND FINISH Car park beside St Margaret's Loch, Holyrood Park. NT 278 741

HOW TO GET THERE From the city centre, the easiest means of getting there is by foot via the Palace of Holyroodhouse. From elsewhere, enter the park via the Meadowbank entrance and park in the car park on the left.

WALK DIRECTIONS
Take the footpath beside the loch that climbs up towards the ruins of St Anthony's Chapel. Just before the final steep climb to the chapel, turn left on to a thin path that traverses back above St Margaret's Loch and the car park. When just beyond the car park, turn right on to a wide, grassy track and climb up and over Whinny Hill.

On the far side of Whinny Hill, cross the valley through which the main tourist route passes from Dunsapie Loch to

Arthur's Seat. Continue ahead and a little to the right and climb up to the large, pyramidal cairn on the top of a hill (Crow Hill). From here, there are stupendous views of the east of Edinburgh, East Lothian and the Firth of Forth.

Descend the steep, south side of Crow Hill to the top of the crags overlooking Duddingston Loch (a bird sanctuary). Turn right on the narrow path that runs along the top of the crags. Just before the path begins to descend steeply, turn right, up a gully, to reach the top of Nether Hill, then on directly ahead to the summit of the highest hill in the park, Arthur's Seat (251 m / 823 ft, triangulation point, viewfinder).

Take the main path off the steep section of Arthur's Seat, then go left (west) at a fork and descend steeply into the broad valley (Hunter's Bog) between Arthur's Seat and Salisbury Crags. Follow the path around the steep base of Arthur's Seat to the saddle at the southern end of Salisbury Crags. Turn right and follow the crags around the perimeter of the park until level with Holyrood Palace. Just beyond this point, climb up to the ruins of St Anthony's Chapel, then descend to St Margaret's Loch and the car park.

2. EDINBURGH'S CANAL

ORDNANCE SURVEY MAP NO	LANDRANGER 66
	PATHFINDER 407
DISTANCE FROM EDINBURGH	2 KM (1 ML)
WALKING DISTANCE	7½ KM (4½ ML)
AMOUNT OF CLIMBING	NEGLIGIBLE
ESTIMATED TIME	2¼ HR

DESCRIPTION The Union Canal was originally built to transport coal from the West Lothian mines to the centre of Edinburgh. It starts at the canal basin in Fountainbridge and runs all the way to Falkirk, but nowadays the section at Wester Hailes runs through a pipe beneath the houses and can no longer be followed. However, the towpath beside the remaining section within the city makes for a very pleasant and easy stroll. Although never far from a main road or houses, the canal is shielded by trees for most of its length and attracts considerable bird life, so the walker can easily relax and forget the urban environment.

START Haymarket Railway Station, Edinburgh. NT 240 732
FINISH Wester Hailes Shopping Centre. NT 201 700

HOW TO GET THERE By car, drive out of Edinburgh along the Lanark Road (A70) and turn right into Wester Hailes Road to reach the shopping centre. Park in the large car park at the back, between the cinema and the railway station. Take a train (ScotRail) or bus (SMT C5, C55; LRT 33) to Haymarket. Alternatively, start the walk in the city centre and take the train or bus described above back to the start.

WALK DIRECTIONS
Walk to the right of the Haymarket public house along Morrison Street. Pass the traffic lights and take the next

WALK 2: EDINBURGH'S CANAL

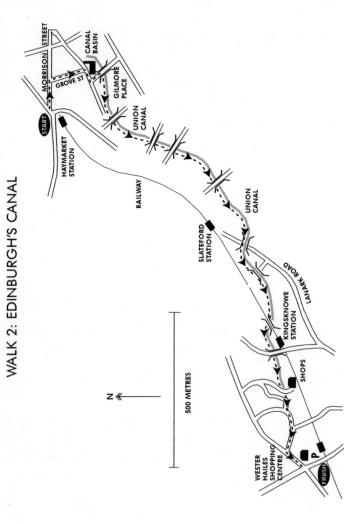

right, Grove Street. At the end of this road, turn right for a few paces along a main road then left into Gilmore Place to reach the canal. Go left to view the canal basin and canoe course, then turn around and follow the canal back across Gilmore Place.

From here it is a straightforward but fascinating stroll beside the canal, beneath bridges and over aqueducts, until it can be followed no further. Climb the steps here and cross a road, then descend to a footpath. Follow this past a block of flats, then a police station, to reach another road.

Walk along the road to a bend in another, more major, road and turn left. On reaching a roundabout, go straight across. At a T-junction, turn left to reach the Wester Hailes Shopping Centre.

WALK 3: EDINBURGH'S OLD RAILWAY LINES

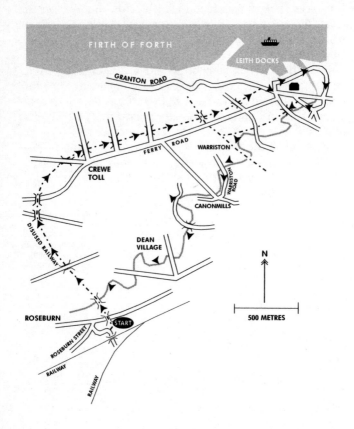

3. EDINBURGH'S OLD RAILWAY LINES

ORDNANCE SURVEY MAP NO	LANDRANGER 66
	PATHFINDER 407
DISTANCE FROM EDINBURGH	3½ KM (2 ML)
WALKING DISTANCE	17 KM (10½ ML)
AMOUNT OF CLIMBING	NEGLIGIBLE
ESTIMATED TIME	5 HR

DESCRIPTION This is a long but easy walk from Roseburn to Leith, following an old railway line and returning along another disused railway track and the Water of Leith Walkway. The route can be shortened by 3½ km by cutting through Warriston to the Water of Leith, or by joining the route at any of its many access points.

START AND FINISH Russell Road, Roseburn, Edinburgh. NT 233 729

HOW TO GET THERE By car, take the A8 past Haymarket to Roseburn. Turn left into Roseburn Street and immediately left again into Russell Road. Park close to the railway bridge. Or take a bus (LRT 26, 31, 36, 63, 85, 86; MB 38; SMT 16, 18, 37) to Roseburn, walk back to the railway bridge and climb the nearby steps to join the route a little north of that described below.

WALK DIRECTIONS
Go through the gate close to the railway bridge and follow the old railway track (now a walk and cycle path) north, over Roseburn Terrace and the Water of Leith then past the backs of houses, colleges and offices. After 3 km the track swings round to the right. After a further 2 km, go over a crossroads of paths and continue ahead for a further 300 m to a track departing to the right. This is the short-cut to the Water of Leith. The main route continues directly ahead. At

a fork go left and finally emerge on to a main road close to the docks in Newhaven. Go right, then left at the traffic lights into Leith Docks and past *Britannia*. Follow the road around to the right, pass the government buildings, then turn right, cross the Water of Leith and follow it upstream, past a floating restaurant and over a main road, to the next bridge (Sandport Place). Cross and continue upstream on the Water of Leith Walkway. Just beyond the next bridge, where the river disappears to the left, go straight ahead on an old railway track. After 500 m the river will reappear.

At a fork, follow the signpost to 'Canonmills'. After a kilometre you will emerge on to a road next to a supermarket. Turn right for a few paces then right again. At the clock tower, move on to a minor road beside the river to regain the Water of Leith Walkway. Cross a footbridge and continue upstream on a path, then a road round a bend to a junction. Go left for a few paces to a bridge and descend steps to rejoin the river.

At the end of this path, cross a main road and take the minor road opposite, then a path beside the river to St Bernard's Well (an old mineral spring). From here follow an asphalt path beside the river to the very high Dean Bridge. Pass beneath then climb up a minor road (Miller Row) and down Hawthorn Bank, past Elizabethan-style houses, to a footbridge. Cross over and follow the river as far as a high stone viaduct. Climb the steps on the left and go right along the old railway track used earlier, to return to the start.

4. COLINTON DELL

ORDNANCE SURVEY MAP NO	LANDRANGER 66
	PATHFINDER 420 & 407
DISTANCE FROM EDINBURGH	5 KM (3 ML)
WALKING DISTANCE	6½ KM (4 ML)
AMOUNT OF CLIMBING	60 M (200 FT)
ESTIMATED TIME	2 HR

DESCRIPTION Although within Edinburgh, there is hardly a building to be seen on this walk; just the sounds and sights of running water and an abundance of bird life. The route winds its way through the valley of the Water of Leith to the charming village of Colinton and returns via a disused railway track (including a long tunnel) and part of the Union Canal. There are lots of things to see and do along the route and several picnic sites.

START AND FINISH Slateford Railway Station, Edinburgh. NT 224 712

HOW TO GET THERE Frequent bus services (LRT 4, 28, 44; SMT 66) or train (ScotRail) to Slateford Station. By car, take the Slateford Road (A70) to Slateford and park in Chesser Avenue opposite the station.

WALK DIRECTIONS
Walk away from the city centre along Slateford Road and into Lanark Road for a little way to the Tickled Trout pub. Here join the signposted path behind the pub and follow it upstream along the Water of Leith. Just after passing a white house, go a little to the left to a paved lane and turn right to pass Redhall Mill (now a private residence). Just beyond the mill, descend a few steps to continue on the path beside the river. A little further along there is a weir. Cross the bridge here and continue upstream, then climb some more steps to

WALK 4: COLINTON DELL

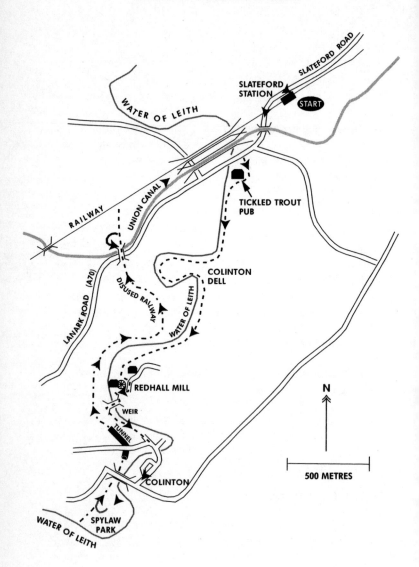

Dell Road. Walk along the road, past a church and cemetery (well worth a visit), over a road bridge across the river and up Spylaw Street into Colinton.

Colinton is well worth exploring, but to continue the route enter Spylaw Park via the gate (signposted 'Spylaw House') near the top of Spylaw Street. Follow the path round to the left, under the high road bridge and over the river, then past Spylaw House. Stay on the path as it ascends to the right to join a wide track (a disused railway). Follow this track to the right, back under the high bridge, then through a long tunnel. Stay on the track as it follows Colinton Dell, high above the Water of Leith, then bears round to the left, away from the river, and reaches a footbridge over a busy main road.

Cross the bridge and continue a little further to a bridge over the Union Canal. Cross this bridge and immediately turn left. Descend to the canal and follow it beneath the footbridge and on, past an old iron boat, to an aqueduct. Cross the aqueduct and continue beside the canal a little further to a second aqueduct. Do not cross this one, but descend the steps to the left, back to Slateford Road. Turn left for Slateford Station.

WALK 5: HERMITAGE OF BRAID & BLACKFORD HILL

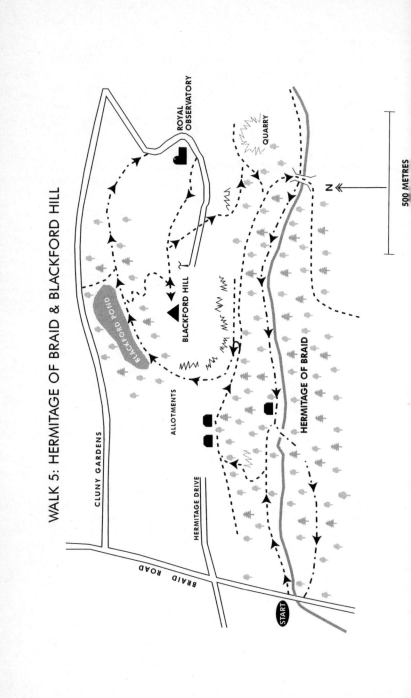

ROYAL OBSERVATORY

QUARRY

BLACKFORD POND

BLACKFORD HILL

ALLOTMENTS

CLUNY GARDENS

HERMITAGE OF BRAID

HERMITAGE DRIVE

BRAID ROAD

START

N

500 METRES

5. HERMITAGE OF BRAID & BLACKFORD HILL

ORDNANCE SURVEY MAP NO	LANDRANGER 66
	PATHFINDER 407
DISTANCE FROM EDINBURGH	5 KM (3 ML)
WALKING DISTANCE	5½ KM (3½ ML)
AMOUNT OF CLIMBING	130 M (430 FT)
ESTIMATED TIME	1¾ HR

DESCRIPTION An easy walk through a popular nature reserve and beauty spot close to the heart of Edinburgh. The early part of the route passes through the wooded glen that is the Hermitage of Braid, but then gradually climbs to the summit of Blackford Hill – from which there are stupendous views over Edinburgh to the Castle and Arthur's Seat and beyond to the Firth of Forth. Deep within the Hermitage of Braid there is a Visitor Centre, toilets and a tea-room (Sundays only).

START AND FINISH Braid Road, Morningside, Edinburgh. NT 244 702

HOW TO GET THERE Frequent bus services (LRT 11, 15; WS 100; LOW 315) to Greenbank Crescent then walk east through Braidburn Terrace to the start. By car, drive south along Lothian Road then Morningside Road. At the traffic lights go straight ahead into Braid Road. Park on the side of the road, just beyond the mini-roundabout.

WALK DIRECTIONS
Pass through the gap in the stone wall to enter the Hermitage of Braid Nature Reserve. Immediately turn left to pass through a wooden kissing gate and follow the path along the left bank of Braid Burn. After 500 m (if you reach the toilets you've gone 50 m too far), turn left through a gap in the wall and ascend the wooden steps to an old dovecot.

Turn right in front of this and follow the path through the woods, above some crags and over some rocks. Then turn right on to another path near some houses. This path runs beside a wooden fence, then past a meadow to a stone wall. Pass through a gap in the wall on the left and reverse direction on a track. Follow this round to the right, pass some allotments on the left, then into some woods and past Blackford Pond and an entrance gate. The path now ascends behind some houses to join a road. Follow the road up to the Royal Observatory and take any of the many tracks past the observatory and along the ridge to the summit of Blackford Hill (539 m / 1,768 ft, triangulation pillar, viewfinder, bench).

From the summit head back towards the observatory, but turn right just beyond the radio mast. Descend diagonally on a grassy track, over a tarmac track, and on to the tops of some crags. Walk around to the right of the crags and descend again to a fence marking the top of an old quarry. Turn right and follow the dirt path down into the woods where it meets a more substantial path. Go left, downhill, to a wooden bridge over the burn. Do not cross, but descend to the left to the burn, then pass beneath the bridge. From here it is a very straightforward but pleasant stroll along a track, following the burn upstream all the way to the starting point.

6. WATER OF LEITH WALKWAY — SAUGHTON TO LEITH

ORDNANCE SURVEY MAP NO	LANDRANGER 66
	PATHFINDER 407
DISTANCE FROM EDINBURGH	5 KM (3 ML)
WALKING DISTANCE	10 KM (6 ML)
AMOUNT OF CLIMBING	NEGLIGIBLE
ESTIMATED TIME	3 HR

DESCRIPTION A fascinating walk through the centre of Edinburgh following the Water of Leith Walkway to the river outlet into Leith Docks. Lots to see on the way. Asphalt or good dirt paths throughout.

START Saughton Park, Edinburgh. NT 222 721
FINISH Leith Docks, Edinburgh. NT 271 766
BUS LINK LRT 22 or 25

HOW TO GET THERE By car, drive along Dalry Road, then Gorgie Road, to Saughton Park and park in the car park just within the park. There are also frequent bus services (LRT 22, 25).

WALK DIRECTIONS
Cross the main road and follow the Balgreen Walkway downstream. Pass beneath a railway bridge then cross the Water of Leith and continue downstream, past Murrayfield Stadium, to a quiet residential road. Go straight ahead along the road for a short distance, then first left to reach a busy main road. Cross over at the traffic lights and walk up Roseburn Cliff for a few paces, then turn left back on to a footpath beside the river.

Continue downstream, passing beneath a high bridge, then alongside a weir, then passing through a gap in a stone

WALK 6: WATER OF LEITH WALKWAY – SAUGHTON TO LEITH

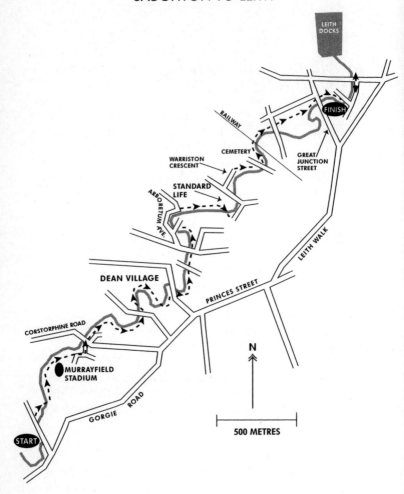

wall. Cross the footbridge on to the left bank and go beneath another high bridge and along into Dean Village. Cross the river again and turn left on to a cobbled road past Elizabethan-style houses. Go straight across a crossroads into Miller Row and so back down to the river. Pass beneath Dean Bridge and back on to the walkway.

Shortly after passing St Bernard's Well, pass beneath a bridge and continue beside the river to a main road. Cross over, turn left over the bridge and immediately descend the steps to the right on to a riverside path. At the next bridge, go left then right into Arboretum Avenue and around the bend; then through a gate to regain the walkway. Just before the Standard Life building, cross the river and follow a road to the left, to a main road. Turn left then right into Warriston Crescent. At the end of this road, climb some steps on to an old railway track and go left for 400 m to a gap in the stone wall on the right. Pass through, walk down to the river and continue downstream, past a park and through a small tunnel beneath a railway.

Shortly thereafter there is a junction of paths. Go straight ahead along a disused railway track. The river soon disappears off to the right but reappears after 500 m. Continue beside the river, beneath a bridge (Great Junction Street) to the next bridge (Sandport Place). Cross the river here and follow The Shore into Leith. After exploring this interesting area, retrace your steps to the Great Junction Street bridge. Climb the steps to the top of the bridge and take the bus back to Saughton Park.

WALK 7: HAPPY VALLEY – EASTER CRAIGLOCKHART HILL

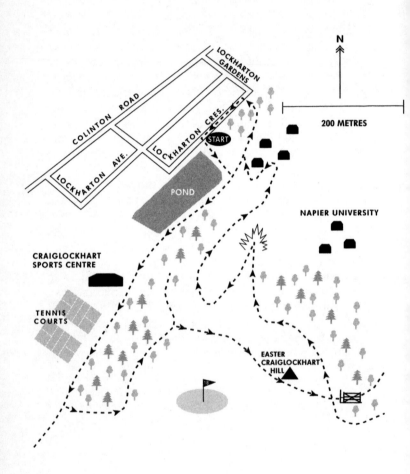

7. HAPPY VALLEY – EASTER CRAIGLOCKHART HILL

ORDNANCE SURVEY MAP NO	LANDRANGER 66
	PATHFINDER 407
DISTANCE FROM EDINBURGH	5½ KM (3½ ML)
WALKING DISTANCE	2 KM (1½ ML)
AMOUNT OF CLIMBING	80 M (260 FT)
ESTIMATED TIME	¾ HR

DESCRIPTION This small Urban Wildlife Site has, for years, been known locally as 'Happy Valley'. Although in the midst of Edinburgh suburbs, one can easily forget the urban environment. Here there are wet areas, hilly scrub areas, dense woodland and open grassland. All this attracts a variety of bird and animal life and makes for a very pleasant walk. A free map of the reserve is available from the nearby sports centre.

START AND FINISH Lockharton Crescent, Craiglockhart, Edinburgh. NT 231 709

HOW TO GET THERE By car, drive along Lothian Road. Continue through Tollcross and Bruntsfield, to the foot of Bruntsfield Place at Holy Corner. Turn right on to Colinton Road. Lockharton Crescent is on the left, just beyond Boroughmuir RFC (Meggetland). Park in Lockharton Crescent close to the pond. By bus, take LRT 10, 27, 45 or 47.

WALK DIRECTIONS
Enter the nature reserve through the gate in the railings. Walk along the edge of the pond to a T-junction and turn right. Keep to the lower path beside the pond. Pass the sports centre and tennis courts. On reaching a stone wall with a path going straight ahead, turn left up a muddy track through trees. At the top of the climb follow the path round

to the left and on to a fork with a stone marker. Go right, following the arrow towards Rock No. 5. After a few paces, leave the woods and climb a grassy track up a gorse-covered hill. At the top there is a bench, a rock with a number 5 on it and a splendid view over western Edinburgh.

Continue on the path running parallel to some railings to a gate in a stone wall with a distinctive arrow and woodland beyond. Do not pass through the gate, but turn left on to a narrow path that follows the stone wall downhill. At the end of the stone wall there is another path and a rock bearing a number 6. Go straight ahead through some trees for a short distance, then along a grassy track to a rocky prominence and a view over the city.

Turn back along the grassy track but do not re-enter the woods. Instead, bear right and ascend slightly over rough grassland. Then descend through gorse to Rock No. 8. Turn right following the arrow to Stone No. 9. After a short distance, pass Stone No. 9 before descending steeply to a gate in a stone wall. Pass through and turn left. Follow the path as it swings round to the right, past some houses, then go down a few steps on to a track. Turn right. At a fork, go left for a few paces then pass through a gate in the railings back on to Lockharton Crescent. Turn left to return to the start.

8. THE BRAID HILLS

ORDNANCE SURVEY MAP NO	LANDRANGER 66
	PATHFINDER 420 & 407
DISTANCE FROM EDINBURGH	6½ KM (4 ML)
WALKING DISTANCE	5 KM (3 ML)
AMOUNT OF CLIMBING	165 M (540 FT)
ESTIMATED TIME	2 HR

DESCRIPTION This is an invigorating walk across gorse-covered hills, around a golf course and through a wooded glen; all within the City of Edinburgh. From the highest point there are superb views of the Pentland Hills and across the city to the Firth of Forth and beyond to the hills of Fife. There are good paths throughout and nothing beyond the capabilities of a walker of average fitness.

START AND FINISH Car park situated on Braid Hills Drive. NT 700 253

HOW TO GET THERE Head south through Morningside. Just over a kilometre beyond Morningside Post Office, up Comiston Road, turn left into Braid Hills Road, which becomes Braid Hills Drive. Then, just beyond the houses, turn right into the car park. By bus (LRT 11 or 15; WS 100; or LOW 315) go to Braid Hills Drive and walk up to the car park.

WALK DIRECTIONS
Walk along the bridleway of orange-coloured gravel heading west, parallel to the road. This ascends for a short distance then traverses through gorse, swings left then ascends again, passes a house and ends just inside the entrance to a golf course. Step through the entrance gate on to the road and turn left. At the end of the road, take the footpath beside the green railings to the back of the houses

WALK 8: THE BRAID HILLS

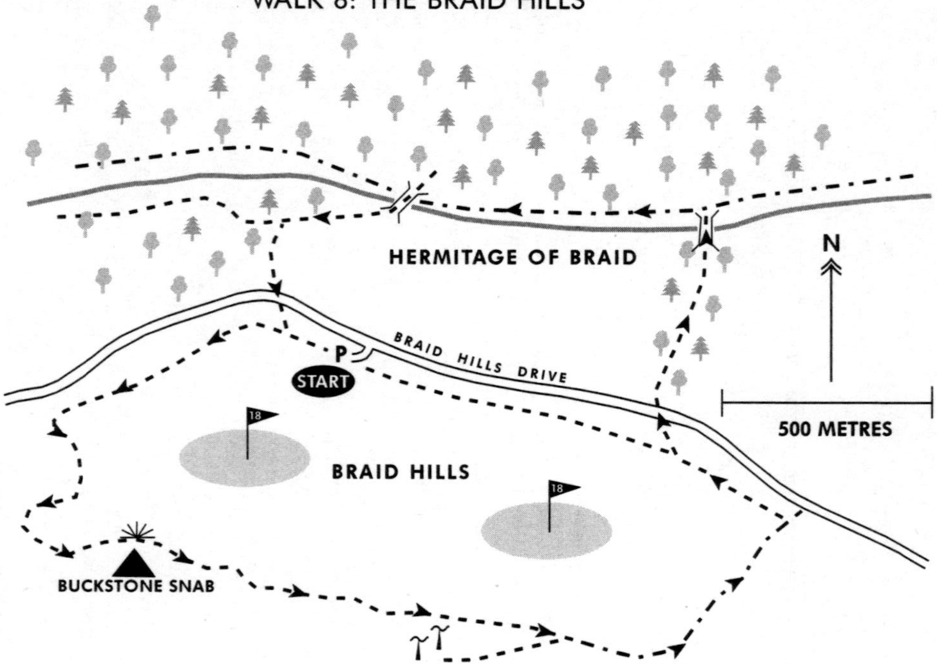

HERMITAGE OF BRAID

BRAID HILLS

BRAID HILLS DRIVE

START

P

BUCKSTONE SNAB

N

500 METRES

and turn right on to another orange-coloured bridleway. This path passes the backs of houses, then swings left and climbs steeply through gorse-covered hills. Near the summit, where the track bears right, go straight ahead on a footpath to the top of Buckstone Snab (208 m / 682 ft, triangulation pillar, viewfinder, benches, superb views).

Continue in the same easterly direction, passing to the left of two radio masts. Then join a dirt track and follow it around the edge of the golf course to a tarmac road. Just before the road, turn left on to a bridleway. This ascends a little, after which it descends to a gate on to the road on the right. Cross the road and take the Howe Dean Path opposite, down through the trees, beside a small burn, to a bridge over the more substantial Braid Burn. Turn left on to the track that follows the burn upstream, passing an old quarry on the right.

On reaching the next bridge across the burn, cross over and climb a flight of steps. Then follow the path between railings, along the edge of a woodland, to a T-junction of paths. Go left and ascend a short distance, then cross again the main road crossed earlier. Take the thin path opposite for a few paces up to a bridleway. Turn left to return to the car park.

WALK 9: CORSTORPHINE HILL

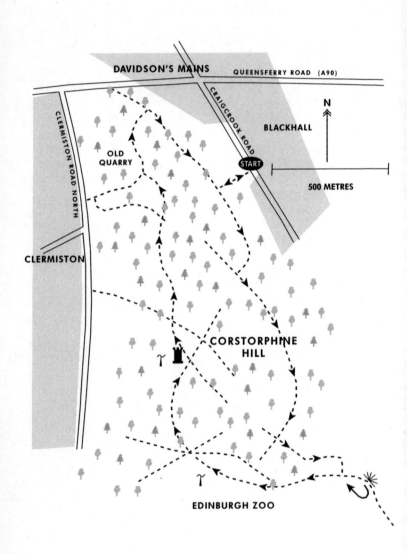

9. CORSTORPHINE HILL

ORDNANCE SURVEY MAP NO	LANDRANGER 66
	PATHFINDER 407
DISTANCE FROM EDINBURGH	6½ KM (4 ML)
WALKING DISTANCE	5 KM (3 ML)
AMOUNT OF CLIMBING	170 M (560 FT)
ESTIMATED TIME	2 HR

DESCRIPTION A pleasant stroll through deciduous woodland popular with dog walkers. There are superb views over Edinburgh and the Firth of Forth. You may also catch a glimpse of zebras or other exotic creatures as you pass the perimeter fence of Edinburgh Zoo.

START AND FINISH Craigcrook Road, 500 m from the junction with Queensferry Road, Blackhall, Edinburgh. NT 209 746

HOW TO GET THERE By car, take the Queensferry Road (A90) to Davidson's Mains and turn left at the traffic lights into Craigcrook Road. Park on the side of the road, approximately 500 m from the traffic lights, close to Hillpark Green. Or, by bus, LRT 13 from Charlotte Square.

WALK DIRECTIONS
There is a footpath between the fields leading up to the woodlands just a little north of Hillpark Green. Take this up to the woods. On reaching a T-junction with another path, go left. At the top of a flight of wooden steps, turn left along another path as far as a junction of several footpaths. Turn left again and follow the path along the edge of the woods, above a golf course. This path appears to end at the golf course perimeter fence but it is possible to climb up to the right, past a large boulder, to some metal railings (perimeter fence of Edinburgh Zoo). Here, go left for 50 m,

through a stone arch, to a wooden bench and a superb view.

Turn around and return to the point where the route joined the metal railings, but now continue directly ahead alongside the zoo fence. At a fork, take the left path to stay beside the zoo fence. Pass a transmitter mast on the left (within the zoo) then descend a few wooden steps to another junction of paths. Take the only ascending path (directly ahead) across a small open area, towards another radio mast. Continue the gradual ascent through the woods to the radio mast and nearby Clermiston Tower.

Walk past the tower and continue north along the top of the ridge on any of the many undulating paths. Do not descend too far to the left or you will end up on Clermiston Road. Eventually, the path will meet the fence of an old quarry. Follow the path beside the fence and descend until another path is reached, with a wooden fence and houses directly ahead. Go right here and follow the eastern edge of the woods back to the path ascending from Craigcrook Road and return to the start.

10. RIVER ALMOND & CAMMO PARK

ORDNANCE SURVEY MAP NO	LANDRANGER 65
	PATHFINDER 406
DISTANCE FROM EDINBURGH	6½ KM (4 ML)
WALKING DISTANCE	9 KM (5½ ML)
AMOUNT OF CLIMBING	95 M (310 FT)
ESTIMATED TIME	3 HR

DESCRIPTION A wooded river valley with cataracts and waterfalls, a country park with the ruins of a once great house, farm land beside a quieter stretch of river and a short section along a country lane which provides panoramic views of the surrounding countryside. There are good paths throughout but they can be muddy in places. Note that this walk passes close to Edinburgh Airport where several low flying aircraft will be encountered. Some may find this intrusive while others, particularly children, may find it exciting.

START AND FINISH Cramond Brig Hotel, Cramond Bridge. NT 179 755

HOW TO GET THERE Frequent bus service from Edinburgh (MB 45, 46, 47, 48; SMT 43). By car, take the A90 (Queensferry Road). Just beyond the Cramond Brig Hotel (on the right), turn right off the main road and park on the minor road close to the hotel.

WALK DIRECTIONS
Cross the old Cramond Bridge (constructed 1687) and turn right at a white cottage to join the River Almond Walkway. Bear right and descend some steps to reach the river itself then follow it upstream, passing beneath the new Cramond Bridge. Go 200 m beyond the bridge and then, just before

WALK 10: RIVER ALMOND & CAMMO PARK

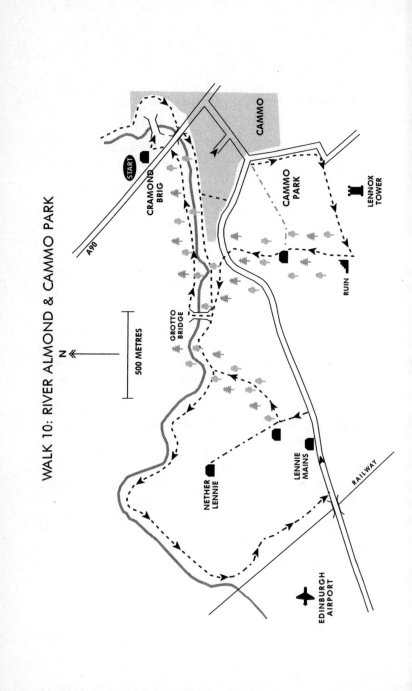

N

500 METRES

START

CRAMOND BRIG

A90

CAMMO

CAMMO PARK

LENNOX TOWER

RUIN

GROTTO BRIDGE

NETHER LENNIE

LENNIE MAINS

RAILWAY

EDINBURGH AIRPORT

the riverside path drops into a gully, turn left along the top of the gully, past the backs of houses, to reach a residential road. Follow this road round to Cammo Road then turn right to reach the entrance of Cammo Park.

Just before the entrance gates, turn left, over a small bridge, on to a path that runs parallel to a road. After 500 m you will reach a small car park on the right. Walk across the car park and through a gate on to a path along the edge of the park. From here, Lennox Tower can be seen over to the left. On reaching the ruins of an old house, turn right. Continue past a small pond and on to the remains of Cammo House. Behind the ruins take the path that leads to a wooden gate, then continue straight ahead, across open ground beyond. Descend to the right to emerge from Cammo Park on to a country lane.

Enter the woods opposite through a gap in the wooden fence and walk down to Grotto Bridge (an old stone bridge spanning the River Avon) and the nearby cataracts. Do not cross the bridge but continue upstream for a further 2 km. This path winds its way through woodland beside the river, then leaves the woods and follows the river across farmland until it reaches a railway bridge over the river with Edinburgh Airport just beyond. Turn away from the river and follow a sandy road beside the railway up to a tarmac road.

Follow the road to the left. Just beyond a white cottage on the brow of a hill, turn left towards Nether Lennie. At the cottages, turn right on to a path that passes between fields then through woodland. Follow it down to the river and the path used earlier. Go downstream, back to Grotto Bridge. Cross the bridge this time and continue downstream all the way back to Cramond Brig Hotel.

WALK 11: CRAMOND FORESHORE

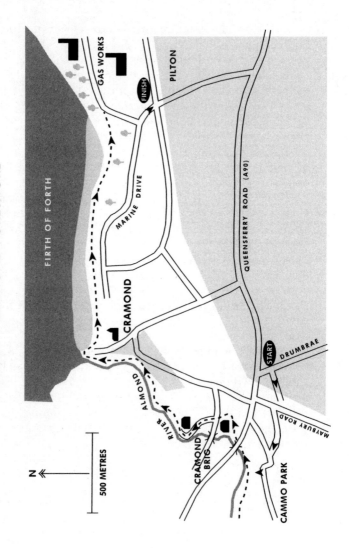

11. CRAMOND FORESHORE

ORDNANCE SURVEY MAP NO	LANDRANGER 66
	PATHFINDER 406 & 407
DISTANCE FROM EDINBURGH	7½ KM (5 ML)
WALKING DISTANCE	9 KM (5½ ML)
AMOUNT OF CLIMBING	60 M (200 FT)
ESTIMATED TIME	2¾ HR

DESCRIPTION A pleasant walk beside the River Almond followed by a stroll along the foreshore with splendid views across to Cramond Island and Fife. The church and maltings at Cramond are well worth exploring. Paths are gravel or asphalt throughout, except the first part along the river which can be muddy. Note that there are several flights of steps on the river section. Toilets and tea-rooms may be found at Cramond and Silverknowes.

START Bus stop at the north end of Drumbrae, Edinburgh. NT 189 748
FINISH Bus stop at the west end of West Granton Road, Pilton, Edinburgh. NT 207 762
BUS LINK LRT 32 or 52. (32 runs from Pilton to Drumbrae, while 52 runs in the opposite direction).

HOW TO GET THERE Frequent bus services (FS 55; LRT 82; MB 47; SMT 43) from the centre of Edinburgh. By car, take the Queensferry Road (A90) to Drumbrae and park in one of the residential streets.

WALK DIRECTIONS
Walk along Barntongate Avenue (opposite the bus stop). At no. 40, turn right on to a footpath that passes behind the houses, then up a few steps to a busy main road. Cross over and walk along Cammo Gardens (opposite the Garden Centre). At the end, turn left into Cammo Road and follow

this round a bend and past the entrance to Cammo Park. Just beyond the next bend, turn right on to a narrow footpath (next to a lane) and follow it down to the river. Go downstream, beneath a high road bridge, then climb a few steps and turn left to a white cottage.

Do not cross Cramond Old Bridge (although it is worth having a look at) but continue ahead along Dowie's Mill Lane to a weir. Rejoin the footpath here and follow it beside the river, up and down steps and past another weir and a sailing club. Proceed to Cramond Maltings and the point where the Almond joins the Forth. There are toilets and refreshment places in this vicinity.

From here walk along the foreshore, past another tea-room and toilet, to the Granton Gas Works. Go right along West Shore Road. At a T-junction, go left to a roundabout then left to the bus stop in West Granton Road.

12. WATER OF LEITH WALKWAY — BALERNO TO CRAIGLOCKHART

ORDNANCE SURVEY MAP NO	LANDRANGER 66
	PATHFINDER 419 & 420
DISTANCE FROM EDINBURGH	13 KM (8 ML)
WALKING DISTANCE	8½ KM (5½ ML)
AMOUNT OF CLIMBING	NEGLIGIBLE
ESTIMATED TIME	2½ HR

DESCRIPTION This entire route follows a dirt track (sometimes muddy) which was once a railway but is now the Water of Leith Walkway. The first half of the walk closely parallels a busy road, while the second half delves deep into the City of Edinburgh — but this can hardly be believed, for the absence of buildings and roads, the many trees and the sounds of birds and water rushing over waterfalls and weirs give a totally different impression.

START Balerno High School, Bridge Road, Balerno. NT 163 666
FINISH Arnott Gardens, Craiglockhart, Edinburgh. NT 215 703
BUS LINK LRT 43 or 44 or SMT 66

HOW TO GET THERE By car, take the Lanark Road (A70) to Balerno and park in one of the residential streets beyond the High School. There are also frequent bus services to either end of the walk (LRT 43, 44; SMT 66).

WALK DIRECTIONS
Walk back up the road a few paces, then turn right on to a disused railway track that is now the Water of Leith Walkway. The track soon meets the river and follows the left bank downstream. After a further 600 m, pass Kinnard Farm on the right, then cross the river and follow the right bank. Pass beneath a road bridge and go past Kinleith Industrial Estate on the left (notice here the original rail

WALK 12: WATER OF LEITH WALKWAY – BALERNO TO CRAIGLOCKHART

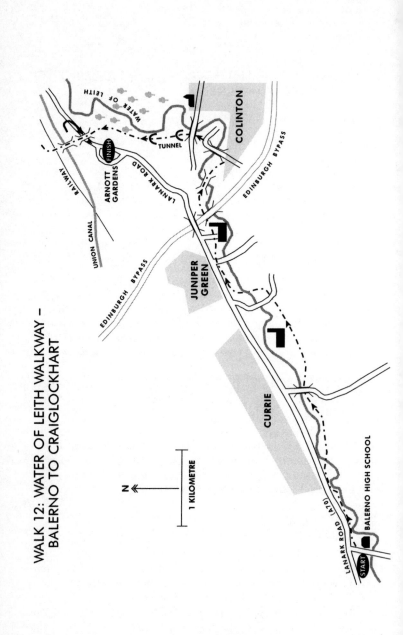

tracks leading into the warehouses). Follow the track over a road then across the river, back on to the left bank. On reaching a road with an industrial complex on the right, pass the entrance to the factories before bearing right back on to the dirt track and going beneath the City Bypass high overhead.

Stay on the track beside the river. Soon the track crosses to the right bank then ends at a road. Turn left and use the road to cross the river, then immediately turn left once more to regain the old railway track. Shortly hereafter the track passes Spylaw Park from where paths lead up to Colinton. Continue straight ahead along the old railway track, passing beneath a high road bridge then through a tunnel. From here the track continues to follow the Water of Leith but high above the river.

Eventually the track swings round to the left, away from the river, then suddenly ends at a footbridge across a busy main road. Cross over. Ahead is another bridge crossing the Union Canal. Turn right before the canal bridge and descend a few steps on to the main road. Pass beneath the footbridge and continue along the road for a short distance to Arnott Gardens.

WALK 13: INCHCOLM ISLAND

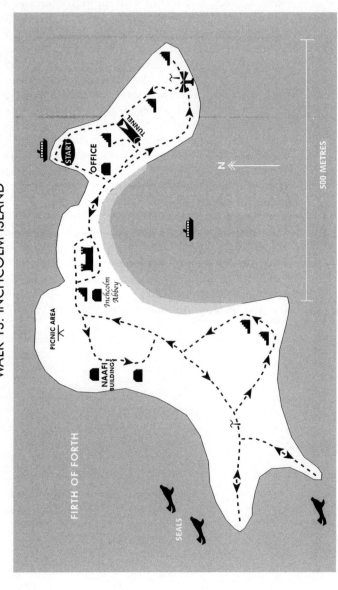

FIRTH OF FORTH

SEALS

PICNIC AREA

NAAFI BUILDINGS

Inchcolm Abbey

START

OFFICE

TUNNEL

N

500 METRES

13. INCHCOLM ISLAND

ORDNANCE SURVEY MAP NO	LANDRANGER 66
	PATHFINDER 394
DISTANCE FROM EDINBURGH	14½ KM (9 ML)
WALKING DISTANCE	3½KM (2 ML)
AMOUNT OF CLIMBING	135 M (440 FT)
ESTIMATED TIME	1¼ HR

DESCRIPTION A unique walk on an island in the Firth of Forth. There are superb views of the Bridges, the Firth of Forth and the coast of Fife; the best preserved medieval monastery in Scotland; and resident colonies of seals, puffins, kittiwakes and many other sea birds. There are also toilets, a gift shop and a small museum, but there are no refreshments.

The island, property of Historic Scotland, is reached by private boat or by the *Maid of the Forth* ferry from South Queensferry or North Queensferry. A small admission charge is incorporated in the ferry fare, or is payable to the resident Custodian if you are using your own marine transportation. The ferry operates from Easter until mid-October with two trips per day during the summer. The usual time ashore is 1½ hr: sufficient for a brisk walk over the entire island plus exploration of the abbey.

Seals and sea birds are best seen from the east end of the island – take binoculars. Please note that nesting birds may become aggressive during the nesting season (June–July). There may be periods when this is such a problem that access to parts of the island has to be restricted. If you find that you are being bombarded, a stick held above the head may provide protection.

START AND FINISH Inchcolm Island Quay. NT 191 827

HOW TO GET THERE By car, take the A90 towards the Forth

Road Bridge. Just beyond Cramond Bridge, take the slip road to South Queensferry. Park in the esplanade car park close to the ferry slipway opposite the Hawes Inn. Alternatively, take either the bus (MB 47) or train (ScotRail) to Dalmeny Station and walk along the path beside the railway down to the Hawes Inn.

WALK DIRECTIONS
Pass the shop and museum then climb to the left. At a fork go right, following a path along the cliff top, past a navigation light, to some derelict war-time buildings and views down the Firth of Forth. Return to the light, climb the adjacent steps and follow the path past more military relics. Then descend left and pass through a tunnel. At the tunnel exit, a detour to the right will lead to the highest point on this part of the island. Returning to the tunnel exit, follow the path back down to the museum then across to the abbey.

Either walk through or around the abbey, then pass the hermit's cell and picnic area and follow the path up to the mast on the eastern part of the island. Just beyond the picnic area, a path to the left passes some old NAAFI buildings then rejoins the main path. From the mast, a path extends out on to the eastern promontory; another descends steeply to the left down to the rocks at sea level. Care should be taken on both of these paths, especially if you are accompanied by adventurous children.

The return is via the outward path, or via a thin path around some old gun emplacements over to the right.

14. DALMENY ESTATE

ORDNANCE SURVEY MAP NO	LANDRANGER 65
	PATHFINDER 406
DISTANCE FROM EDINBURGH	15 KM (9 ML)
WALKING DISTANCE	10 KM (6 ML)
AMOUNT OF CLIMBING	NEGLIGIBLE
ESTIMATED TIME	3 HR

DESCRIPTION A pleasant walk along good paths (right-of-way) through the wooded estates of Dalmeny House, then by ferry (small charge) across the River Almond to Cramond. There are superb views of the Forth bridges and across the firth to Fife and the open sea. In spring, the estates are a mass of snowdrops. Note that dogs are not permitted on this route.

START Dalmeny Railway Station. NT 139 779
FINISH Cramond Bridge. NT 180 759
BUS LINK SMT 43 or MB 47

HOW TO GET THERE Frequent train (ScotRail) and bus service (SMT 43, X43; MB 47) from Edinburgh to Dalmeny Station. By car, take the A90 (Queensferry Road), following signs for the Forth Road Bridge. At Cramond Brig Hotel, turn right and park on the old road close to the hotel. Cross the old Cramond Bridge and turn right at the white cottage on to the River Almond Walkway. Pass beneath the new Cramond Bridge then climb up to the main road. Walk back towards Edinburgh for a few paces to a bus stop and catch a bus to Dalmeny Station.

WALK DIRECTIONS
Walk along the footpath beside the railway and through the woods. Then descend steeply to the Hawes Inn (a haunt of

WALK 14: DALMENY ESTATE

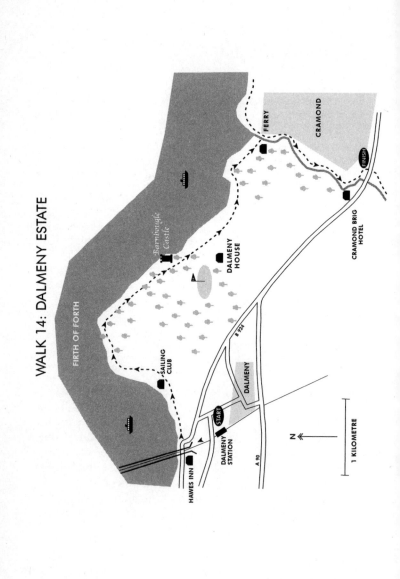

FIRTH OF FORTH

Barnbougle Castle

DALMENY HOUSE

SAILING CLUB

FERRY

CRAMOND

FINISH

CRAMOND BRIG HOTEL

B 924

DALMENY

START

DALMENY STATION

HAWES INN

A 90

N

1 KILOMETRE

Robert Louis Stevenson and inspiration for some of his novels). Cross the road to the lifeboat station, turn right and follow the dirt track beside the water to pass beneath the Forth Bridge. A kilometre further along, pass a sailing club then enter Dalmeny Estate via Long Craig gate. A notice-board here indicates the operating times of the ferry. It takes at least two hours to walk to the ferry from this point.

Follow the track through the woods. After a kilometre, pass some agricultural land on the right then re-enter the woods. Continue along the track, round the headland of Hound Point, then beside some sandy beaches to Barnbougle Castle. Originally the seat of the medieval crusading family of Moubray, this was later owned by the Earls of Rosebery; but when the third Earl was drenched by sea water coming in through his bathroom window during a storm, he decided to build Dalmeny House, further away from the water. Beyond the castle, follow the signs marking the right-of-way across the golf course and gardens in front of Dalmeny House. Continue along a grassy track through woods and over small streams to Cramond Ferry. Ringing the bell beside the river will summon the ferryman.

On the far side of the river it is a straightforward walk upstream to the old Cramond Bridge.

NORTHERN REGION

WALK 15: NORTH QUEENSFERRY

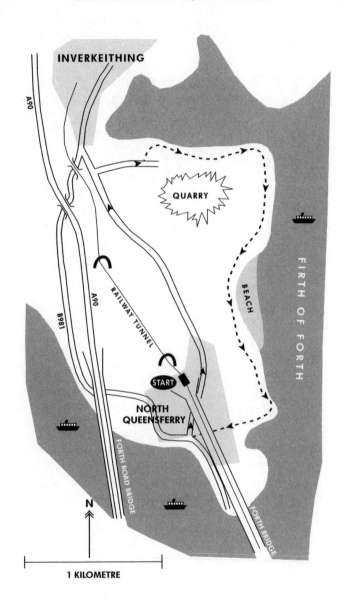

15. NORTH QUEENSFERRY

ORDNANCE SURVEY MAP NO	LANDRANGER 65
	PATHFINDER 394
DISTANCE FROM EDINBURGH	22 KM (14 ML)
WALKING DISTANCE	5 KM (3 ML)
AMOUNT OF CLIMBING	A FEW STEEP BUT VERY
	SHORT CLIMBS
ESTIMATED TIME	1¾ HR

DESCRIPTION A circular, mostly coastal walk around the North Queensferry peninsula. May be combined with a walk around the old town of North Queensferry or a visit to Deep Sea World (a massive aquarium with underwater tunnel).

START AND FINISH North Queensferry Railway Station. NT 131 809

HOW TO GET THERE Take a train (ScotRail) from Edinburgh or ferry (summer only) from South Queensferry (to Deep Sea World). By car, cross the Forth Road Bridge and take the first exit. Follow signs for 'Deep Sea World'. In the centre of North Queensferry, at the war memorial, turn left up The Brae. At the top, pass beneath a railway bridge then enter the station car park.

WALK DIRECTIONS
Leave the station car park and turn sharp left (north). Follow this quiet road past a few houses, then through some quite attractive rural countryside. On the right, as the road descends towards Inverkeithing, there is a viewing area of a very large man-made hole in the ground. Continue downhill. At the large 'Comfort' factory turn right into Cruikness Road. At the end of this short road, take the footpath (Fife Coastal Path) on the left of the quarry entrance.

This path follows the edge of an old harbour then swings right and hugs the coast. The first part of the coast is rocky but later there is a sandy bay. Shortly after leaving the beach, at the top of a rise, take a short detour to the left to gain a splendid view of the Forth Bridge. Continue on the main path for a short distance further to emerge in the centre of North Queensferry. Turn right to return to the railway station. Alternatively, follow the town heritage trail (there is a map diagonally across the road) or turn left and back on yourself to visit Deep Sea World.

Walking in the shadow of the Forth Bridge

16. LARGO LAW

ORDNANCE SURVEY MAP NO	LANDRANGER 59
	PATHFINDER 374
DISTANCE FROM EDINBURGH	62 KM (39 ML)
WALKING DISTANCE	6 KM (4 ML)
AMOUNT OF CLIMBING	310 M (1,015 FT)
ESTIMATED TIME	2½ HR

DESCRIPTION A steep climb from the sea at Lower Largo, birthplace of Alexander Selkirk (on whom Robinson Crusoe was based) to the summit of Largo Law, the highest point in the east of Fife. From the summit there are stunning views over the whole of Fife and the Firth of Forth. Note that the climb is more strenuous than it looks from the bottom.

START AND FINISH Foreshore car park, Lower Largo, Fife. NO 422 026

HOW TO GET THERE Bus service from Edinburgh (FS 57). By car, cross the Forth Road Bridge and drive north along the M90 motorway. At Junction 2A turn right on to the A92 to Kirkcaldy. At a roundabout just beyond Kirkcaldy, take the A915 (signposted 'Leven'). At Leven, follow the signs for St Andrews so as to avoid Leven town centre. On reaching a left-hand bend in Lundin Links, turn right to Lower Largo. Follow the road down to the sea then turn left. Pass over the bridge close to the harbour and continue along a narrow winding road, past a statue of Robinson Crusoe, to a car park on the left, close to the sea.

WALK DIRECTIONS

Climb the steps at the rear of the car park and go right along an old railway track (now the Largo to Elie Walkway). After a few paces, turn left on to a footpath through a narrow

WALK 16: LARGO LAW

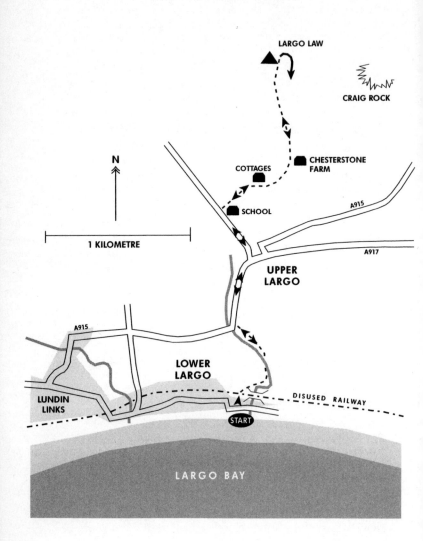

wooded valley (Serpentine Walk) to a main road (A915). Go uphill along the road to Upper Largo.

At Upper Largo, take the first road to the left (just beyond a garage) and follow it uphill for 300 m to a school on the right. Turn right between the school and the adjacent cemetery. Pass through a gate. Follow the path along the edge of a field, then a track past some cottages, to a farm (Chesterstone). Follow the track left through the farm, passing between two large barns. At the back of the right-hand barn, at a signpost, turn uphill on a rough stone track. Pass through a gate at the top of the track. Continue to climb steeply directly ahead on a path, through gorse bushes, to the first summit of Largo Law. From here descend into a small valley, cross a stile over a fence and climb up to the highest summit of Largo Law (290 m / 951 ft, cairn, triangulation pillar).

The return route is exactly the same as the ascent. Unfortunately no variations are permitted.

WALK 17: FIFE COAST –
ABERDOUR TO KINGHORN

N

2 KILOMETRES

A921

BURNTISLAND

BEACH

KINGHORN

FINISH

SILVERSANDS BAY

START

ABERDOUR

RAILWAY

A921

17. FIFE COAST – ABERDOUR TO KINGHORN

ORDNANCE SURVEY MAP NO	LANDRANGER 66
	PATHFINDER 395
DISTANCE FROM EDINBURGH	28 KM (17 ML)
WALKING DISTANCE	10 KM (6 ML)
AMOUNT OF CLIMBING	NEGLIGIBLE
ESTIMATED TIME	3 HR

DESCRIPTION An easy walk along part of the Fife Coastal Path. It may be combined with the Inverkeithing to Aberdour (Walk 18) route to make a total distance of 20 km (12 ml). The walk passes Aberdour Harbour then climbs over some cliff tops. It then crosses the beautiful Silversands Bay. Beyond the bay the path runs very close to the sea, so expect to get wet if the sea is choppy. Later the route passes a none too pleasant aluminium works, then winds its way through Burntisland and finally crosses the sands to Kinghorn. On this last section, it may be necessary to detour on to the road if the tide is high.

START Aberdour Railway Station, Fife. NT 191 854
FINISH Kinghorn, Fife. NT 267 866
BUS LINK FS 57

HOW TO GET THERE Train or bus from Edinburgh (FS 57, ScotRail). By car, cross the Forth Road Bridge then take the second exit (Junction 1 of the M90 motorway). Follow the A921 to Aberdour and park in one of the town's car parks or on a side street.

WALK DIRECTIONS
Walk east along the main road. Just after a bend, turn left and follow Shore Road down to the harbour. Walk to the sailing club then turn left on to a path beside a small café. Follow this path then a minor road, past a house and a

hotel, to the cliffs at Hawcraig Point. Retrace your steps as far as the house, then ascend a minor road for a short distance to an open area on the right. From here take the path along the cliff top then descend to Silversands Bay.

Cross the bay then take the way-marked path along the shoreline between the rocks and the railway. Pass through a tunnel and continue on the path beside the railway, through woodland then past an aluminium works, to emerge on to a road in the suburbs of Burntisland. Turn right. Pass beneath a railway bridge before climbing some steps on the left. Take the path between some houses then a minor road to a T-junction. Go left, through a gate in the old town wall, then descend some steps to the right to reach the centre of Burntisland.

At the end of the main street turn right to return to the sea-front. Take the path along the top of the beach to an underpass beneath the railway. From here, if the tide allows, cross the sands to Kinghorn. If this is impossible, pass beneath the railway and follow the road to Kinghorn (or take a bus from here back to Aberdour).

18. FIFE COAST – INVERKEITHING TO ABERDOUR

ORDNANCE SURVEY MAP NO	LANDRANGER 65
	PATHFINDER 394
DISTANCE FROM EDINBURGH	28 KM (17 ML)
WALKING DISTANCE	10 KM (6 ML)
AMOUNT OF CLIMBING	90 M (300 FT)
ESTIMATED TIME	3¼ HR

DESCRIPTION This walk follows part of the Fife Coastal Path along the Firth of Forth for most of its route. It can easily be combined with the Aberdour to Kinghorn (Walk 17) route to make a total distance of 20 km (12 ml). The walk passes through wooded areas, open grassland and a few built-up areas, but always clings closely to the coast – often close enough to get wet! There are good paths throughout.

START Inverkeithing Railway Station. NT 131 833
FINISH Aberdour Railway Station. NT 191 854
BUS/TRAIN LINK FS 57 or ScotRail

HOW TO GET THERE Train or bus from Edinburgh (FS 57, ScotRail). By car, cross the Forth Road Bridge and leave the M90 motorway at the second exit (Junction 1). Follow the A921 to Aberdour, park in one of the town's car parks or quiet streets close to the railway station and take the train or bus to Inverkeithing.

WALK DIRECTIONS
Follow the railway south. At a road bridge over the railway, descend a few steps and continue beside the railway for a short distance to a fork. Go left along a road beside a burn, across a main road, then beside the burn once more, following it round to the right. Turn left at a blue footpath signpost. Pass by a sports ground then, at the end of a row

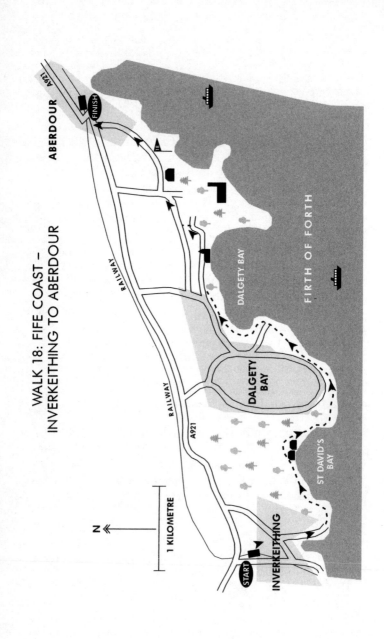

WALK 18: FIFE COAST –
INVERKEITHING TO ABERDOUR

ABERDOUR

A921

FINISH

RAILWAY

RAILWAY

DALGETY BAY

DALGETY BAY

FIRTH OF FORTH

ST DAVID'S BAY

A921

N

1 KILOMETRE

START

INVERKEITHING

of houses, pass between boulders and follow the path along the coast.

The path clings to the shoreline as far as St David's Bay where there is a new housing development. Climb slightly to the left to pass the entrance to the 'village' then pass through a gap in a stone wall and continue along the coastal path. Soon more new houses are reached. Pass by the front of these to regain the coastal path. At Dalgety Bay Sailing Club take the track through the woods, then the path along the shoreline around Dalgety Bay.

When beyond the houses, stay on the main path. Do not climb the stile on the right. On reaching a ruined church, join a tarmac road. At the next woodland there is a large white sign with a semi-circular arrow. Go left here, still following the road. After 300 m, turn left on to a path between fields for 100 m, then right on to another minor road. Follow this through an underpass. Continue past St Colme House, then alongside a golf course, before eventually emerging on to a main road in Aberdour opposite the Woodside Hotel. Turn right to reach the bus stop and railway station.

WALK 19: PITTENCRIEFF PARK, DUNFERMLINE

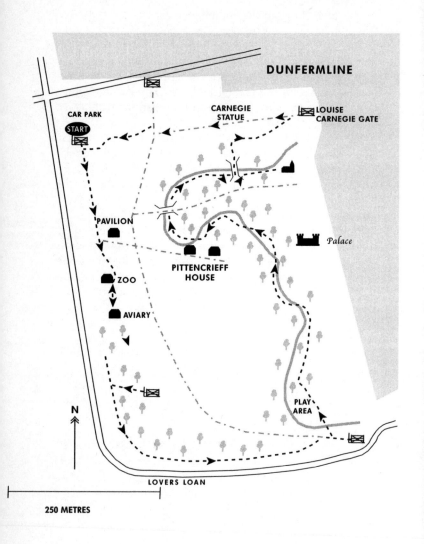

DUNFERMLINE

CAR PARK
START

CARNEGIE STATUE

LOUISE CARNEGIE GATE

PAVILION

ZOO

AVIARY

PITTENCRIEFF HOUSE

Palace

PLAY AREA

N

LOVERS LOAN

250 METRES

19. PITTENCRIEFF PARK, DUNFERMLINE

ORDNANCE SURVEY MAP NO	LANDRANGER 65
	PATHFINDER 394
DISTANCE FROM EDINBURGH	28 KM (17 ML)
WALKING DISTANCE	2½ KM (1½ ML)
AMOUNT OF CLIMBING	NEGLIGIBLE
ESTIMATED TIME	1 HR

DESCRIPTION Although short and in an urban park, this route is well worth walking. There are gardens and lawns, woodlands and a scenic wooded, narrow glen. You will also find a pavilion, glasshouse, museum, small zoo and aviary. The park itself was originally the private grounds of Pittencrieff House but it was purchased and bequeathed to the people of Dunfermline by Andrew Carnegie, Dunfermline's famous son and benefactor. While in the area, the town of Dunfermline is well worth exploring, especially the Abbey, Palace, Abbot House and St Margaret's Cave.

The route described is only a suggestion, for there are various paths throughout the park and several notice-boards with maps and local information.

START AND FINISH Pittencrieff Park car park, Dunfermline. NT 084 874

HOW TO GET THERE By car, cross the Forth Road Bridge and follow the signs for Dunfermline. At the large roundabout beneath a railway viaduct, go left. When this road turns left, go straight ahead into Lovers Loan. Follow this minor road around to the right alongside a stone wall. Just before the traffic lights, turn right into the car park. There is also a frequent rail (ScotRail) and bus service (MB 54, 55; FS 56, 58) from Edinburgh to Dunfermline.

WALK DIRECTIONS

Enter the park via the gate in the corner of the car park and follow a track beside a wall to the pavilion. Continue in the same direction, now on a path, to the zoo and then on to the aviary. From here it is necessary to retrace one's steps for a few paces before continuing on along the edge of some woodlands. Pass through a small gate on the right and walk through the woodlands to a tarmac path. Go left along this path, past a park entrance gate then a children's play area, into the 'glen'.

Follow the path as it meanders through the glen, frequently changing from one side of the burn to the other. The path passes beneath a road bridge, then reaches a small stone bridge across the burn. Climb right here, up a zigzag path, to a road. Go left for a couple of paces then head back down to the stone bridge. Cross over and climb out of the glen. At the top is the impressive Louise Carnegie Gate. Take the path heading towards Andrew Carnegie's statue. Pass the statue then continue on to a stone wall and take the path beside the wall back to the car park.

20. LOCHORE MEADOWS COUNTRY PARK

ORDNANCE SURVEY MAP NO	LANDRANGER 58
	PATHFINDER 384
DISTANCE FROM EDINBURGH	36 KM (22 ML)
WALKING DISTANCE	10 KM (6 ML)
AMOUNT OF CLIMBING	180 M (590 FT)
ESTIMATED TIME	3½ HR

DESCRIPTION A circular walk around Loch Ore within the Lochore Meadows Country Park. The area was once devoted to coal mining with accompanying bings and winding gear. However, all that has now been cleared and the area planted with grass and trees. The western part of the loch, near the start of the route, is a nature reserve with abundant bird life. The far side of the loch, close to the Park Centre, is used for various forms of water sport. The paths and terrain vary considerably; in some places there is asphalt while in others there are rocks or grass tracks. Many of the paths can be very muddy.

START AND FINISH Lochore Meadows Country Park, western entrance. NT 152 949

HOW TO GET THERE By car, take the A90 across the Forth Road Bridge and on to the M90. At Junction 4 turn right. Pass straight through Kelty. At the T-junction on the far side of this town, turn left. Then, at a left-hand bend, turn right on to a minor road (signpost 'Lochore Meadows Country Park') leading to a small car park for Park visitors. Those using public transport may take bus FS 56 to Ballingry and start and finish the walk there.

WALK DIRECTIONS
Pass through the gate adjacent to the car park and follow a tree-lined track for 600 m to a junction of footpaths. Go left

WALK 20: LOCHORE MEADOWS COUNTRY PARK

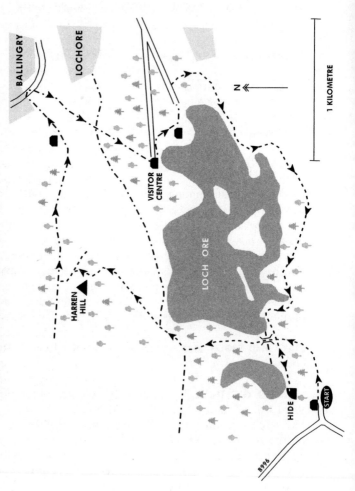

for 100 m to the Kon Lipphardt hide with its splendid view of aquatic bird life; then retrace your steps to the junction. Turn left, cross a wooden bridge and follow a footpath through woodland to an asphalt road. Go right along the road, around a bend, then turn off left on to a gravel track ascending through more woodlands (Harren Hill Wood). The path becomes progressively steeper and narrower as it rises. Just beyond the summit, bear left on to a track for a short distance, then pass through a gate to reach a gravel track.

Go right along this track. After a kilometre you will pass the old winding tower away to the right. Shortly thereafter, at the outskirts of Ballingry, turn right to cross a bus turning circle. Turn right again, over a stile, and on to rough grazing land. Follow the overhead electricity cables across the grassland to some trees, then bear left to reach a minor road. Cross diagonally to a kissing gate and follow the path past a winding tower and old locomotive, then pass car parks to reach the Park Centre (information, toilets and refreshments).

From the Park Centre follow the loch shore to the Water Sports Centre. Pass through the car park behind the building. Head away from the water on a path, then an asphalt road. After a short distance along the road, turn right on to a footpath over a footbridge. This path crosses some rocky outcrops beside the edge of the loch before it reaches a meadow. Cross the grassland roughly parallel with the loch shore, passing a couple of copses of trees, then enter woodlands to return to the junction of paths crossed earlier. Turn left to return to the car park.

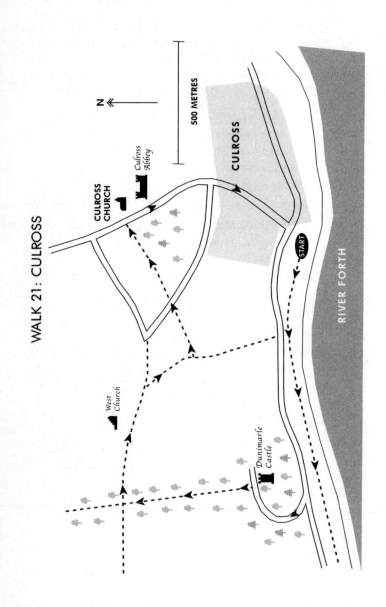

WALK 21: CULROSS

N

500 METRES

CULROSS CHURCH

Culross Abbey

CULROSS

START

West Church

Dunimarle Castle

RIVER FORTH

21. CULROSS

ORDNANCE SURVEY MAP NO	LANDRANGER 65
	PATHFINDER 393
DISTANCE FROM EDINBURGH	38 KM (24 ML)
WALKING DISTANCE	5 KM (3 ML)
AMOUNT OF CLIMBING	70 M (230 FT)
ESTIMATED TIME	2 HR

DESCRIPTION A short walk through rolling agricultural land with superb views across the Forth. Many sites of considerable historical interest *en route*, especially in Culross where many buildings have been renovated and may be visited. The entire route follows right-of-ways.

START AND FINISH car park near the water just west of the centre of Culross. NS 984 859

HOW TO GET THERE Take the A90 across the Forth Road Bridge. At Junction 1 of the M90 motorway, turn off on to the A985 heading west. After 11 km (6½ ml), turn left at roundabout and follow the B9037 through Torryburn to Culross. By bus, use service MB 52, 54 or 55 to Dunfermline, then MB 14 to Culross.

WALK DIRECTIONS
Head west along the bank of the River Forth following the grassy path beside the railway then, later, through gorse bushes. Turn right at the first opening in the gorse bushes, cross the road and walk up Dunimarle Castle access road towards the castle. At the top of the hill, just as the castle comes into view, bear left along a grassy track behind some trees then left again along a drive heading away from the castle. Pass between monkey puzzle trees and on into a wilderness area.

At a footpath signpost for West Kirk, turn right. After 100 m you will reach the ruins of West Kirk and cemetery (well worth exploring). Continue along the path to a group of gates. Here, bear right on a path between fences, then left at the signpost for Culross Abbey. On reaching a road, pass through the gate opposite and walk along the edge of a field to a second road. Follow this road downhill, past Culross Church and the Abbey, and on through the narrow streets of Culross to the waterfront. Turn right to return to the car park.

Woodland snowdrops

22. LOCH GLOW

ORDNANCE SURVEY MAP NO	LANDRANGER 58
	PATHFINDER 384
DISTANCE FROM EDINBURGH	38 KM (24 ML)
WALKING DISTANCE	8 KM (5 ML)
AMOUNT OF CLIMBING	250 M (820 FT)
ESTIMATED TIME	3 HR

DESCRIPTION A pleasant hill ramble around Loch Glow and over some of the Cleish Hills. The section along the south bank of the loch and over the moorland beyond can be very boggy. Good walking boots are essential. There are a few fences to step over. Be careful to do no damage.

START AND FINISH Car park near Loch Glow. NT 100 955

HOW TO GET THERE By car, cross the Forth Road Bridge then follow the M90 motorway to Junction 4. Head west on the B914 for 1¾ ml, then turn right on to a minor, single-track road for a further 1¾ ml. The car park is on the left through a wooden gate with a signpost for Loch Glow. There is no public transport to this area.

WALK DIRECTIONS

Go along the forest road to Loch Glow then turn left to walk along the south bank. There is a boggy path just above the water's edge; or a muddy (fisherman's) path closer to the water. At the end of the trees on the left, go over the stile close to the water then climb up on to the moorland and bear away from the loch, heading towards some higher ground in the near distance. From this high point it is possible to see Dumglow, with Black Loch at its base, over to the right and a small hill directly ahead with some ruins near the summit. Bear right to avoid the worst of the boggy moorland and head for the ruins. On arrival you will find a

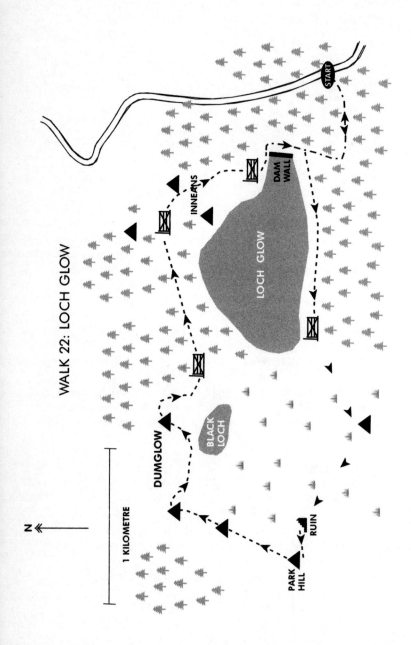

WALK 22: LOCH GLOW

N

1 KILOMETRE

START

INNEANS

DAM WALL

LOCH GLOW

DUMGLOW

BLACK LOCH

PARK HILL

RUIN

line of raised ground heading uphill. Follow this to the top. Turn right to walk parallel to the boundary fence of some woodlands and surmount another small hill. Descend into a small valley, carefully climb over the wall and fence, then climb a steeply ascending path directly ahead to a cairn. Still on the path, go right to follow a fence down and across a watershed to the base of Dumglow. Climb over the fence and scramble up the steep western ridge to the summit (379 m / 1,243 ft, triangulation pillar, cairn).

Follow the most prominent path down, bearing round to the right (southeast), to a forest boundary fence with a stile. Climb over the stile and walk down the forest ride ahead to the far side of the forest and another fence. Climb over the fence. Follow the path directly ahead between (or over) some small knobbly hills (The Inneans).

Gradually descend the ridge to the right, down to Loch Glow and the dam wall. Cross the stile and bridge over the loch outlet to reach the forest road used earlier and follow this back to the car park.

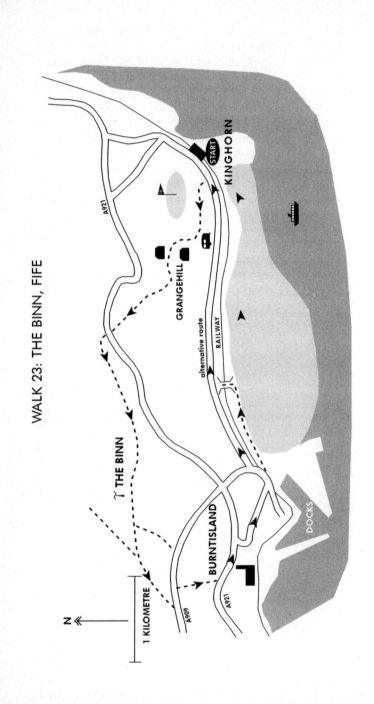

WALK 23: THE BINN, FIFE

N

1 KILOMETRE

THE BINN

BURNTISLAND

A909

A921

GRANGEHILL

RAILWAY

alternative route

KINGHORN

START

A921

DOCKS

23. THE BINN, FIFE

ORDNANCE SURVEY MAP NO	LANDRANGER 66
	PATHFINDER 395
DISTANCE FROM EDINBURGH	39 KM (24 ML)
WALKING DISTANCE	11 KM (7 ML)
AMOUNT OF CLIMBING	180 M (590 FT)
ESTIMATED TIME	4 HR

DESCRIPTION The Binn is the prominent hill on the Fife coast that supports the area's television transmitter. Being so prominent, it provides spectacular views of the Firth of Forth and the Bridges. The route up passes through varied agricultural and forestry land, while the return route passes through Burntisland (cafés, shops, toilets) and across an extensive sandy bay.

START AND FINISH Kinghorn, Fife. NT 265 865

HOW TO GET THERE Frequent train service from Edinburgh (ScotRail; GNER) or bus (FS 57). By car, cross the Forth Road Bridge. At Junction 1 of the M90 motorway, turn right on to the A921. At a roundabout near Burntisland, go straight ahead (still on the A921) then take the next road to the right into Kinghorn and park in any of the town's many car parks.

WALK DIRECTIONS
From the centre of Kinghorn, walk west along the main road. At Kinghorn Golf Course, turn right to reach the clubhouse, then turn left and follow a gravel track across the golf course to a caravan park. Continue along the track round to the right, past Grangehill, to some farm buildings. Turn left and follow the track to a main road. Go left for a few paces then cross the road, pass through a gate and follow the gradually ascending footpath to the left for a little

more than a kilometre to a high gate and fence. Pass through the gate and continue directly ahead, over a stile, then uphill, along the edge of a field, to the summit of The Binn.

Continue in the same direction along the edge of the field, then take the path that heads away from the sea over bumpy grassland to a track. Go left downhill along the track to a main road. Go left along the road for a short distance. Turn right on to a path beside an electricity sub-station. Descend through the woodlands then past a few houses to a road. Go left, pass the aluminium works, then turn right to reach the centre of Burntisland.

Go left along the main street of Burntisland. At its end turn right and head for the sea. Take the path along the top of the beach to a pedestrian underpass beneath the railway. From here, if the tide allows, cross the sands to Kinghorn. If this is impossible, pass beneath the railway and follow the road (or take a bus) back to Kinghorn.

24. VANE FARM NATURE RESERVE

ORDNANCE SURVEY MAP NO	LANDRANGER 58
	PATHFINDER 384
DISTANCE FROM EDINBURGH	39 KM (24 ML)
WALKING DISTANCE	1½ KM (1 ML)
AMOUNT OF CLIMBING	130 M (430 FT)
ESTIMATED TIME	1 HR

DESCRIPTION Vane Farm Nature Reserve (owned by the Royal Society for the Protection of Birds) and the adjacent Loch Leven are major 'stop-over' points for migratory birds. The woodland walk through the reserve is short, but full of interest, and has superb views over Loch Leven. Along the way there are frequent information points that amply describe the vegetation and local bird life. A picnic area is situated at the end of the route. The walk may easily be combined with a visit to the RSPB Centre (small admission charge). There is also a shorter 'wetland' walk nearby.

START AND FINISH Vane Farm Nature Reserve, Fife. NT 160 990

HOW TO GET THERE By car, take the A90 across the Forth Road Bridge and on to the M90. Leave at Junction 5 and follow the signs for the Vane Farm Nature Reserve. There is a car park next to the Visitor Centre.

WALK DIRECTIONS
Check-in at the Visitor Centre. (They usually charge for entry but often waive the fee if you tell them that you are merely walking on the hill.) Take the path at the back of the building and head uphill. This path soon swings round to the right and passes through mixed deciduous woodland. Later it passes a hide then turns left. At Information Point No. 10, where the route passes from woodland to heather-

WALK 24: VANE FARM NATURE RESERVE

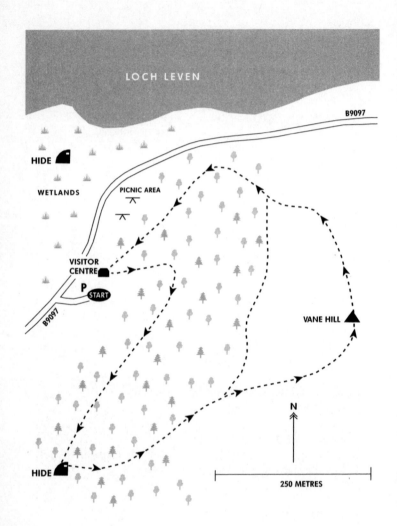

covered moorland, take the right-hand path (uphill) to a superb view over Loch Leven. The large island in the foreground is St Serf's Island. The ruins on the island were a monastery and abbey built 800 years ago. The distant, tree-covered island is the one on which Mary, Queen of Scots was held captive. Continue on the path directly ahead to descend back to the Visitor Centre.

Interested locals? A typical scene of cattle in the countryside

WALK 25: CARDENDEN GLEN

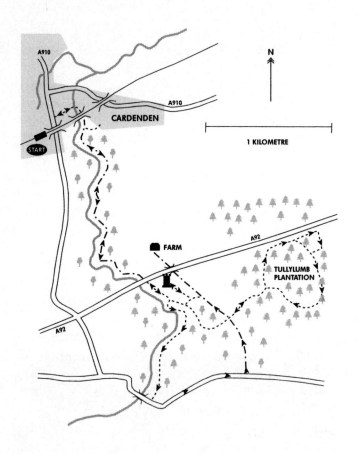

25. CARDENDEN GLEN

ORDNANCE SURVEY MAP NO	LANDRANGER 58
	PATHFINDER 385
DISTANCE FROM EDINBURGH	40 KM (25 ML)
WALKING DISTANCE	10 KM (6 ML)
AMOUNT OF CLIMBING	90 M (300 FT)
ESTIMATED TIME	3¼ HR

DESCRIPTION This is a fairly easy walk along a winding, wooded glen; then a short road walk followed by a circuit within a coniferous forest (Tullylumb Plantation); then back through the glen. There are good tracks and paths although they can be muddy in places.

START AND FINISH Cardenden Railway Station, Fife. NT 217 949

HOW TO GET THERE By car, cross the Forth Road Bridge and head north on the M90. At Junction 2A, turn east on to the A92 and follow the signs for Cardenden. Park in the railway station car park. The easiest method of public transport from Edinburgh is the train (ScotRail) to Cardenden.

WALK DIRECTIONS
From the railway station car park, walk along the road beneath the railway for a few paces, then turn right on to an asphalt footpath. Follow this back under the railway. At a fork, go right and ascend to a track. Follow this track along the route of the burn on the right. Soon, the houses (and rubbish) are left behind and the route meanders through woodlands following the stream. At one point the track turns right and crosses a tributary but it never crosses the main water course. Do not take any of the many side paths and tracks. Two kilometres on, shortly after passing beneath a high road bridge, you will reach a fork in the tracks. Take

the right-hand track to stay beside the burn.

On reaching a minor road, turn left and follow the road for a kilometre, past an open area on the left and round a double bend on a small incline. Shortly after the road becomes straight, turn left on to another dirt track. Follow this to the point where it is crossed by another track (there are gates on either side). Here, turn on to the forestry track to the right. After a few paces, at a fork, go left on to a path. Follow this through the forest. At one point the path passes close to a busy main road before reaching the edge of the woodland and swinging right and uphill. At the top of the short incline bear right and continue until another forestry track is reached. Go left along this track and you will return to the point where the forest was entered. Turn right on to the continuation of the track used earlier.

Once you emerge from the forest, go left for a few paces and descend some steps. Follow the path at the bottom for 100 m to the remains of a tower, then return to the steps. Descend into the glen and follow the burn back to the start.

26. KNOCK HILL & SALINE HILL

ORDNANCE SURVEY MAP NO	LANDRANGER 58
	PATHFINDER 384
DISTANCE FROM EDINBURGH	42 KM (26 ML)
WALKING DISTANCE	8 KM (5 ML)
AMOUNT OF CLIMBING	260 M (850 FT)
ESTIMATED TIME	3 HR

DESCRIPTION A fairly strenuous but short hill walk. It follows a track on to Knock Hill, but from there the route passes over very rough grazing land with only a thin path. There are fantastic views over the Forth valley and across to the Ochil Hills. Hill-walking boots are recommended for this route.

START AND FINISH Lay-by on A823 close to entrance to Knockhill Racing Circuit. NT 064 945

HOW TO GET THERE By car, cross the Forth Road Bridge and take the M90 to Junction 4 then the B914 towards Saline. After 2 ml, at a fork, go right. After another 2 ml, at a crossroads, turn right again. Park in the lay-by on the right just beyond the entrance to Knockhill Racing Circuit.

WALK DIRECTIONS
Walk along the access road to the racing circuit. At the entrance continue straight ahead, across a cattle grid, and up the road towards a house. Just before the house, turn left and follow a track to the summit of Knock Hill (364 m / 1,194 ft, triangulation pillar, radio masts).

Leave the summit heading southwest towards the small valley between Knock Hill and Saline Hill. Carefully descend the least steep section in a zigzag fashion, aiming for the highest part of the saddle. Here, step across a small burn then go left along a farm track which passes through

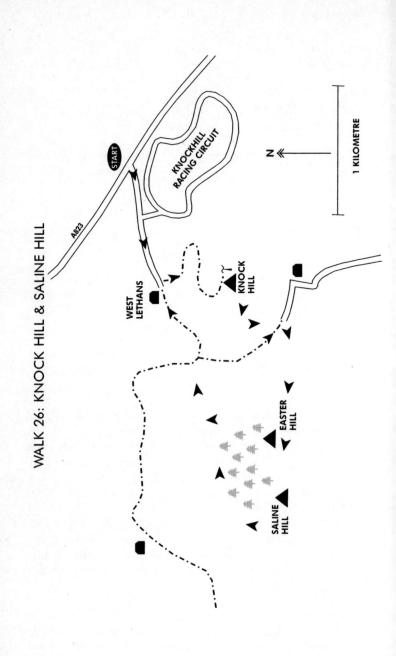

WALK 26: KNOCK HILL & SALINE HILL

A823

START

KNOCKHILL RACING CIRCUIT

WEST LETHANS

KNOCK HILL

EASTER HILL

SALINE HILL

N

1 KILOMETRE

the valley. On reaching a low dry-stone wall and fence, turn right and follow the fence up over Easter Cairn. Continue beside the fence, past a woodland, to the summit of Saline Hill (359 m / 1,178 ft, cairn).

Turn right and follow the edge of the trees down the side of the valley. At the corner of the tree plantation turn right and continue along the edge of the woods. At the next corner of the plantation turn left, away from the trees, and descend beside a dry-stone wall to a gate.

Continue by turning right and following a second wall as far as another gate and a footpath signpost for 'West Lethans'. Follow the signposted direction to West Lethans farm, pass the farmhouse then walk along the farm access road back to the starting point.

WALK 27: BENARTY HILL, FIFE

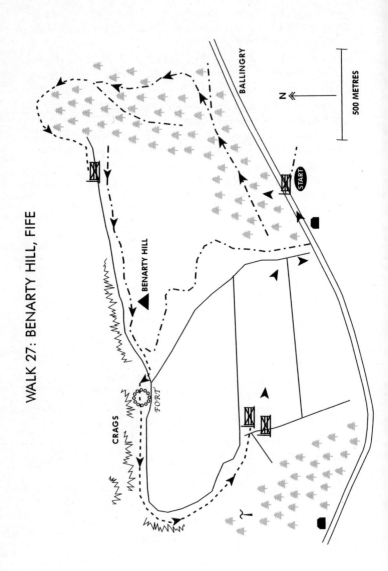

BALLINGRY

START

BENARTY HILL

CRAGS

FORT

N

500 METRES

27. BENARTY HILL, FIFE

ORDNANCE SURVEY MAP NO	LANDRANGER 58
	PATHFINDER 384
DISTANCE FROM EDINBURGH	43 KM (27 ML)
WALKING DISTANCE	7 KM (4½ ML)
AMOUNT OF CLIMBING	360 M (1,180 FT)
ESTIMATED TIME	2¾ HR

DESCRIPTION A hill walk along the top of an escarpment with stunning views of Lochs Leven and Ore. If there is a northerly or easterly wind then you will probably be accompanied by gliders sailing quietly overhead. Hill-walking boots are recommended for this route.

START AND FINISH Minor road, one mile southeast of the village of Ballingry, Fife. NT 159 970

HOW TO GET THERE By car, cross the Forth Road Bridge and follow the M90 motorway to Junction 5. Turn right. At a T-junction, turn right again then left on to a minor road towards Ballingry. After 1¾ ml, park on the side of the road beside a farm track on the right (limited space) or in Ballingry and walk back. It is also possible to take bus FS 56 to Ballingry and walk along the road to the start.

WALK DIRECTIONS
There are some wooden steps ascending through the forest opposite the farm track and gate. Climb up these to a forest track and nearby seat with a splendid view over Loch Ore. Follow the track to the right (downhill), past a sheep-grazing area, as far as a fork. Take the left (uphill) fork and swing round to the left above the village of Ballingry. When you reach the forest boundary and the track doubles back upon itself, go directly ahead, over a fence, on to rough grassland.

Follow the edge of the forest downhill a little, then round to the left. Step over another fence on the left and climb the steep, grassy bank ahead to a dry-stone wall and another fence with heather-covered moorland beyond. Follow the wall away from the forest for a few paces to a stile. Cross over and continue beside the wall on a thin track through heather, then over rough moorland grass to the highest point of Benarty Hill (356 m / 1,168 ft, triangulation pillar).

From this high point, the nearby dry-stone wall clings to the top of the escarpment above Loch Leven. Continue on the track beside the wall until it reaches a gully and bears off to the left. (For a short-cut, stay on the track downhill to a road, then go left to return to the start.) To continue the main route, leave the track and climb the steep path directly ahead beside the wall. On the top there is another dry-stone wall, this time with an electric fence. Step over the wall to the right and continue in the same direction to climb over a few small hills (the remains of an ancient fort).

A little beyond these small hillocks you will reach another electric fence, this time with a stone stile. Cross over and continue along the top of the escarpment around the western end of Benarty Hill. In this area there are a number of red signs warning of the shooting range lower down. Follow this line of signs, descending a short, steep section, towards another woodland. Stay close to the fence on the left. When two gates are reached, go through the left-hand gate and follow the path close to the fence on the right for a few paces. Here leave the fence, cross a small burn and traverse around the base of a small hill to reach another dry-stone wall. Follow this downhill, through two gates, to a road. Go left for a short distance to return to the start.

28. BISHOP HILL ABOVE LOCH LEVEN

ORDNANCE SURVEY MAP NO	LANDRANGER 58
	PATHFINDER 372
DISTANCE FROM EDINBURGH	45 KM (28 ML)
WALKING DISTANCE	9 KM (5½ ML)
AMOUNT OF CLIMBING	470 M (1,550 FT)
ESTIMATED TIME	4 HR

DESCRIPTION A hill walk overlooking Loch Leven. The route starts on an undulating path along the bottom of an escarpment followed by a long, steep climb to the top which is rewarded with magnificent views in all directions. One may even hear the occasional whistles as gliders soar just above one's head. Hill-walking boots are recommended for this route.

START AND FINISH The Well, Scotlandwell. NO 185 016

HOW TO GET THERE By car, cross the Forth Road Bridge and take the M90 to Junction 5, then right on to the B9097. Pass the Vane Farm Nature Centre. At a T-junction, turn left and immediately left again. Look for the signpost for the 'well' in the centre of Scotlandwell and park at the end of the lane beside the well.

WALK DIRECTIONS
Walk back to the main road and turn left. Just outside the village, turn right up some steps on to the Tetley Trail, a way-marked path that undulates through deciduous woodland then across open moorland. At the point where the path zigzags down 10 m to a gate into the village of Kinneswood, turn right and climb steeply up a shoulder to join a higher transverse path. Follow this path to the left, passing above, then through, bracken. When it reaches a gully the path becomes a little overgrown but is still present.

WALK 28: BISHOP HILL ABOVE LOCH LEVEN

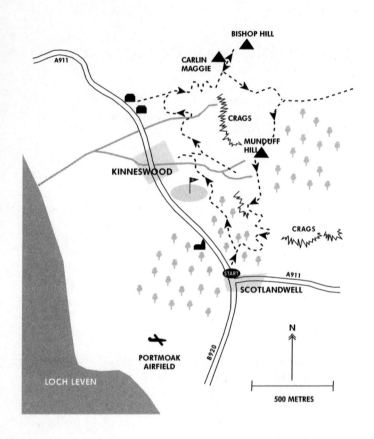

Follow it to the top of the gully then continue to traverse the hillside to a gate in a stone wall. Descend diagonally across grassland to a fence, then walk alongside the fence to a gate. Here go right on to a track that ascends steeply up the escarpment. On reaching the top, turn left off the track on to a path which leads past Carlin Maggie (a pillar of rock off the edge of the escarpment) and on to the summit of Bishop Hill (461 m / 1,512 ft, cairn).

Turn around and retrace your steps back as far as a stone wall. Climb over the gate through the wall and follow a grassy track away from the edge of the escarpment. Where the track passes through another wall, bear right and head for the high point with a prominent cairn (Munduff Hill).

Leave this summit, heading southwest and descend along the edge of some woods. Stay on the path as it leaves the trees, crosses grassland, passes through another woodland, then descends in a zigzag fashion to join the Tetley Trail just above Scotlandwell church. Go left to return to the start.

WALK 29: THE TETLEY TRAIL, SCOTLANDWELL

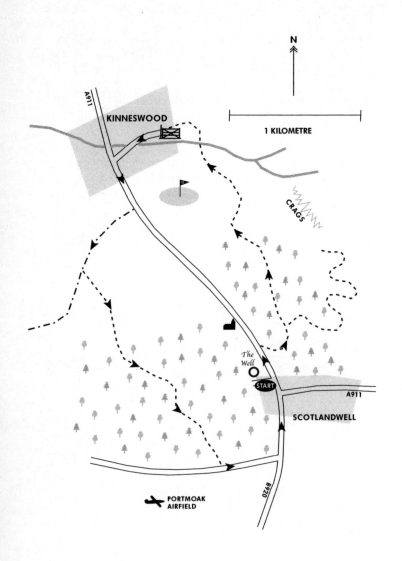

29. THE TETLEY TRAIL, SCOTLANDWELL

ORDNANCE SURVEY MAP NO	LANDRANGER 58
	PATHFINDER 372
DISTANCE FROM EDINBURGH	45 KM (28 ML)
WALKING DISTANCE	6 KM (4 ML)
AMOUNT OF CLIMBING	150 M (500 FT)
ESTIMATED TIME	2 HR

DESCRIPTION This delightful walk through varied terrain follows well-maintained and way-marked paths throughout. Support for the maintenance of the path has been given by Tetley Tea, hence its name. There are fine views across Loch Leven, an internationally famous bird sanctuary. There are also occasional whistles as gliders soar overhead.

START AND FINISH The Well, Scotlandwell. NO 185 016

HOW TO GET THERE By car, cross the Forth Road Bridge and take the M90 to Junction 5, then right on to the B9097. Pass the Vane Farm Nature Centre. At a T-junction, turn left and immediately left again. Look for the signpost for the 'well' in the centre of Scotlandwell and park at the end of the lane beside the well.

WALK DIRECTIONS

Go back to the main road and turn left. Just outside the village, turn right up some steps on to the Tetley Trail, a way-marked path that undulates through deciduous woodland then traverses open moorland above a golf course and beneath the towering White Craigs. Eventually, the path zigzags down for 10 m and passes through a gate to enter the village of Kinneswood.

Walk down a lane to reach a busy main road in the centre of the village and turn left. Just beyond the village, at a footpath signpost, turn right on to a farm road. Take the first turn to the left and follow a gravel track, then a grassy track and finally a footpath. This passes along the edge of fields, then through Portmoak Moss Forest, before finally emerging on to a road a little south of Scotlandwell. Turn left to return to the well.

Walking through snow in the Lomond Hills

30. ROYAL HUNTING GROUNDS, LOMOND HILLS

ORDNANCE SURVEY MAP NO	LANDRANGER 58
	PATHFINDER 373
DISTANCE FROM EDINBURGH	50 KM (31 ML)
WALKING DISTANCE	11 KM (6½ ML)
AMOUNT OF CLIMBING	190 M (625 FT)
ESTIMATED TIME	4 HR

DESCRIPTION A moorland walk around several reservoirs amidst the Lomond Hills. The area hereabouts was very popular for hunting in the days when Falkland Palace was occupied by royalty. The route itself is very scenic and reasonably easy, as it follows established tracks for most of its length. Note that the area around the top of Harperleas Reservoir is quite boggy and the track above the reservoir has been churned up by many hooves.

START AND FINISH Holl Reservoir near Leslie, Fife. NO 224 035

HOW TO GET THERE By car, cross the Forth Road Bridge and follow the M90 motorway to junction 5. Turn right and follow signs to Vane Farm Nature Reserve. Beyond Vane Farm, at a T-junction, turn left. After 2½ ml, turn left to cross the River Leven and immediately right on to the A911 towards Leslie. With almost another mile, turn left on to a track to Holl Reservoir and park in the adjacent car park. There is no public transport serving this walk.

WALK DIRECTIONS
From the car park, continue along the road beside Holl Reservoir. Do not turn right towards the dam wall, but continue ahead going uphill past a blue-green post. At the top of the incline, take the left fork and continue along a track over moorland, then through the woods beside Harperleas

WALK 30: ROYAL HUNTING GROUNDS, LOMOND HILLS

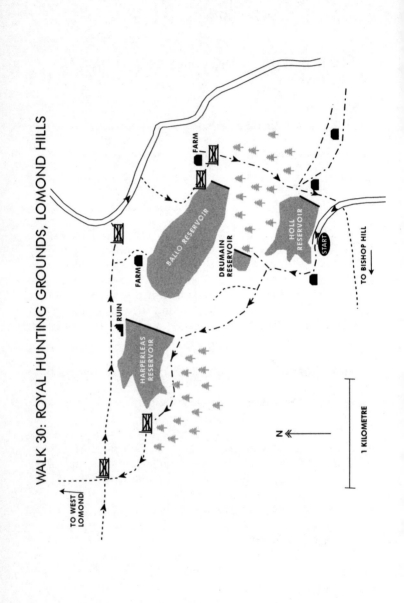

FARM

BALLO RESERVOIR

HOLL RESERVOIR

DRUMAIN RESERVOIR

START

TO BISHOP HILL

FARM

RUIN

HARPERLEAS RESERVOIR

TO WEST LOMOND

N

1 KILOMETRE

Reservoir to a small weir (inlet to the reservoir). Here climb a stile over a dry-stone wall and turn left on a path beside the wall. Follow this across the watershed towards West Lomond. Just before the path begins to climb steeply, at a junction of footpaths, turn right over another stile over a stone wall and follow the grassy track beyond.

This track passes above Harperleas Reservoir to the ruins of a house just above the dam wall. From here the track gradually becomes more substantial. After passing a white-walled farm on the right, the track gradually ascends and finally reaches an asphalt road. Walk right along the road for 700 m to a footpath signpost. Turn right and follow the footpath over a small rise, then down to a green angler's bothy beside Ballo Reservoir. Turn left and follow the signposted path beside the reservoir.

On approaching a farm, bear right through a gate and along a fenced pathway around the farm. At the end of the path, turn right on to a track and follow it downhill, through woodlands, back to Holl Reservoir. Cross the weir and dam wall. Turn right to return to the car park.

WALK 31: DOLLAR GLEN

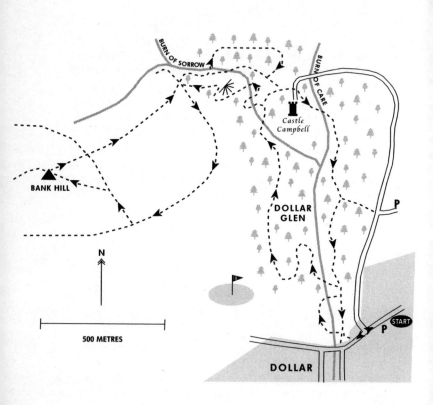

BURN OF SORROW

BURN OF CARE

Castle Campbell

BANK HILL

DOLLAR GLEN

N

500 METRES

P

START

P

DOLLAR

31. DOLLAR GLEN

ORDNANCE SURVEY MAP NO	LANDRANGER 58
	PATHFINDER 383
DISTANCE FROM EDINBURGH	53 KM (33 ML)
WALKING DISTANCE	6½ KM (4 ML)
AMOUNT OF CLIMBING	180 M (590 FT)
ESTIMATED TIME	2¼ HR

DESCRIPTION This is a walk not to be missed. Dollar Glen is in the care of the National Trust of Scotland. It is a deep, heavily wooded ravine in the hillside through which the Burn of Care and the Burn of Sorrow tumble over many cascades and waterfalls – making it one of the most beautiful glens in Scotland. As if this were not enough, at the top of the glen is the haunting and foreboding Castle Campbell (Historic Scotland, small admission charge, tearoom) and the views from the top of Bank Hill are quite phenomenal.

START AND FINISH Hillfoot car park, Dollar. NS 965 984

HOW TO GET THERE By car, cross the Forth Road Bridge and take the M90 motorway to Junction 4, then the B914 to Saline and the B913 to Dollar. At the T-junction in Dollar, turn right then left at the brown sign for Castle Campbell. At the top of this road, turn right and go a little uphill (past the road to Castle Campbell) to Hillfoot car park on the right.

WALK DIRECTIONS
Walk back down the hill until just beyond the road to the castle. Turn right on to a path between houses that leads to the lower, park-like part of the glen and follow a burn upstream (either side). Shortly after entering a woodland,

cross a new wooden footbridge to reach the left side of the burn and follow a twisting path up the glen. On reaching the castle cross the burn and climb the far bank. Here turn off the path leading to the castle and take another path heading upstream. This path crosses the burn three more times before diverging away from the water and climbing to the top of a ridge, where there is a bench seat overlooking the glen.

Take the ascending path behind the bench. At the top of this short climb, leave the National Trust by passing through a gate on to open hillside. Immediately turn left on to a path that follows a fence round to the left of Bank Hill. When Dollar and a golf course come into view and the path is crossed by another, turn right on to the second path and climb to the top of the ridge. Here turn left to join a steeply ascending path on to the summit of Bank Hill (344 m / 1,128 ft, large cairn of loose rocks).

Leave the summit of Bank Hill on a path that heads towards the distant Whitewisp Hill (the one to the left of the tree-covered hill). At the bottom of the descent, cross a path that leads to the wooden gate used earlier and continue down to a burn. Follow the burn downstream, crossing to the far side at the first footbridge. Stay on this path down to Castle Campbell, then pass through the wooden gate to the left of the castle entrance and follow a winding path all the way back down to the bottom of the glen.

32. RUMBLING BRIDGE GORGE

ORDNANCE SURVEY MAP NO	LANDRANGER 58
	PATHFINDER 384
DISTANCE FROM EDINBURGH	53 KM (33 ML)
WALKING DISTANCE	1½ KM (1 ML)
AMOUNT OF CLIMBING	NEGLIGIBLE, BUT MANY
	STEPS
ESTIMATED TIME	¾ HR

DESCRIPTION A short, easy and very pleasant walk through a famous beauty spot. Well-maintained paths follow the course of the river Devon as it cascades and falls through this spectacular, rocky gorge.

START AND FINISH car park behind Rumbling Bridge Nursing Home. NT 016 997

HOW TO GET THERE By car, cross the Forth Road Bridge and take the M90. At Junction 5 turn left on to the B9097. At the T-junction with the A977 turn left. After a further 3 ml, turn right to Rumbling Bridge. The car park is behind the large yellow building on the right, just after crossing the bridge.

WALK DIRECTIONS
Walk around the back of the nursing home to a signpost indicating the direction to the gorge; descend the steps through the garden. At the bottom, cross a path and pass a notice-board, then descend more steps to discover a superb view of the gorge. Return to the main path and follow it upstream past the many cataracts and waterfalls. Pass the first footbridge encountered and continue upstream to a second footbridge. Cross this bridge then follow the gorge back downstream to a wooden kissing gate. Pass through and continue to a main road. Go right along the road, over

WALK 32: RUMBLING BRIDGE GORGE

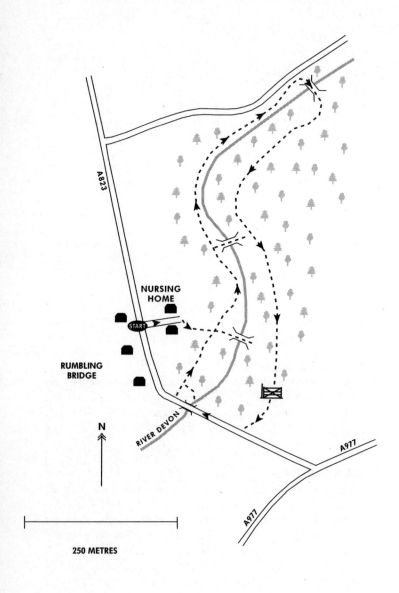

A823

NURSING
HOME

START

RUMBLING
BRIDGE

N

RIVER DEVON

A977

A977

250 METRES

a bridge, then right through a metal gate and on to another footpath. A deviation to the right here will provide an interesting view of the stone bridge. Continue along the path, beside the river, to the notice-board and then return to the car park.

Heading towards East Lomond

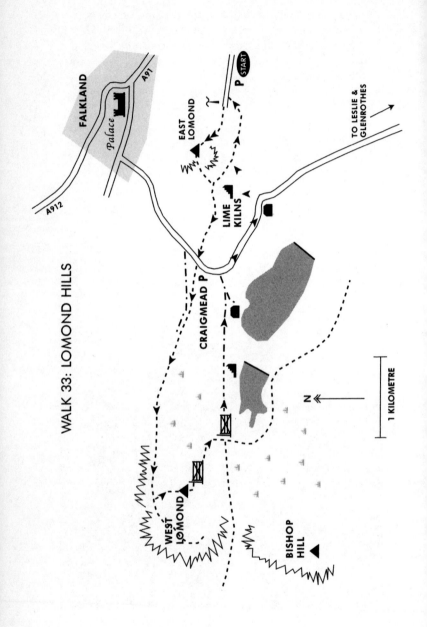

WALK 33: LOMOND HILLS

FALKLAND

Palace

A91

A912

EAST LOMOND

LIME KILNS

CRAIGMEAD P

TO LESLIE & GLENROTHES

WEST LOMOND

BISHOP HILL

N

1 KILOMETRE

P START

33. LOMOND HILLS

ORDNANCE SURVEY MAP NO	LANDRANGER 58 & 59
	PATHFINDER 372 & 373
DISTANCE FROM EDINBURGH	60 KM (37 ML)
WALKING DISTANCE/	14 KM (9 ML) / 8 KM (5 ML)
SHORT VERSION	
AMOUNT OF CLIMBING	450 M (1,500 FT) /
	290 M (950 FT)
ESTIMATED TIME	5 HR / 3 HR

DESCRIPTION A hill walk over the two highest hills in Fife. From the summits it is possible to see the entire Kingdom of Fife. However, hill mist is very common so be sure to take adequate clothing, a map and a compass. Also, the route is very rugged and good hill-walking boots are essential.

START AND FINISH East Lomond car park near Falkland, Fife. NO 252 059

HOW TO GET THERE By car, cross the Forth Road Bridge, follow the M90 motorway to Junction 2A, then the A92. Pass Kirkcaldy and Glenrothes. Turn left towards Falkland on the A912 for a mile, then turn left on a single-track road up to the car park at the base of East Lomond. There is no public transport to this walk.

WALK DIRECTIONS
From the car park, take the signposted footpath beside the radio masts. Follow the path up the shoulder then climb steeply on to the summit of East Lomond (424 m / 1,393 ft, triangulation point).

Descend an equally steep path on the far side to join a track just above some old lime workings. Follow this track down to an asphalt road and Craigmead car park. Take the path at the rear of the car park, over a stile, then left up a grassy track beside a stone wall. Stay on the track for 3½ km to the base of West Lomond and a sign to the left marking a closed path. Continue along the track a little further, to its highest point, then turn left and climb steeply on to the summit of West Lomond (522 m / 1,712 ft, triangulation pillar, cairn, several stone enclosures).

Head off the summit in the direction southsouthwest (204°). The path down is just as steep as the path up. By a stone wall, electric fence and signpost at the bottom of the steep part, turn left and follow the wall for 200 m to a stile. Climb over and turn left on to a fairly thin path over small, heather-clad hills, then descend steeply to a junction of paths. Turn left, climb a stile over a stone wall and walk along a grassy track above Harperleas Reservoir. Once beyond the first reservoir the track gradually becomes more substantial. After passing a white-walled farmhouse on the right, the track gradually ascends and finally ends at an asphalt road.

Turn right and walk along the road for a little more than a kilometre. Pass a house on the right then, at a bend, climb a stile on the left and ascend steeply to a marker post. (Other than the marker post, there is nothing to indicate the route, so follow the arrow on the post in a straight line across the grazing land.) On reaching a stile over another stone wall, climb over and head across to some old lime workings. Bear right and follow an ascending path over grazing land to where two stone walls meet. Climb over and follow the track on the far side, around the base of East Lomond, back to the car park.

SHORT VERSION Begin and finish at Craigmead car park (on the Leslie–Falkland road) and miss out East Lomond. This saves 6 km.

34. THE CHAIN WALK, EAST NEUK OF FIFE

ORDNANCE SURVEY MAP NO	LANDRANGER 59
	PATHFINDER 374
DISTANCE FROM EDINBURGH	64 KM (40 ML)
WALKING DISTANCE	9 KM (6 ML)
AMOUNT OF CLIMBING	70 M (230 FT)
ESTIMATED TIME	3 HR

DESCRIPTION This scenic coastal route includes a particularly exciting section around the base of some cliffs which, when the tide is in, is only passable by perilously hanging out over the raging sea holding on to chains secured to the cliff face. It is not for the faint-hearted! However, there is a detour for the less adventurous and for when a high tide makes passage impossible.

START AND FINISH Elie, Fife. NT 496 998

HOW TO GET THERE By bus from Edinburgh use service FS 57. By car, cross the Forth Road Bridge and head north on the M90. At Junction 2A, turn east on to the A92. At the roundabout just beyond Kirkcaldy, turn on to the A915 to Leven then follow signs for St Andrews. At Upper Largo, continue directly ahead on to the A917 to Elie. There are several car parks and other parking areas in Elie. Parking and starting in Earlsferry will shorten the walk by 2 km.

WALK DIRECTIONS

Walk down to the harbour and turn right (west) along a road above the foreshore, then between buildings to a beach. Cross the sand, then climb up to another road and turn left. Pass some cottages and continue directly ahead on a grassy track between a stone wall and a cliff top. At a corner, turn right on to a path over rough grassland down to a golf course and a large sandy bay. From here the cliffs

WALK 34: THE CHAIN WALK, EAST NEUK OF FIFE

of Kincraig Point and a huge cave may be seen on the far side of the bay. Cross to the cliffs by either walking over the sands or following the path along the top of the beach. The detour that avoids the chain section climbs steeply up the cliffs at this point.

To continue the main route, clamber over the rocks at the base of the cliffs. Soon a well-worn path in the rock will become evident. Follow this, climbing over progressively steeper rocks and round a precipice to an inlet which leads to an enormous cave and the first of the chains. Holding on to the chain, descend then transverse the vertical wall. There are footholds but some are far apart. Cross the loose rocks that slope up to the cave, then climb out towards the sea on a small rocky promontory. Straddle across to the far wall, then climb up and over and continue on the path around the peninsula. There are several more ascents and descents requiring the use of chains. On reaching flat, rocky ground with a deep narrow channel running into the cliff face, turn back and climb the steep grassy bank to the cliff top.

Walk across to two wooden benches and proceed down the path ahead, following it along the edge of a field to a caravan park. Walk through the park to the entrance, then take the road to the right. At a T-junction, turn left on to a track. Pass by a farm (Grangehill) then bear right. Pass some cottages and take the sandy track over the golf course. Turn right then left to pass through Earlsferry to Elie.

DETOUR At the start of the cliffs take the path up the steep, grassy bank to an old fortification. Walk along the cliff top, past a triangulation point and mast on Kincraig Hill, and down to rejoin the main route.

SOUTHERN REGION

WALK 35: IN THE STEPS OF ROBERT LOUIS STEVENSON

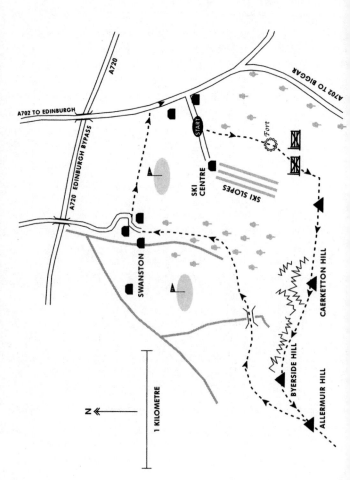

35. IN THE STEPS OF ROBERT LOUIS STEVENSON

ORDNANCE SURVEY MAP NO	LANDRANGER 66
	PATHFINDER 420
DISTANCE FROM EDINBURGH	9 KM (5 ML)
WALKING DISTANCE	7 KM (4½ ML)
AMOUNT OF CLIMBING	440 M (1,443 FT)
ESTIMATED TIME	3 HR

DESCRIPTION A short but steep hill walk close to Edinburgh, providing a wonderful panorama over Edinburgh and the Firth of Forth. Robert Louis Stevenson spent much of his childhood in the picturesque village of Swanston (through which the route passes) and loved to wander on these hills. There are good paths throughout but good walking or mountain boots are advisable. For a small fee, one can take a slightly different ascent and use the chair lift (this may be used by walkers as well as by skiers).

START AND FINISH Lay-by just inside Hillend Country Park (or at the Ski Centre). NT 250 670

HOW TO GET THERE By car, take the A702 through the Edinburgh suburbs of Morningside and Fairmilehead. Just beyond the Edinburgh Bypass, turn right into Hillend Country Park. By bus, use service LRT 4.

WALK DIRECTIONS
Walk along the grassy bank, away from the Park entrance, until you are just beyond the trees on the left. Turn left and climb steeply up the ridge between the trees and the artificial ski slopes to a small summit (an ancient fort). Continue climbing to a fence that traverses the hill at the same level as the top of the ski slopes. Here there are two stiles. Go over the right-hand stile and climb the steep, zigzag path directly ahead to a large cairn, fence and stone

wall. Turn right and follow the wall a little downhill, then up to another large cairn on the summit of Caerketton Hill (478 m / 1,567 ft). Continue beside the wall and fence, down into a gully, then up over a lesser hill (Byerside Hill) and on along the top of the crags to the summit of Allermuir Hill (493 m / 1,617 ft, triangulation pillar, view indicator).

Turn around. Bear a little left and take the steeply descending path off Allermuir Hill, then pass below some crags and scree to a golf course. Follow the well-worn path along the top of the golf course, then alongside a small burn down to the village of Swanston.

Pass through the village. Where the road bends left, go straight ahead, through a gate and past a footpath signpost on to a path between a golf course and agricultural land. On reaching a main road, turn right and walk along the road for 300 m to return to the entrance to Hillend Country Park.

36. LOANHEAD, LASSWADE & POLTON

ORDNANCE SURVEY MAP NO	LANDRANGER 66
	PATHFINDER 420
DISTANCE FROM EDINBURGH	9½ KM (6 ML)
WALKING DISTANCE	6½ KM (4 ML)
AMOUNT OF CLIMBING	50 M (160 FT)
ESTIMATED TIME	2 HR

DESCRIPTION An easy ramble on established paths across fields, through woodlands and alongside the River North Esk in a scenic area close to Edinburgh.

START AND FINISH car park near crossroads in centre of Loanhead. NT 283 656

HOW TO GET THERE By car, take the A701 to the Edinburgh Bypass then turn left to Loanhead. At the traffic lights in the centre of Loanhead, turn left and immediately left again into a car park beside a disused railway. There are also frequent bus services from Edinburgh (LRT 87, 87A; SMT C70).

WALK DIRECTIONS
Walk away from the centre of Loanhead, past the old railway station (now a private residence) and along a path beside some old railway sidings to a road. Cross over and take the track to Loanhead Hospital. At the hospital entrance, continue straight ahead on a path along the edge of a field and beside a small stream. Halfway along the field, step left through a gap in the hedge and continue on the far side of the burn. Pass through a wooden gate into woodlands then follow a gravel track. When a busy road comes into view, turn right on to another track that runs parallel to the road until it reaches another road. Cross over, go right for a few paces then first left into a lane behind some houses. Follow this to Lasswade Cemetery and the

WALK 36: LOANHEAD, LASSWADE & POLTON

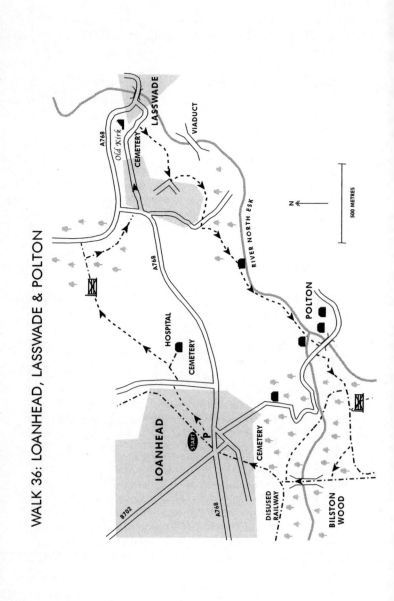

remains of the old kirk (worth a visit). Then go downhill. Halfway down, turn right on to a steeply ascending footpath. Follow this along the ridge, which overlooks the river North Esk with its weir and a viaduct that once carried a railway to the Polton paper mills.

At the end of this path, turn left on to another path that winds around to the right beside a stone wall. At a fork beside a wooden barrier, keep right and continue beside the wall. On reaching a country lane, cross over and take the footpath opposite. The first section of this path descends quite steeply and some of the sloping concrete slabs can be very slippery when wet, so take particular care here. Follow the path past a field where horses frequently graze. Continue past a house, then close to the river, to the tiny village of Polton.

Go right along the road for a few paces, then left through a gap in a stone wall and up some steps on to a knife-edge ridge. Down below to the left is the River North Esk and remains of paper mills; to the right, out of sight in the woodlands, is Bilston Burn. On reaching a dirt track, continue straight ahead along the edge of Bilston Woods. Near the end of the woodlands, enter the woods and follow the inner edge of the woods. Cross a stile to reach an old railway track.

Turn right and cross the recently renovated railway viaduct over Bilston Glen. On the far side, bear right along an old railway track that, at the time of writing, still has some of the tracks in place (this section is soon to be converted to a proper footpath). Clamber up the right embankment on to a path beside a stone wall, then on to the Loanhead Cemetery access road. Follow this road back into the centre of Loanhead.

WALK 37: THE MAIDEN CASTLE & BILSTON WOODS

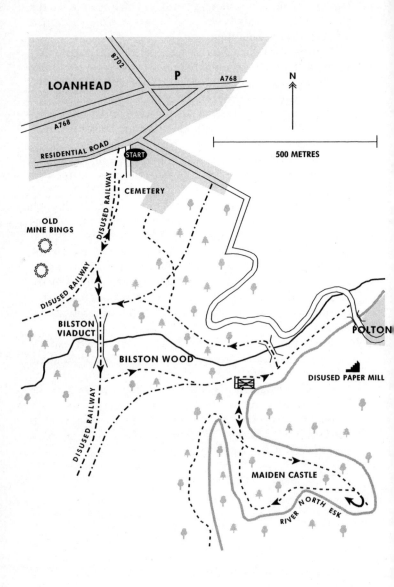

37. THE MAIDEN CASTLE & BILSTON WOODS

ORDNANCE SURVEY MAP NO	LANDRANGER 66
	PATHFINDER 420
DISTANCE FROM EDINBURGH	11 KM (7 ML)
WALKING DISTANCE	5 KM (3 ML)
AMOUNT OF CLIMBING	135 M (440 FT)
ESTIMATED TIME	1¾ HR

DESCRIPTION The Maiden Castle is not a real castle at all, but a small hill almost completely surrounded by a river so that it may seem like a castle. However it is rich in tales of fairies and goblins. The walk itself will take you through dense woodlands and open farmland, along a knife-edge ridge, into a riverine gorge and over a recently restored Victorian railway viaduct. There is a site close to the river that is very suitable for a picnic. Note that the path along the ridge is eroded in places. Take care not to fall, or to cause further erosion. Note also that the track through the woods can be very muddy.

START AND FINISH Loanhead, Midlothian. NT 283 656

HOW TO GET THERE Frequent bus service from Edinburgh (LRT 87; SMT C70). By car, take the A701 towards Penicuik. Just beyond the Edinburgh Bypass, turn left to Loanhead. At the traffic lights in the centre of Loanhead, turn left and immediately left again to reach a car park.

WALK DIRECTIONS
Return to the traffic lights and cross to the statue of a horn opposite. Cross the green then, at the police station, go straight ahead. Just before the road crosses an old railway, turn left towards a cemetery. At the entrance gates, step right and follow a narrow path which runs beside the cemetery wall then along an old railway track. On reaching

an open area, bear left and cross the recently renovated Bilston Viaduct. At the far end, turn left on to a path along the inner edge of a woodland.

Where this path emerges on to a track, turn left. Just beyond the field on the right, turn right through a gate (or over the adjacent stile) on to a path across rough grassland; then along a knife-edge ridge; then steeply down through gorse bushes to a narrow neck of land between two arms of the River North Esk. The area ahead is the Maiden Castle. Continue directly ahead until you reach the water's edge with cliffs on the far side – a good picnic spot.

After exploring the various paths over the Maiden Castle, retrace your steps back up through the gorse to the gate and stile encountered earlier. Turn right and follow the track round to the left, then steeply downhill through Bilston Woods to a stone bridge. Cross over and go left, still on the track, now climbing the far side of the glen. At a fork near the top of the ascent, go left on a path to return to Bilston Viaduct. Climb up on to the old railway track and return to the start via the outward route.

38. THE DALKEITH CIRCUIT

ORDNANCE SURVEY MAP NO	LANDRANGER 66
	PATHFINDER 420
DISTANCE FROM EDINBURGH	11 KM (7 ML)
WALKING DISTANCE	8 KM (5 ML)
AMOUNT OF CLIMBING	50 M (160 FT)
ESTIMATED TIME	2¾ HR

DESCRIPTION This fascinating circular route includes a sixteenth-century estate with rhododendrons, ornamental trees and ice house, mixed woodland and many remnants of past industry. Regrettably, it is necessary to walk along the busy A7 road for a short part of the route.

START AND FINISH Dalkeith, Midlothian. NT 332 674

HOW TO GET THERE Frequent bus service from Edinburgh (LRT 3, 30, 82; SMT 79, 80; LOW 30, 95). By car, take the Dalkeith Road (A68) and park in one of the free car parks in the town centre.

WALK DIRECTIONS
From the centre of town, head south on the A68, past a supermarket, garage and school. Cross the River South Esk then take the second entrance on the right. Follow the track to the river then walk upstream, past an old stone bridge, into woodlands. This path meanders beside the river for 1½ km before reaching a main road (B703). On the way you will pass Newbattle Abbey (now a college) on the far side of the river, a footbridge and an ice house.

On approaching the road, duck beneath a large black pipe then climb some steps and cross the road. Pass through an old stone gateway opposite to enter Lady Lothian's Plantation. Walk across to the river, then climb a steep bank to the left to join a more substantial footpath through the

WALK 38: THE DALKEITH CIRCUIT

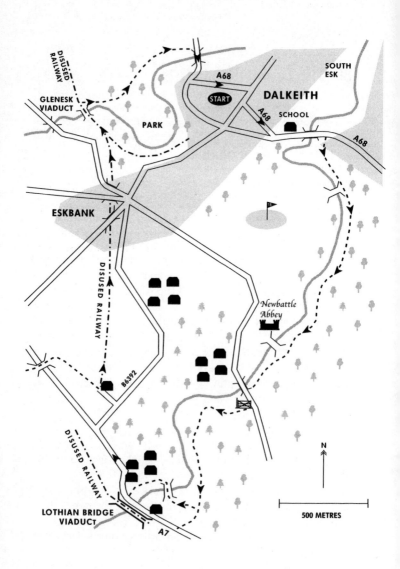

DISUSED RAILWAY

GLENESK VIADUCT

PARK

A68

START

DALKEITH

SOUTH ESK

SCHOOL

A68

A68

ESKBANK

DISUSED RAILWAY

B6392

Newbattle Abbey

N

DISUSED RAILWAY

LOTHIAN BRIDGE VIADUCT

A7

500 METRES

woodlands. Just before reaching another busy road (you should hear the traffic ahead), turn right and descend to the river. Cross the new bridge over the river and go left to emerge on to the main road (A7) opposite Lothian Bridge – an impressive 23-span viaduct. This viaduct was built by the North British Railway in the 1840s and, until the line closed in 1969, carried the steam express trains to London.

Turn right and follow the road round a bend to a roundabout. Turn right on to the B6392 then first left down a lane, past some cottages, to Hardengreen Farm. At the farm, go left for a few paces then right on to a tarmac track. This track follows the route of the 'Innocent Railway' along which horse-drawn trains once plied between Lothian Bridge and Edinburgh.

At the end of the asphalt track, pass beneath a stone bridge. Climb some steps on the right to reach the old Eskbank Station (now a private residence). Walk along to a main road and go right to reach a roundabout. Take the first exit left (B6392). Just beyond the last house on the right, turn right on to a path and descend back on to the old railway track. Follow this across Glenesk Viaduct then immediately turn right and climb some steps.

After a short distance, where steps descend into Ironmills Park, turn left and follow a stone wall along the edge of woods above the Park to reach a main road (A68). Turn right and follow a path that runs parallel to the road to return to the centre of Dalkeith.

WALK 39: THE HEART OF MIDLOTHIAN – SOUTH ESK VALLEY

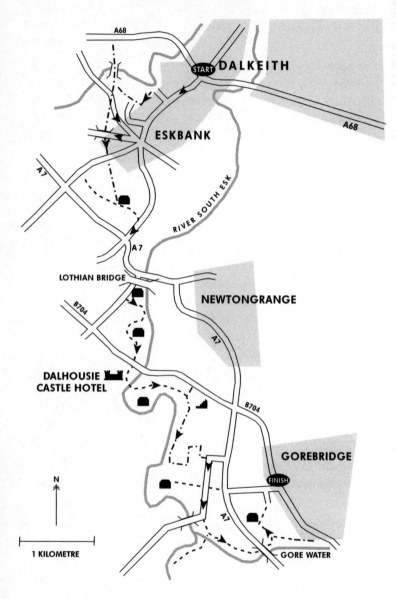

39. THE HEART OF MIDLOTHIAN — SOUTH ESK VALLEY

ORDNANCE SURVEY MAP NO	LANDRANGER 66
	PATHFINDER 420
DISTANCE FROM EDINBURGH	11 KM (7 ML)
WALKING DISTANCE	11 KM (7 ML)
AMOUNT OF CLIMBING	190 M (623 FT)
ESTIMATED TIME	3¾ HR

DESCRIPTION An interesting walk through a variety of terrain following rights-of-way for almost its entire length. If the short section from Dalhousie Castle to the ruined church is too overgrown or wet to permit passage, use the adjacent B704.

START Centre of Dalkeith. NT 332 673
FINISH Gorebridge. NT 341 621
BUS LINK SMT 80

HOW TO GET THERE By car, take the Dalkeith Road to Dalkeith and park in one of the town's many car parks. Alternatively, use one of the frequent bus services from Edinburgh (LOW 30; LRT 3, 30, 82; SMT 79, 86).

WALK DIRECTIONS
Walk southeast along the High Street then Eskbank Road. Just beyond the park on the left, turn right over an old railway bridge and immediately left on to an asphalt path. Follow this to an open area close to a viaduct and bear left along a disused tarmac road. At a right-angle bend, climb the bank directly ahead on to a main road. Cross over, go left to a roundabout then first right (towards 'Loanhead'). After a few paces, at the Eskbank Trading Store, turn left, past a house (once Eskbank Station), then descend right on to an old railway track (now a tarmac path). At the end of

this path, turn left then right, along a lane, to a main road. Go right along the road to a roundabout then left along the A7, round a bend, to a huge stone viaduct (Lothian Bridge).

Turn right beneath the viaduct. Just beyond a cottage on the left, turn left on to a dirt track to descend to the River South Esk. Now follow a path through trees beside the river to a farm surrounded by a high stone wall. Walk around the farm, then along the farm access road to a main road. Just before the road, turn left on to the Dalhousie Castle Hotel access road.

At the entrance to the hotel grounds, pass through a gap in a wall on the left and follow a path (right-of-way) around the perimeter of the lawns then over a bridge across the river. Immediately turn left on to a thin path through rhododendron bushes above the river, then uphill to a small area of rough grassland. Cross to a gate and turn right on a track: this passes the ruins of Old Cockpen Church then descends a little and runs above the South Esk. Stay on the track as it swings left, away from the river. When the track ends at a high bank, go left along the bottom of the bank. At the highest point, climb over the bank then pass between grazing pastures to reach a farm track. Turn right. At a minor road go right, passing beneath a low bridge, until the road turns and crosses the South Esk (Trotter's Bridge).

Enter Gore Glen just before the bridge. After a few paces, take a left fork and follow the Gore Water (a tributary of the South Esk) for 800 m. Pass with the burn beneath a high road bridge, then immediately climb steeply up to a track. Follow this to the left, past a house, and on to some sports fields, a road and a new residential area. At a T-junction, turn right and walk along Engine Road to reach the Hunters Tavern and main road in Gorebridge.

40. PENTLAND HILLS

ORDNANCE SURVEY MAP NO	LANDRANGER 66
	PATHFINDER 419 & 420
DISTANCE FROM EDINBURGH	13½ KM (8½ ML)
WALKING DISTANCE	12½ KM (8 ML)
AMOUNT OF CLIMBING	695 M (2,280 FT)
ESTIMATED TIME	5 HR

DESCRIPTION This route follows the main ridge of hills through the Pentland Hills. There is a fair amount of climbing but it is not too difficult; the going is quite easy and the scenery is fantastic. It may be completed by anyone of reasonable fitness and without any special knowledge. But be warned, the wind on the tops can be very chilling – even in summer – so take a sweater and a windproof anorak. Good walking boots are essential. Beware also, the return leg is along an asphalt track sometimes used by fast-moving mountain bikes.

START AND FINISH Car park beside the Countryside Information Centre, Flotterstone. NT 234 631

HOW TO GET THERE By bus, use service WS 100. By car, take the A702 through the Edinburgh suburbs of Morningside and Fairmilehead to the Edinburgh Bypass (A720). Continue on the A702 for a further 3 ml to Flotterstone. Turn right and pass the Flotterstone Inn to reach the car park. This is a very popular area, so arrive early or park closer to the main road.

WALK DIRECTIONS
Walk along the tree-lined lane, past the Countryside Information Centre, to a bend in the road to the right. Here, leave the road through a gate on the left. Pass through a picnic site and cross the footbridge over a small burn. Turn

WALK 40: PENTLAND HILLS

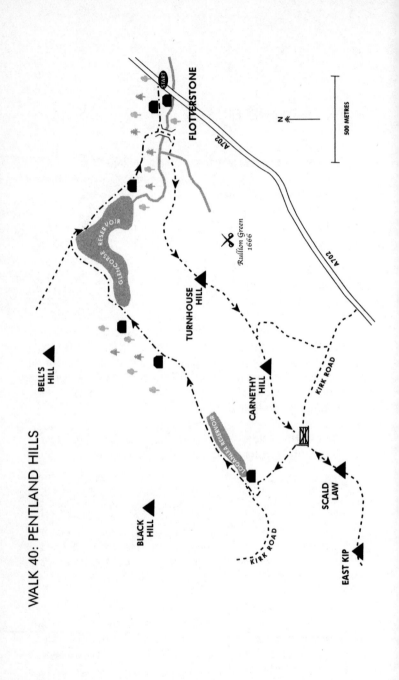

FLOTTERSTONE

START

A702

A702

N

500 METRES

Rullion Green
1666

GLENCORSE RESERVOIR

LOGANLEA RESERVOIR

BELL'S HILL

BLACK HILL

TURNHOUSE HILL

CARNETHY HILL

KIRK ROAD

KIRK ROAD

SCALD LAW

EAST KIP

right. After a few paces, ford a small burn then climb the ridge that separates two streams. From here, follow the path all the way up to the summit of Turnhouse Hill (506 m / 1,660 ft). Continue straight ahead (southwest), down a ridge and across a col between hills. Then go up another ridge to the top of Carnethy Hill (576 m / 1,889 ft, cairn – it is thought to have been used for sun worship in the distant past, but was definitely used as a wind shelter by the author in the not-too-distant past).

From the summit, bear a little right (westerly) to descend the shoulder of the hill down to the saddle between Carnethy Hill and Scald Law. Across this saddle runs a very well-worn path, the Kirk Road, so named because it was once used by Balerno residents to reach their church in Penicuik. Cross the Kirk Road, climb the stile over a fence and proceed steeply up the path directly ahead to the summit of Scald Law (579 m / 1,899 ft, triangulation pillar, highest point in the Pentland Hills).

Turn around and descend back to the stile on the Kirk Road. Turn left and follow the path down into a broad valley with an isolated farmstead (The Howe). Cross the valley floor and stream then turn right. Pass the farmhouse and follow an asphalt track past Loganlea Reservoir, then Glencorse Reservoir, before finally arriving back at Flotterstone.

WALK 41: THE FORGOTTEN GLEN, ROSLIN

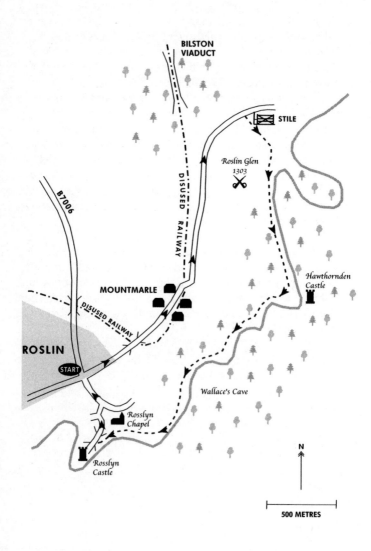

BILSTON
VIADUCT

STILE

B7006

DISUSED RAILWAY

Roslin Glen
1303

MOUNTMARLE

Hawthornden
Castle

DISUSED RAILWAY

ROSLIN

START

Wallace's Cave

Rosslyn
Chapel

Rosslyn
Castle

N

500 METRES

41. THE FORGOTTEN GLEN, ROSLIN

ORDNANCE SURVEY MAP NO	LANDRANGER 66
	PATHFINDER 420
DISTANCE FROM EDINBURGH	14 KM (9 ML)
WALKING DISTANCE	6 KM (4 ML)
AMOUNT OF CLIMBING	150 M (500 FT)
ESTIMATED TIME	2¼ HR

DESCRIPTION This route passes through the lower part of Roslin Glen. This part of the glen is particularly scenic and was very popular amongst poets, walkers and picnickers 100 years ago, but nowadays seems to have been forgotten by most people. It is also steeped in history. One of the biggest battles against the English (32,000 combatants) was fought here in 1303; Robert the Bruce hid in caverns beneath Hawthornden Castle; William Wallace in another; and General Monck's forces camped here on their way north. Towards the end of the route is Rosslyn Castle and, nearby, the beautiful and mysterious Rosslyn Chapel. The chapel is open to the public (small admission charge) and is well worth a visit.

START AND FINISH Roslin, Midlothian. NT 272 632

HOW TO GET THERE Frequent bus service from Edinburgh (LRT 87A; SMT 315). By car, take the A701 towards Penicuik. Two miles beyond the Edinburgh Bypass, turn left at a roundabout on to the B7006 to Roslin. Park on the side of a road in the village.

WALK DIRECTIONS
At the Old Original Roslin Inn, turn left (northeast) into Manse Road. Beyond the houses continue on the track straight ahead to Mountmarle Research Station. Walkers are permitted to pass through; but do not leave the road and do

keep any dogs on a tight lead. On the far side, follow the track through a gap in an old railway embankment, then past fields and woodlands to a gate and stile on the right.

Climb over and follow the path through rough grass, then gorse, along a knife-edge ridge. Descend a steep section and at the bottom turn right on to a path that leads across to a wooden gate close to the river. Climb over the gate and continue along a path which heads upstream and gradually rises through woodlands. Just over the top of this incline it is possible to glimpse Hawthornden Castle through the trees on the far side of the gorge. Stay on the most prominent path, following it down to the river's edge for a while, then going back up into the woods and finally out on to a sloping meadow below Rosslyn Chapel. Directly ahead is Rosslyn Castle.

Walk across to the foot of the castle ramparts and turn right to pass beneath a high archway. Take a few more paces, then turn right and climb a flight of steps to the castle access road. Follow this uphill, turning right at a cemetery, to a T-junction. Turn right here to visit the chapel, or left to return to Roslin village.

42. PENICUIK TO ROSLIN RAILWAY WALK

ORDNANCE SURVEY MAP NO	LANDRANGER 66
	PATHFINDER 420 & 434
DISTANCE FROM EDINBURGH	14 KM (9 ML)
WALKING DISTANCE	8½ KM (5½ ML)
AMOUNT OF CLIMBING	135 M (443 FT)
ESTIMATED TIME	2¾ HR

DESCRIPTION A fascinating walk beside the River North Esk on an old railway track, now a walking and cycling track, then through the upper section of the scenic Roslin Glen. Along the way are traces of past industry, railway tunnels, a viaduct, the remnants of a gunpowder mill, a castle and Rosslyn Chapel – one of the most beautiful and mysterious buildings in Scotland.

START Penicuik Town Hall (red-stone building with clock in the centre of Penicuik). NT 236 599
FINISH The village of Roslin, Midlothian. NT 272 632
BUS LINK SMT 141 or 315

HOW TO GET THERE By car, take the A701 towards Penicuik. Two miles beyond the Edinburgh Bypass, turn left at a roundabout on to the B7006 to Roslin. Park in the street and take the bus to Penicuik. Bus SMT 315 serves both Roslin and Penicuik.

WALK DIRECTIONS
Head west along the High Street, round the bend to the left into Bridge Street and downhill to a bridge over the River North Esk. Turn left just before the bridge. Then turn right over a footbridge across the river and on to a footpath. This path passes two ponds then runs beside the river for a short distance before joining an old railway track. Follow the track past the remains of an old paper mill on the left, then

WALK 42: PENICUIK TO ROSLIN RAILWAY WALK

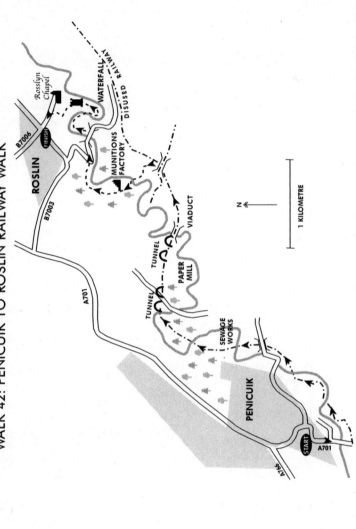

through a gate. From here the track is asphalt as far as a sewage works, then becomes dirt again. Follow the track round a bend, past the remains of a station, over the river and through a tunnel.

At the far end, take the signposted path past a paper mill. Rejoin the railway track and follow it through a second tunnel and over a viaduct, then up a long, straight gradual incline. When the track passes beneath a road bridge, pass underneath and immediately turn left up a few steps, and through a gate to enter the Roslin Glen Nature Reserve. Follow the path down to the river and over a bridge. From here the main path leads through the glen; but it is more interesting to descend the steps on the right and walk through the old gunpowder mill before rejoining the main track. When steam trains ran along the top of the cliffs, the track was enclosed in a tunnel of corrugated iron to prevent sparks from locomotives igniting the gunpowder. However, you will see from the occasional blackened wall that accidents still sometimes happened.

When a road is reached head towards the river, cross it and immediately turn left. Follow the river around a flat area (now a car park but it once contained linen bleach fields). Cross the footbridge over the river and turn right to continue beside the river as far as a waterfall. Now retrace your steps for a few paces then head up towards the castle, stepping through a break in the wall on the right to reach an old yew tree beside the castle dungeons. Walk around the base of the castle then through a high archway. Ascend the steps to the right and follow the road up, past a cemetery, to a T-junction. Turn right to visit the Chapel, or left to reach Roslin.

WALK 43: GORE GLEN

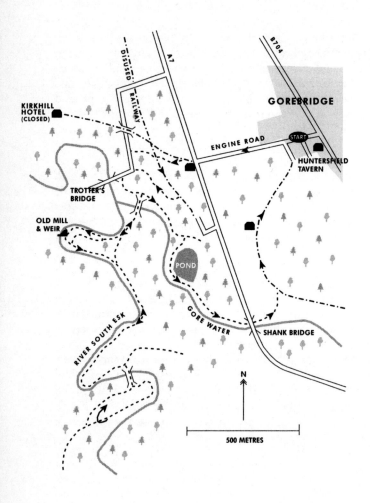

KIRKHILL
HOTEL
(CLOSED)

DISUSED RAILWAY

A7

B704

GOREBRIDGE

ENGINE ROAD

START

HUNTERSFIELD
TAVERN

TROTTER'S
BRIDGE

OLD MILL
& WEIR

POND

RIVER SOUTH ESK

GORE WATER

SHANK BRIDGE

N

500 METRES

43. GORE GLEN

ORDNANCE SURVEY MAP NO	LANDRANGER 66
	PATHFINDER 420
DISTANCE FROM EDINBURGH	16 KM (10 ML)
WALKING DISTANCE	6 KM (4 ML)
AMOUNT OF CLIMBING	90 M (295 FT)
ESTIMATED TIME	2 HR

DESCRIPTION This is a beautiful woodland walk beside the River South Esk and Gore Water. Along the River South Esk there is a small meadow which makes an ideal site for a picnic but everything must be carried in and all litter carried out again. Note that this walk can be considerably shortened by starting and finishing at Trotter's Bridge.

START AND FINISH Gore Glen car park off Engine Road, Gorebridge. NT 339 621

HOW TO GET THERE By car, follow the A7 then B704 to Gorebridge. At the Huntersfield Tavern, turn right into Engine Road then second left to reach the car park. There are also frequent bus services from Edinburgh to Gorebridge (LRT 30; SMT 80).

WALK DIRECTIONS
Walk down Engine Road, carefully cross the busy A7 and take the gravel road directly opposite. A few paces beyond the cottage, turn left into the forest on a path that parallels the road for a short distance then swings left on to what was once a railway line. After a further 100 m, where the track leaves the denser part of the forest, turn right on to a path beside a fence. Follow this downhill, round to the right, then down a flight of steps to a road bridge (Trotter's Bridge) over the River South Esk.

Do not cross the bridge but turn left through a gate on to

a footpath. After a few paces, at a fork, turn right to cross the Gore Water (a tributary of the South Esk). Follow the path beside the main river. Here there is a choice: take either the main path above the river, or the narrower path by the water's edge. The latter is more interesting as it passes through an old mill, but care is required when negotiating the second building because part of the river flows through it. The two paths rejoin just beyond the mill.

Whichever path is chosen, stay beside the river. Follow the twists and turns of the river, past some rock outcrops, to an old stone bridge. Cross over and explore the flat, open area beyond (an ideal picnic spot).

From here retrace your steps as far as the footbridge over the Gore Water, then turn right and follow the path beside the Gore Water. The path leaves the stream near a small weir but, if you keep right, you will soon regain the water. Follow the stream beneath a high road bridge then climb steeply to the left up to a track. Go left, over an old bing and past an isolated house, back to the car park.

44. THE GOREBRIDGE CIRCULAR RAMBLE

ORDNANCE SURVEY MAP NO	LANDRANGER 66
	PATHFINDER 420 & 434
DISTANCE FROM EDINBURGH	16 KM (10 ML)
WALKING DISTANCE	15½ KM (10 ML)
AMOUNT OF CLIMBING	370 M (1,200 FT)
ESTIMATED TIME	6 HR

DESCRIPTION Long and challenging but very rewarding. The route passes through agricultural land, woodland and along river banks. There are some splendid views *en route* and two castles, Crichton and Borthwick, the former of which is open to visitors.

The entire route follows rights-of-way except the final section along a disused railway track, the thirty-metre portion between Gore Water, and the farm cottages, and the section through Currie Wood. The Currie Wood route described is the proposed diversion of the right-of-way which presently passes through the adjacent farm and horse-grazing area and has been causing disruption to farming activities.

Please note that some sections of this route have been infrequently used of late and have become overgrown. Some exploration may be required. Also, there are a couple of burns to cross, a few stiles that have fallen into disrepair and some new fences that have been erected without stiles. When climbing over these fences take care not to damage yourself or the landowner's property.

It is recommended that walkers wear boots and some form of protection to the legs from nettles.

START AND FINISH Gore Glen car park off Engine Road, Gorebridge. NT 339 621

HOW TO GET THERE By car, follow the A7 then B704 to Gorebridge. At the Huntersfield Tavern turn right into

WALK 44: THE GOREBRIDGE CIRCULAR RAMBLE

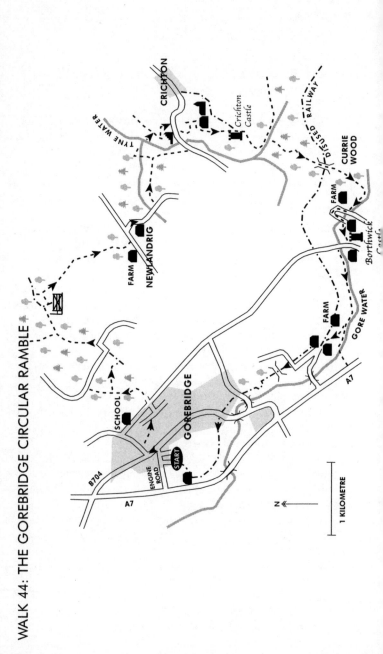

Engine Road, then second left to reach the car park. There are also frequent bus services from Edinburgh to Gorebridge (LRT 30; SMT 80).

WALK DIRECTIONS

Return to Engine Road and walk through the lane opposite to reach the main road through Gorebridge. Cross to the road opposite and turn right on to a footpath along a green. At the end, go right then left along residential roads, then over a grassy embankment and a road. Carry on through a metal gate and along a footpath up to an open cast mine. Follow the path around to the left of the mine. On entering some woodlands, turn right and ascend out of the woods, then left along a track for a few paces to a bend in a minor road. Go straight ahead, along the road, for 50 m. At the next bend go straight ahead, between metal posts, on to a footpath into more woodlands.

At a fork go right (left leads to a cultivated field). Gradually ascend out of the woods on to the top of a ridge, where a track will be encountered. Turn back along the track for a few paces towards a gate; then turn left over rough grass then through a little gorse, past a corner of a field and a stile, into a coniferous woodland. Passage here may appear difficult but there is a way through – just follow the old stone wall on the left. On the far side of the woods cross an old stile and turn right. Descend along the edge of fields, over a farm track and down into woodlands, then past a poultry farm to the tiny village of Newlandrig.

Go left along the road then next right. After 700 m, just beyond a bridge over a small burn, turn left into woodlands. The path here may be difficult to distinguish but it generally follows a gradually descending track, now overgrown with trees, along the edge of the woodland. On reaching a fence, turn left and descend steeply to a small burn. Step over and follow the burn out of the woodland. Cross a small flood plain (following a stone wall) to a larger burn. Use the stepping stones to ford it, then ascend to the right. At a track go right again and, just before an old lime kiln, go left up to a road. Cross into the woodlands opposite, bear right then swing left and climb steeply. At the top, go right along a track towards a house; then right, then left to circumnavigate the house. Continue along the path to Crichton Castle.

Descend past the castle chapel and go over a small burn to a second burn. Follow this for a few paces, then leave the path and step across the burn. Walk across a flat area of rough grassland to a grassy embankment with a path rising up to a wooden gate. Climb up to the gate and go around to the left, through gorse and bracken, to the corner of a fenced grazing pasture. Follow the right-hand edge of this grazing land to an old railway bridge. Cross over and bear right, following a hedgerow along the edge of more grazing land, over a small hill, then down into a woodland (Currie Wood). Continue downhill through the woods, following a fence on the right. When the fence turns right. When the fence turns right continue straight ahead for another 10 m to reach a more substantial path. Follow this to the right. On reaching the edge of the woodland after a steep descent, double back left beside a fence. Turn right through a pedestrian gate and on alongside the edge of a farm to a minor road.

Go right along the road, then left at a high stone wall and left again at the next corner of the wall. Follow this lane over a burn (Gore Water) then, at the entrance to a house, climb a stile to the right and walk across grazing land beneath Borthwick Castle to a road. Use the road bridge to cross the Gore Water. Then go left on to a path between the stream and a fence. From here the right-of-way roughly follows the course of the Gore Water. After 1½ km, just as farm buildings come into sight up to the right and the fence ends, leave the Gore Water and gradually ascend on a track across grazing land, past a large tree, towards some houses. Pass the houses and join a road at a hairpin bend. Head uphill. Halfway up the ascent, shift on to an old railway track on the right.

After a further 700 m the track crosses some open ground before entering a thickly wooded area. Further passage is impossible but a short detour to the left will soon return you to the railway track and easier going. (Nowadays it is difficult to imagine, but this track once carried the express trains from Edinburgh to London). Continue along the railway, past a station (now a restaurant) and over a low stone wall, then past the backs of houses and beneath bridges before emerging back into the countryside. Soon the traffic on the busy A7 can be heard through the trees to the left. On reaching an isolated house, turn right and follow another track back to the car park.

45. CURRIE WOOD

ORDNANCE SURVEY MAP NO	LANDRANGER 66
	PATHFINDER 434
DISTANCE FROM EDINBURGH	22 KM (14 ML)
WALKING DISTANCE	2 KM (1 ML)
AMOUNT OF CLIMBING	100 M (328 FT)
ESTIMATED TIME	1 HR

DESCRIPTION A short and easy but fascinating wander through a wooded glen owned and managed by the Woodland Trust. There are many minor paths within the woodland most of which are quite thin and eventually peter out. However, the route described follows paths of good quality, with steps, bridges and raised walkways over most of the difficult sections. Please note that there is only sufficient space to park two or three cars close to the start of the walk.

START AND FINISH Currie Wood, near Borthwick Castle. NT 371 597

HOW TO GET THERE Take the A7 south until close to Gorebridge. Just beyond the second turn-off to Gorebridge, turn left on to a minor road and follow it towards Borthwick Castle (round a hairpin bend, sharp right at next junction then right at a crossroads). Just before the castle, as the road crosses a disused railway track, turn left on to a single-track road and follow this downhill, past a high stone wall and a farm. Park in the small car park by the scout hut.

WALK DIRECTIONS
Go through the gate on the left-hand side of the burn into the woodland. Follow the path above the burn to two pedestrian gates. Pass through and turn left, following a

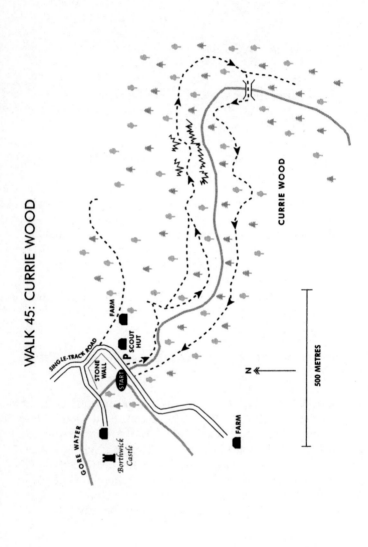

WALK 45: CURRIE WOOD

CURRIE WOOD

SINGLE-TRACK ROAD

FARM

SCOUT HUT

STONE WALL

START

GORE WATER

Borthwick Castle

FARM

N

500 METRES

path beside a farm. After a few paces turn right and back on oneself to climb steeply into the woodland.

A little beyond the top of the climb, the path divides into an upper and a lower path. Either path may be taken, as they rejoin further along. Beyond where the two paths rejoin, the path passes above some crags then gradually descends to a footbridge across the burn.

Cross over and follow an undulating path downstream through the trees, across small streams and gullies, and back through the glen to the start.

WALK 46: SCALD LAW & THE KIPS

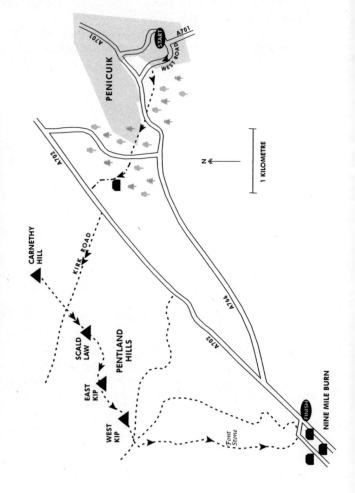

46. SCALD LAW & THE KIPS

ORDNANCE SURVEY MAP NO	LANDRANGER 66
	PATHFINDER 419 & 420
DISTANCE FROM EDINBURGH	22 KM (14 ML)
WALKING DISTANCE	11½ KM (7 ML)
AMOUNT OF CLIMBING	580 M (1,900 FT)
ESTIMATED TIME	4½ HR

DESCRIPTION A superb hill and ridge walk over Scald Law (579 m), highest of the Pentland Hills. Note that this route is more arduous than most of the routes described in this book. Also, the weather conditions on the hill can be very different to those in the valley below. It can be extremely windy and very cold on higher grond, even in summer, so wear suitable clothing and stout footwear.

START Penicuik Town Hall (red-stone building with clock in the centre of Penicuik). NT 236 599
FINISH Nine Mile Burn. NT 177 577
BUS LINK WS 100

HOW TO GET THERE Frequent bus service to Penicuik (LRT 81, 87; SMT 315, 64, 65; LO 62; WS 100) but less frequent service (WS 100) to Nine Mile Burn. By car, take the A702 (the Carlisle road). Turn right 8½ ml beyond the bypass into the village of Nine Mile Burn. Park in the village, walk back to the main road and take the link bus to the starting point in Penicuik.

WALK DIRECTIONS
Head west. At a bend in the main road continue directly ahead into West Street and follow it round to the right. Just beyond Craigiebield House Hotel, turn left on to a path beside some trees. At a road, take the signposted footpath diagonally opposite through woods. On reaching houses,

cross the road and continue straight ahead on an asphalt path leading across the green through the housing estate to another road. Cross the small green opposite and enter another woodland. Continue directly ahead, over an asphalt road and along a dirt road, still through the woods, to a farm.

Pass unobtrusively through the farm and on to a main road (A702). Go left along the road for 500 m to a stile and a footpath signpost on the right. Climb over the stile and cross a boggy area; then follow the grassy path, a little to the left, into the gully between Carnethy Hill (right) and Scald Law (left). This is the Kirk Road, a pass across the Pentlands once used by Balerno residents to reach their church in Penicuik. At the top of the pass, turn left over a stile (electrified fence) and climb steeply to the summit of Scald Law (579 m / 1,899 ft, triangulation pillar).

Leave the summit in a southwesterly direction. At a fork just below the summit, descend to the right on a peat path to a saddle. Climb over the two cone-shaped hills of East Kip and West Kip. Below West Kip, at a junction of footpaths, climb over a stile and take the right-hand (ascending) path. After 50 m, turn left on to a broad ridge above a small conifer plantation. Gradually descend along this ridge for 2 km. Halfway down there is a stone with a large depression in it, known as the Font Stone. On reaching a stone wall with adjacent fence and stile, climb over the stile and turn right. At the next fence and stile turn left (not over the stile) and follow the fence to a stone wall. Turn right through a metal gate, then left over another stile and follow the path down to Nine Mile Burn.

47. FALA MOOR

ORDNANCE SURVEY MAP NO	LANDRANGER 66
	PATHFINDER 435
DISTANCE FROM EDINBURGH	26 KM (16 ML)
WALKING DISTANCE ONE-WAY/	8½ KM (5½ ML)/
RETURN	12 KM (7½ ML)
AMOUNT OF CLIMBING	150 M (490 FT)
ESTIMATED TIME	3 HR / 4 HR

DESCRIPTION An easy walk over the bleak expanse of Fala Moor. Many birds of several different species may be seen, especially in the vicinity of the loch.

There are two versions of this route. The return route crosses the moor, makes a loop through grazing land, then returns across the moor. The one-way version (Fala to Heriot) requires private transport to collect walkers from the finish, for there is no public transport connecting the two ends. Alternatively, two groups of walkers could start from opposite ends and exchange car keys when they meet on the moor.

START AND FINISH Forest track near Fala on A68 southeast of Dalkeith. NT 437 608
ONE-WAY FINISH Heriot village on A7 southeast of Dalkeith. NT 403 545

HOW TO GET THERE By car, take the A68 out of Edinburgh and through Dalkeith. Nine miles beyond Dalkeith, after Pathhead, pass the left-hand turn-off to the village of Fala, then turn right (off the A68) on to the gravel forest track and park. By bus, use service LOW 30.

WALK DIRECTIONS
Walk to the gate at the end of the gravel track at the edge of the forest. Pass through the gate and follow the track

WALK 47: FALA MOOR

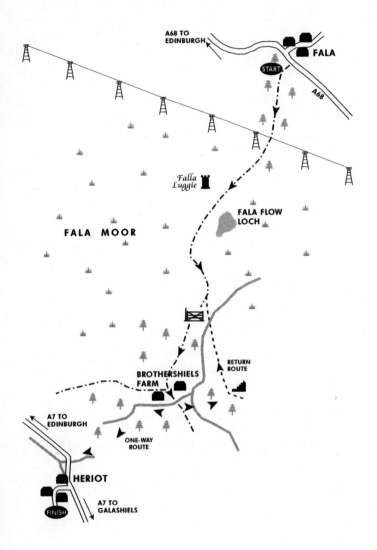

directly ahead, beneath power lines, then up on to the moor. An old peel tower (Fala Luggie) will be passed on the right, followed soon afterwards on the left by Fala Flow Loch. Stay on the track: it crosses the moor, then passes through a gate and descends gently through sheep-grazing land and a line of trees to a farm (Brothershiels). Follow the main track through the farm, then for a few metres uphill as far as two wooden gates opposite each other.

ONE-WAY ROUTE Pass through the gate on the right then cross rough pasture land – keeping parallel with a small burn and a line of telegraph poles on the right – to a line of trees and another gate. Go through the gate. Look for a gate in a stone wall on the skyline a little to the left (about 11 o'clock). Head across rough grassland to this gate, climb over then go right for a few paces. Go through a metal gate and turn left. Now follow the stone wall (and electric fence), then a gully, downhill to a main road (A7). Go left along the road for a few metres, then right to Heriot.

RETURN ROUTE Pass through the left-hand gate. Descend across sheep-grazing land then climb over another gate. Cross a small burn, then climb up to a clump of trees and some ruins (Upper Brotherstone). Turn left and follow a stone wall downhill. Then cross the burn again and join the moorland track used earlier to return to the start.

WALK 48: BLACK LAW & COVENANTER'S GRAVE, PENTLAND HILLS

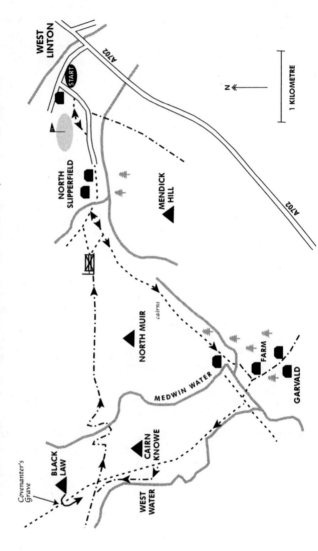

WEST LINTON

START

A702

A702

N

1 KILOMETRE

NORTH SLIPPERFIELD

MENDICK HILL

NORTH MUIR

cairns

FARM

GARVALD

MEDWIN WATER

CAIRN KNOWE

WEST WATER

BLACK LAW

Covenanter's Grave

48. BLACK LAW & COVENANTER'S GRAVE, PENTLAND HILLS

ORDNANCE SURVEY MAP NO	LANDRANGER 72
	PATHFINDER 433
DISTANCE FROM EDINBURGH	29 KM (18 ML)
WALKING DISTANCE	17 KM (9½ ML)
AMOUNT OF CLIMBING	310 M (1,017 FT)
ESTIMATED TIME	5¾ HR

DESCRIPTION An invigorating hill walk of gradual ascents and descents to a covenanter's grave on Black Law at the southern end of the range of Pentland Hills. Most of the route is across heather-clad moorland which can be very boggy in places (so make sure your boots are waterproof). Between North Slipperfield and Garvald the route follows a muddy but easily distinguishable track. However beyond Garvald the path, although a right-of-way and very scenic, is often quite thin, being overgrown with heather. Hence it is not always easy to follow. The return is easy, as it follows a gravel farm track.

START AND FINISH Golf Course, West Linton. NT 141 522

HOW TO GET THERE By car, take the A702 to West Linton and turn right at the far end of the village. Park on the side of the road just beyond the entrance to a golf course. Note that parking space is limited. By bus, use service WS 100 to West Linton then walk the extra kilometre to the Golf Course.

WALK DIRECTIONS
Walk along the farm road towards North Slipperfield. After a few paces, turn right on to a right-of-way across the golf course, then rejoin the road to North Slipperfield. Pass the farm buildings and follow the farm track over a burn then a

little uphill to a footpath signpost and small building. Turn left on to the footpath (a track at this point). Where the main track swings left through a gate, continue straight ahead on a grassy track. Follow this along the right side of the valley, past a few small cairns, then down to pass a copse of trees on the left and a house on the right. Continue on the track straight ahead to a farm.

Pass through the farm, then turn right over a gate and across grazing land to a rickety wooden bridge over a burn (Medwin Water). Cross over and bear left. After a few paces, at a footpath signpost, turn right and follow a gradually ascending path alongside the tumbling waters of another burn (West Water). When the burn swings away to the left, climb up out of the gully and continue straight ahead across open moorland following wooden marker posts. (If you are carrying a compass, head northnorthwest).

As the top of a rise is approached, cut left towards the burn and a new gravel track will be discovered. Walk along this up to a T-junction of tracks and a wooden post. Directly ahead is Black Law. Go right for a few paces then climb up the shoulder of Black Law, following a line of grouse butts. The route of the path and the covenanter's grave is a little to the left of the highest point on Black Law (407 m / 1,335 ft).

Return back down to the gravel farm track and follow it to the left over Medwin Water, then back up on to high moorland. At the next gate, shortly before the valley containing North Slipperfield Farm, bear right down a grassy path to rejoin the path used earlier. Then retrace your steps through North Slipperfield and back to the golf course.

49. THE CORSEHOPE RINGS NEAR HERIOT

ORDNANCE SURVEY MAP NO	LANDRANGER 66
	PATHFINDER 434
DISTANCE FROM EDINBURGH	29 KM (18 ML)
WALKING DISTANCE	8 KM (5 ML)
AMOUNT OF CLIMBING	210 M (689 FT)
ESTIMATED TIME	2¾ HR

DESCRIPTION A fairly easy walk in beautiful Borders hill country, the highlight of which is a very large, ancient fort depicted by several rings of raised earth – the Corsehope Rings. Please note that the early section of this route, through the woodland, is difficult because of fallen trees and some boggy areas; but persevere, as the section is quite short and the rest of the route is easy.

START AND FINISH Bridge on minor road over Heriot Water. NT 409 530

HOW TO GET THERE By car, take the Dalkeith Road (A68) to the Sheriffhall roundabout on the Edinburgh Bypass, then the A7 for a further 11 ml. Turn right on to the B709. Half a mile along, at a right-hand bend, go straight ahead on to a minor road. After a further half mile, park on the side of the road just before a bridge over a river. By bus, take LOW 95 to the B709 turn-off (Heriot) and walk the remaining 1¼ ml to the start.

WALK DIRECTIONS
Cross the bridge and immediately turn right on to a footpath beside the river. Follow the river around to the left, then enter a woodland. It may be necessary to make a few detours or climb over fallen trees, but do not climb up to the left; keep more or less parallel with the river. Before long you will emerge on to a farm track that crosses the river via

WALK 49: THE CORSEHOPE RINGS NEAR HERIOT

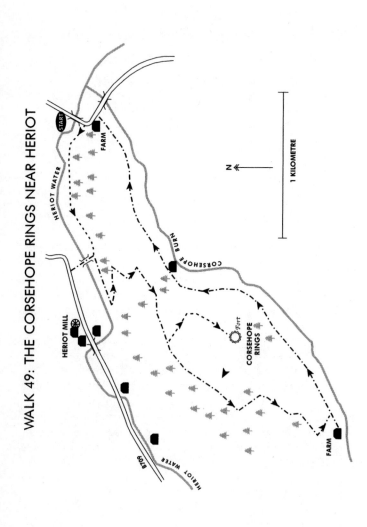

an old wooden bridge. Follow the track beside the river to more woodlands then around a hairpin bend and uphill. Continue around a second hairpin bend and up on to a saddle.

Just as the track begins to descend, at the corner of a line of trees, turn right and follow the tree-line up to a wooden gate. Pass through and continue directly ahead on a track to the base of a hill. Here a less obvious track continues straight ahead, while the main track turns left. Follow the main track left, then gradually right, and up on to the top of the hill (404 m / 1,325 ft, ancient fort).

After exploring the Corsehope Rings, walk across to the far side and follow a fence downhill, across grassland, to a track running along the edge of a woodland. Go left on the track through a gate then enter the woodland. Follow the track around to the left and uphill a little. Continue along the track, out of the forest and gradually downhill, across sheep-grazing land, to a farm. Just before the farm go left on to an asphalt track and follow it all the way through the valley to a road. Go left to return to the bridge and starting place.

WALK 50: GLADHOUSE RESERVOIR

N

1 KILOMETRE

DAM WALL

START

GLADHOUSE RESERVOIR

POND

HUNTLEY
COTTAGE

MOORFOOT
FARM

50. GLADHOUSE RESERVOIR

ORDNANCE SURVEY MAP NO	LANDRANGER 66
	PATHFINDER 434
DISTANCE FROM EDINBURGH	31 KM (19 ML)
WALKING DISTANCE	8½ KM (5 ML)
AMOUNT OF CLIMBING	90 M (300 FT)
ESTIMATED TIME	2¾ HR

DESCRIPTION Gladhouse Reservoir, lying at the foot of the Moorfoot Hills, is not only very scenic but is also a favourite winter spot for wild geese. This is a very enjoyable walk at any time of year. But it is at its best on a cold, sunny day in winter, when the ground crackles underfoot, the water is frozen and the geese are most prolific. Most of the route follows asphalt farm tracks or minor roads, but there is very little traffic and it is easy to walk along the grassy verge.

START AND FINISH Parking place at Gladhouse Reservoir, Midlothian. NT 309 543

HOW TO GET THERE By car, take the A7 out of Edinburgh, over the bypass, and on to the crossroads on the A7 at the southern end of Gorebridge. Turn right on to the B6372 towards Penicuik. At a right-hand corner go straight ahead for a mile then, at a house with a post box, turn left. Follow this road around the reservoir until it turns away to the left. Here turn right on to a farm track. There is a parking place here on the left. Unfortunately, public transport does to serve this area.

WALK DIRECTIONS
Head off away from the road along an asphalt farm track beside the reservoir. At a T-junction, turn right. Do not follow the track into the farm but go straight ahead, through a gate and on to a gravel track past a small pond. Stay on

the track, through another gate, then beside a conifer plantation. At a junction bear right and descend to Huntley Cottage. Pass this house and cross a cattle grid, then follow a track over a burn and on to Moorfoot Farm. Keep right through the farm and leave via the asphalt access road.

On reaching a main road, turn right and walk along the road to the next junction. (There is a post box in the wall on the far side of the road.) Turn right and follow another minor road around the reservoir, passing the dam wall on the way, until you finally return to the starting point.

Gladhouse Reservoir

51. EILDON HILLS, MELROSE

ORDNANCE SURVEY MAP NO	LANDRANGER 73
	PATHFINDER 461
DISTANCE FROM EDINBURGH	33 KM (20 ML)
WALKING DISTANCE	9 KM (5¼ ML)
AMOUNT OF CLIMBING	430 M (1,410 FT)
ESTIMATED TIME	3¼ HR

DESCRIPTION A popular hill walk following a designated and signposted route. There are good paths, superb views and many historical sites. The route and some of the historical sites are more fully described in the Borders Council booklet, *The Eildon Hills*.

START AND FINISH Melrose Railway Station (now a museum). NT 546 339

HOW TO GET THERE By car, take the A68 through Dalkeith and Lauder to Melrose. The station (signposted) is close to the central Market Square. There is a car park next to it. There is also a half-hourly bus service (LOW 62) between Edinburgh and Melrose.

WALK DIRECTIONS
From Market Square, walk south along the B6539 road towards Lilliesleaf. Pass beneath the Melrose Bypass then, in 100 m, turn left on to a footpath between houses. This leads across a burn, up a flight of wooden steps and over a stile then uphill, following a hedge, across agricultural land. After crossing a further three stiles the fields are left behind and the terrain changes to rough grassland and gorse. Follow the path around the base of a hill (North Hill) to a saddle. Turn right and climb to the summit of Mid Hill (422 m / 1,384 ft, triangulation pillar, viewfinder, cairn).

Descend the steep, southern flank of Mid Hill and cross

WALK 51: EILDON HILLS, MELROSE

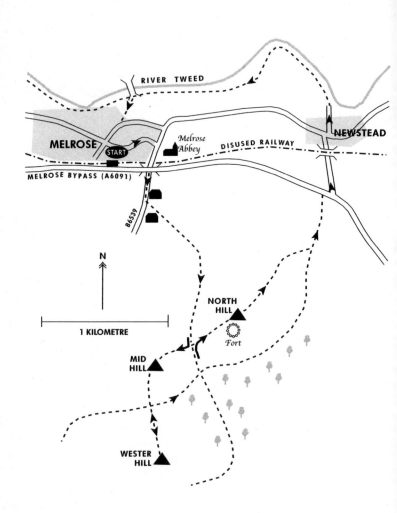

over to Wester Hill (371 m / 1,216 ft). Turn around and traverse around the base of Mid Hill (rather by going back over the top) to return to the saddle between North and Mid Hill. At the saddle, turn right and climb to the top of North Hill (404 m / 1,325 ft, site of Iron Age town and Roman look-out post).

Descend the far side of North Hill, passing through more gorse, to a stile. Climb over and follow the tree-lined track down to a main road. Cross over, go right for a few paces, then left on to a track. At a T-junction just beyond an old railway bridge, turn right (leaving the way-marked route) then left down Claymire Lane into Newstead (an interesting 2,000-year-old village).

Cross the main road (B6361) and walk down Eddy Lane to the River Tweed. Walk upstream, past a dry-stone dyke (Battery Dyke) to a suspension bridge across the river. Do not cross but turn away from the river, crossing a field and a stile, then along a road back into Melrose.

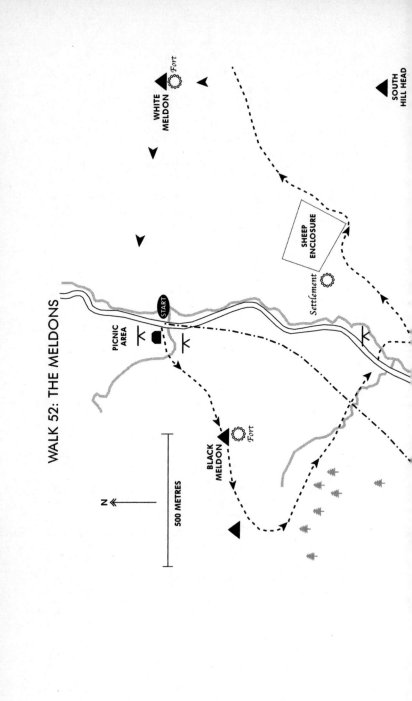

WALK 52: THE MELDONS

N

500 METRES

PICNIC AREA

START

WHITE MELDON — Fort

SOUTH HILL HEAD

SHEEP ENCLOSURE

Settlement

BLACK MELDON — Fort

52. THE MELDONS

ORDNANCE SURVEY MAP NO	LANDRANGER 73
	PATHFINDER 448
DISTANCE FROM EDINBURGH	35 KM (22 ML)
WALKING DISTANCE	6 KM (4 ML)
AMOUNT OF CLIMBING	442 M (1,450 FT)
ESTIMATED TIME	2¾ HR

DESCRIPTION A short, easy walk over the two hills that guard the pass between Eddleston and Lyne. There are superb views over the Tweed valley from both hills and many sites of archeological interest in the area. There are also a number of good picnic sites.

START AND FINISH The Meldons picnic site. NT 212 429

HOW TO GET THERE By car, take the A701 through Penicuik to Leadburn, then the A703 (continuation of the same road). At Eddleston turn right at the sign, 'Lyne via Meldons', and follow this road for 3¾ ml to the top of the pass. Here you will find a car park, picnic site and toilets. There is no public transport available to this walk.

WALK DIRECTIONS
Walk around behind the toilets, cross a burn then climb any of the paths leading up through the bracken directly ahead to the large cairn on the summit of Black Meldon (407 m / 1,335 ft, cairn). Note that the line of rocks just beneath the summit are the remains of the walls of an ancient fort.

From the cairn head west to the second, slightly lower summit. Then turn left and descend the southerly ridge to a small conifer plantation and a stone wall. Follow the wall down to a farm track, cross the track to a gully and follow it the short remaining distance to the road.

Cross the road, adjacent burn and fence. Follow a path

up to the right for 100 m, then left (northeast), gradually climbing, to a large stone-walled sheep enclosure. Just before the enclosure, on the left, is a small rise which is all that remains of an ancient settlement. Continue around the enclosure and up on to a saddle between two hills (White Meldon and South Hill Head). Turn left (north) and climb up the ridge ahead to the top of White Meldon (427 m / 1,400 ft, triangulation point, cairn, ancient fort). Descend towards the west, past the remains of a number of ancient settlements, to return to the road and picnic site.

South Park Wood, Peebles

53. CADEMUIR HILL, PEEBLES

ORDNANCE SURVEY MAP NO	LANDRANGER 73
	PATHFINDER 448 & 460
DISTANCE FROM EDINBURGH	36 KM (22 ML)
WALKING DISTANCE	12 KM (7½ ML)
AMOUNT OF CLIMBING	350 M (1,148 FT)
ESTIMATED TIME	4¼ HR

DESCRIPTION A very scenic ridge walk over low hills overlooking Peebles and the Tweed Valley, then returning along the River Tweed. There are paths along the entire route; but the going on the hill can be quite rough, so stout hill-walking shoes or boots are required. Dog owners should be aware that Cademuir Hill is sheep-grazing land.

START AND FINISH Car park on the south bank of the River Tweed, Peebles. NT 251 402

HOW TO GET THERE Bus service from Edinburgh (LO 62) every 30 minutes. By car, take the A701 south to Peebles. At the roundabout, turn right and pass through the town's main street to a mini-roundabout. Go left, over the bridge across the river, then turn left into a car park beside the river.

WALK DIRECTIONS
From the bend in the road adjacent to the car park, head west along Caledonian Road to a mini-roundabout. Take the road to the left and continue uphill, beyond the residential area, to where the road ends at the gatehouse of Tantah House Estate. Turn right and pass through an iron gate with an adjacent footpath sign. Follow a stone wall as far as a wooden gate on the left. Go through the gate. Climb up to a forest then follow the tree-line uphill, over several mini summits, to a distinctive high point. This appears to be the

WALK 53: CADEMUIR HILL, PEEBLES

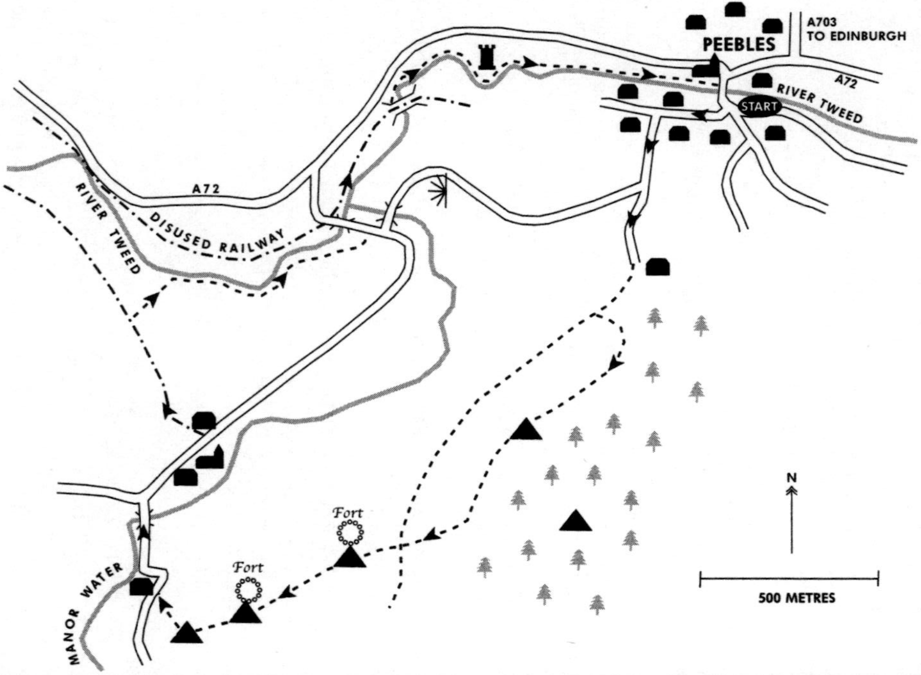

PEEBLES

A703
TO EDINBURGH

A72

RIVER TWEED

START

A72

RIVER TWEED

DISUSED RAILWAY

Fort

Fort

MANOR WATER

N

500 METRES

highest point on Cademuir Hill, but there is an even higher summit hidden within the forest.

Head down to a saddle, leaving the forest behind, then climb the ridge ahead on to the next summit. This hill consists of two small peaks. The higher one on the left has a small cairn. There is also an ancient fort surrounding the summit but it is not easy to see.

Continue in the same direction, descending quite steeply, then climb the next peak along the ridge. Although lower, this next hill seems steeper and more rugged and definitely looks as if it were once a fort. After a short, steep descent off the top, climb the last little knoll on the ridge. From here descend steeply, in a zigzag fashion, towards the right and head for a right-angle bend in the road in the valley below.

Turn right, along the road, then right again at a T-junction. Shortly thereafter, pass a church on the right then turn left, through a pair of white gates, on to a dirt track. Follow this for almost a kilometre to a sign marking the 'Tweed Walk'. Go right here, over a stile and down a grassy track to the river, then downstream to a large stone bridge over the river (Manor Bridge). Cross over and follow the north bank, past Neidpath Castle, all the way back to Peebles.

WALK 54: SOUTH PARK WOOD, PEEBLES

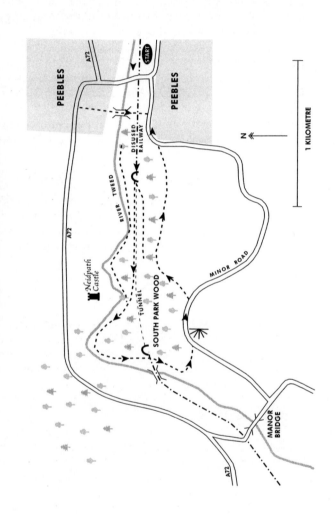

PEEBLES

PEEBLES

A72

START

RIVER TWEED

DISUSED RAILWAY

Neidpath Castle

A72

TUNNEL

SOUTH PARK WOOD

MINOR ROAD

MANOR BRIDGE

A72

N

1 KILOMETRE

54. SOUTH PARK WOOD, PEEBLES

ORDNANCE SURVEY MAP NO	LANDRANGER 73
	PATHFINDER 448 & 446
DISTANCE FROM EDINBURGH	36 KM (22 ML)
WALKING DISTANCE	5 KM (3 ML)
AMOUNT OF CLIMBING	90 M (300 FT)
ESTIMATED TIME	1¾ HR

DESCRIPTION This is a very attractive woodland walk close to the enchanting Borders town of Peebles. There are fantastic views of the Tweed Valley and, on the return, of Peebles and the Moorfoot Hills. All the paths are very good and suitable for all weathers. In fact, the smells of the woodland following rainfall are particularly appealing.

START AND FINISH Car park on the south bank of the River Tweed, Peebles. NT 252 402

HOW TO GET THERE Bus service from Edinburgh (LO 62) every 30 minutes. By car, take the A701 south to Peebles. At the roundabout, turn right and pass through the town's main street. At a mini-roundabout, go left over the Tweed then turn left into the car park beside the river.

WALK DIRECTIONS
Climb over the old railway embankment to reach the river and walk upstream, passing either beneath or over the road bridge, then past a weir to a footbridge. Here, walk away from the river for 100 m and then turn right along an old railway track. On approaching the entrance to a tunnel, gradually ascend the right embankment. (Walking through the tunnel is possible but not recommended.) When you are level with the tunnel entrance, go straight ahead (not left) on a woodland path.

Soon the path joins another coming up from the river.

About here, Neidpath Castle can be seen through the trees and across the river. Continue to a fork before a clearing. Keep right and descend to cross a short section of muddy grassland beside the river before climbing again and re-entering the woodland. A little further and the path meets an old railway track close to where it emerges from the tunnel encountered earlier. In the opposite direction, the railway crosses a stone viaduct over the river. Go straight ahead here (not across the viaduct) back into the woodlands. When the path reaches the edge of the woods with grazing land ahead, turn left and climb steeply, following the edge of the woods to a tarmac road. Here you will find a viewpoint with phenomenal views of the Tweed Valley.

From the viewpoint, follow the road uphill for 200 m then turn left through a wooden gate and take the grassy path beside the woods to a stile. Climb over and follow the path that runs beside a stone wall across grazing land. Continue over another stile and on to join a road that leads back to Peebles.

55. TWEEDDALE

ORDNANCE SURVEY MAP NO	LANDRANGER 73
	PATHFINDER 448 & 446
DISTANCE FROM EDINBURGH	36 KM (22 ML)
WALKING DISTANCE/	13 KM (8 ML)/
SHORT VERSION	6½ KM (4 ML)
AMOUNT OF CLIMBING	110 M (360 FT)/
	50 M (164 FT)
ESTIMATED TIME	4 HR / 2 HR

DESCRIPTION This is a delightful walk through Borders countryside following a designated route along the banks of the River Tweed. Interesting features *en route* include Neidpath Castle, Manor Bridge, a stone railway viaduct and, of course, the ever-present River Tweed. The paths are of good quality throughout and the route is well signposted.

START AND FINISH car park on the south bank of River Tweed, Peebles. NT 252 402

HOW TO GET THERE Bus service from Edinburgh (LO 62) every 30 minutes. By car, take the A701 south to Peebles. At the roundabout, turn right and pass through the town's main street. At a mini-roundabout, go left over a bridge over the Tweed then turn left into a car park beside the river.

WALK DIRECTIONS
Climb over the old railway embankment to reach the river then walk upstream, passing either beneath or over the road bridge. Then pass a weir and a footbridge and continue beside the river, following a path into a woodland. Stay on the path: it clings to the water's edge, crossing rocks and small bridges over streams, then climbs into the woods above the river, allowing glimpses of Neidpath Castle through the trees. On reaching a fork before a clearing, keep

WALK 55: TWEEDDALE

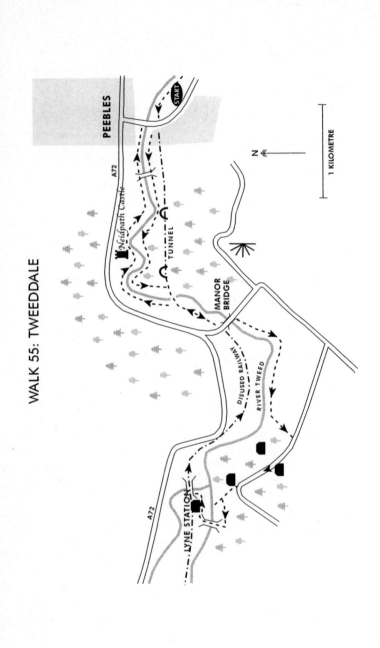

PEEBLES

Neidpath Castle

A72

TUNNEL

MANOR BRIDGE

DISUSED RAILWAY

RIVER TWEED

LYNE STATION

A72

START

N

1 KILOMETRE

right and descend to a short muddy section beside the river. Soon the path climbs again and re-enters the woods before finally emerging close to a stone viaduct across the river. Cross the viaduct and follow the path upstream to Manor Bridge (a substantial stone road bridge across the river).

For a shorter walk, turn around here and follow the north bank of the river back to Peebles.

To continue, cross Manor Bridge and immediately turn right on to another riverside footpath. From here you will climb over several stiles and pass a distinctive, large tree. When the path stops at some woods, turn away from the river and climb over a gate bearing the 'Tweed Walk' bird symbol. Climb the grassy track ahead up to a farm road. Turn right (following the signpost). Follow the road past a farm and adjacent tower, straight ahead, until it turns left close to a cottage on the right. Leave the road here, keeping straight ahead, down a farm track. At a footpath signpost bear left on an ascending path to reach a footbridge across the Tweed.

Cross the river and walk up a farm track, past some cottages, to a burn (Lyne Water). Here, climb some steps up on to an old railway track, then follow the track back past Manor Bridge to the old railway viaduct encountered earlier. Leave the railway track at this point and continue along a path on the north bank of the river. This path follows the river, past Neidpath Castle, all the way back to Peebles.

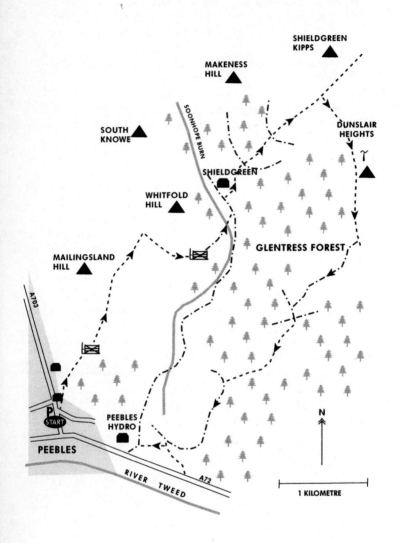

WALK 56: GLENTRESS FOREST & DUNSLAIR HEIGHTS

SHIELDGREEN KIPPS

MAKENESS HILL

SOONHOPE BURN

DUNSLAIR HEIGHTS

SOUTH KNOWE

SHIELDGREEN

WHITFOLD HILL

GLENTRESS FOREST

MAILINGSLAND HILL

PEEBLES HYDRO

N

A703

P START

PEEBLES

RIVER TWEED

A72

1 KILOMETRE

56. GLENTRESS FOREST & DUNSLAIR HEIGHTS

ORDNANCE SURVEY MAP NO	LANDRANGER 73
	PATHFINDER 448
DISTANCE FROM EDINBURGH	37 KM (23 ML)
WALKING DISTANCE/	13 KM (8 ML)/
SHORT VERSION	8 KM (5 ML)
AMOUNT OF CLIMBING	556 M (1,825 FT)/
	250 M (820 FT)
ESTIMATED TIME	5 HR / 3 HR

DESCRIPTION A delightful walk on good paths and tracks through Glentress Forest to the top of Dunslair Heights, the mountain towering over Peebles. The route passes through a mixture of open hillside and thick coniferous forest and there are stupendous views from the summit ridge.

START AND FINISH Car park on Edinburgh Road, Peebles. NT 252 408

HOW TO GET THERE Bus service from Edinburgh (LO 62) every 30 minutes. By car, take the A701/703 south to Peebles. The car park is on the right as you enter the town.

WALK DIRECTIONS
Walk along Edinburgh Road back towards Edinburgh as far as a large house on the right next to a junction with an ascending road (Ven Law High Road). Pass through the high black gate adjacent to the house and walk up the tree-lined track on the far side, past Venlaw Castle Hotel, then out of the forest and on to open hillside. Follow the grass track ahead, past Mallingsland Hill, then around to the right to pass Whitfold Hill, then down towards Glentress Forest. At a fork, go left and over a gate to enter the forest. Follow the gravel track ahead across the valley floor. Go over Soonhope Burn, then up to a prominent, white cottage (Shieldgreen).

For a shorter walk, turn around at this point and follow the gravel track to the left of Soonhope Burn all the way down the valley to the Peebles Hydro.

To continue, pass beneath the house and take the path beside the outbuilding into the forest. This is a long, steeply ascending path through the forest. It crosses two forestry roads before finally emerging from the forest on the summit ridge of the mountain. Turn right and follow a broken dyke up to the radio masts and meteorological station on the highest point of Dunslair Heights (602 m / 1,975 ft).

From here it is downhill all the way back to the car park. Continue in the same southerly direction beside the dyke, past another dyke that disappears off down a shallow gully to the left, then turn right to re-enter the forest on a muddy track that soon reaches a forestry road. Follow the road downhill. After almost 2 km, at a T-junction, go right for 25 m to reach another T-junction. Here, go straight ahead on to a footpath through the trees, round to the left of a clearing, and on to another forestry road. Follow this downhill for a further 2 km to a hairpin bend.

A few paces *beyond* the bend, turn off right on to a steeply descending footpath. This ends quite soon, close to the goods entrance of the Peebles Hydro. Walk down to the main road (Innerleithen Road). Go right as far as a roundabout, then right into Edinburgh Road and so return to the car park.

57. GALASHIELS & THE RIVER TWEED

ORDNANCE SURVEY MAP NO	LANDRANGER 73
	PATHFINDER 461
DISTANCE FROM EDINBURGH	54 KM (33 ML)
WALKING DISTANCE	14½ KM (9 ML)
AMOUNT OF CLIMBING	170 M (558 FT)
ESTIMATED TIME	4¾ HR

DESCRIPTION An easy walk following an old railway track and the picturesque River Tweed to Melrose. The return is partly by the same route, but then detours over Gala Hill from where there are stupendous views over typical Borders country.

START AND FINISH Galashiels Bus Station. NT 493 363

HOW TO GET THERE By car, take the A7 to Galashiels and park in one of the town's car parks. By bus, use service LOW 95.

WALK DIRECTIONS
From the bus station, cross the road via the pelican crossing. Walk behind the church and beneath a metal road bridge, then along an asphalt track that follows the route of an old railway beside a small river. Later, there is an alternative and more interesting parallel path closer to the water for part of the way. After 2 km the main track passes some houses then reaches a road. Here the route is joined by the Southern Upland Way (SUW). Cross the road and continue along the track, over the River Tweed then through trees, until it ends at another road. Cross over and bear left before the Barbour factory. Cross another road and pass through a gate, then follow the SUW footpath beside the river to a huge, metal footbridge.
    Cross the footbridge over the river and turn left to

WALK 57: GALASHIELS & THE RIVER TWEED

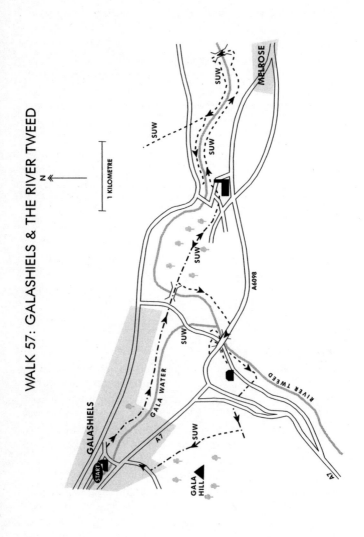

continue on the SUW footpath, now heading upstream. Halfway up a long, straight ascent, leave the SUW by descending back down to the river. Stay beside the river until a road bridge is reached. Just before the bridge, at a fisherman's bothy, go right to reach a road and follow it across the bridge. On the far side, take the road uphill for a few paces; then turn right to rejoin the route used earlier and follow it back to the river crossing.

At the start of the bridge, turn left down some steps on to a public footpath. Follow this beside the river, then past the backs of houses to a major road. Do not cross over. Turn right and use the road to cross the River Tweed. On the far side, turn right on to grassland, descend and pass beneath the bridge. Follow a thin path for a short distance to a wooden fence with houses beyond. Turn left. Scramble down an embankment, over a disused railway track, up the other side then along a minor road back towards the bridge.

Just before the bridge, turn towards the river to rejoin the SUW footpath heading upstream. Follow the SUW markers across the road, up a track, over a main road, up some steps to a third road and then up a farm track into cultivated fields. At the top of the climb, turn left to continue climbing over the shoulder of Gala Hill. Then descend into the suburbs of Galashiels. Leave the SUW where it turns left into Gala Academy and continue straight ahead to return to the centre of town.

WALK 58: THORNYLEE FOREST
NEAR WALKERBURN

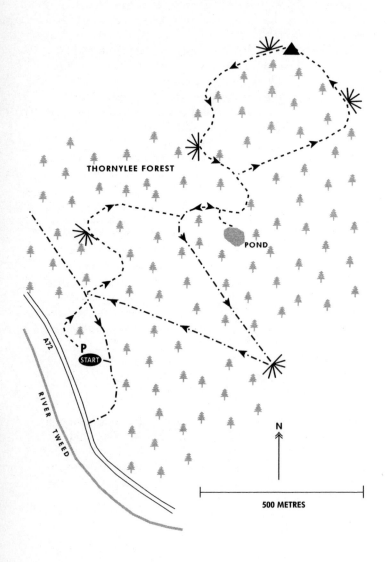

THORNYLEE FOREST

POND

A72

RIVER TWEED

P
START

N

500 METRES

58. THORNYLEE FOREST NEAR WALKERBURN

ORDNANCE SURVEY MAP NO	LANDRANGER 73
	PATHFINDER 460 & 461
DISTANCE FROM EDINBURGH	55 KM (34 ML)
WALKING DISTANCE	4½ KM (3 ML)
AMOUNT OF CLIMBING	260 M (850 FT)
ESTIMATED TIME	2 HR

DESCRIPTION A very pleasant woodland walk in the Tweed Valley following a designated walking route marked by colour-coded sign posts. There are, in fact, four designated routes within the forest. The walk described here is the longest and requires the most climbing; but one could easily follow one of the shorter, less strenuous routes. The entire forest is on a fairly steep hillside, which makes for a lot of climbing to reach the highest point, but also creates many magnificent views of the Tweed Valley and surrounding hills.

START AND FINISH Thornylee Forest, a little east of Walkerburn on the A72. NT 399 368

HOW TO GET THERE By car, take the A703 south through Penicuik to Peebles, then the A72 east towards Galashiels. Thornylee Forest is on the left, 2 ml beyond Walkerburn. There is a car park 200 m along the track leading into the forest. By bus, use service LS 62 from Edinburgh Bus Station to the forest entrance.

WALK DIRECTIONS
Walk over to the large wooden statue and follow the adjacent footpath round to the right and uphill to a junction of forest tracks. Take the higher path, not one of the gravel tracks. Follow this steeply uphill until another forestry track is reached. Go left along the track, past a path leading down

to a small pond on the right, then round to the left and uphill until the track narrows to a path. Turn right here on to a footpath up a bracken-covered cutting marked by a blue-coded signpost and past a stone cairn on the right. At the top, follow the path round to the left and beside a stone wall that marks the perimeter of the forest. From here there are many splendid views over typical Borders hill country; but the best is yet to come.

Continue beside the wall, round to the left and over the highest point of this walk, then downhill and right to re-enter the forest. Part-way down, the path passes over a promontory where there is a small wooden bench and an incredible view up the Tweed Valley. Further downhill you will reach the forest track and junction with the blue marker where you turned off earlier. Continue straight ahead along the forest track, round to the right and past the small pond until the track swings round to the left.

Do not turn off here on to the path used coming up, but continue along the gently descending track. Further down, the track rounds a hairpin bend on the edge of the forest. There are more good views from here and from the rest of the track as it descends. Follow it down to another hairpin bend, where the path used on the ascent is crossed, and on to the car park.

EASTERN REGION

WALK 59: DALKEITH COUNTRY PARK

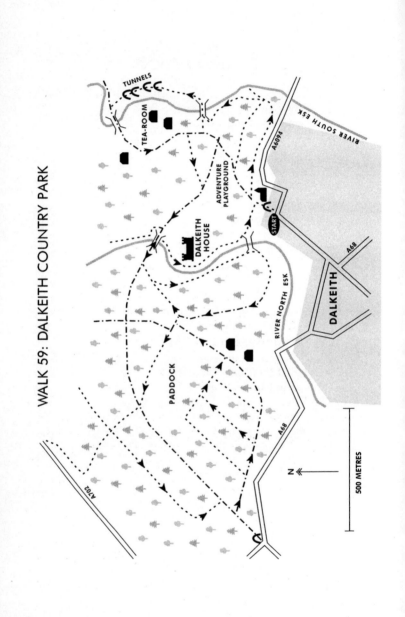

TUNNELS

TEA-ROOM

DALKEITH HOUSE

ADVENTURE PLAYGROUND

PADDOCK

START

RIVER NORTH ESK

RIVER SOUTH ESK

DALKEITH

A6094

A68

A68

A702

N

500 METRES

59. DALKEITH COUNTRY PARK

ORDNANCE SURVEY MAP NO	LANDRANGER 66
	PATHFINDER 420
DISTANCE FROM EDINBURGH	11 KM (7 ML)
WALKING DISTANCE	6 KM (4 ML)
AMOUNT OF CLIMBING	55 M (160 FT)
ESTIMATED TIME	2 HR

DESCRIPTION This walk through Dalkeith Country Park, part of the estate of the Duke of Buccleuch, is full of variety. There are woodlands, rivers, tunnels, a huge conservatory and an adventure playground. Deer, pheasant, squirrels and highland cattle are often seen. There is so much of interest to both young and old alike that a whole day could easily be spent within the park. Note that there is an entry charge of £2 per person during the summer; in winter the park is open to walkers without any charge, but you should take care lest there be a pheasant shoot in progress.

START AND FINISH Main entrance gate to Dalkeith Country Park, Dalkeith. NT 334 677

HOW TO GET THERE Frequent bus service from Edinburgh (LRT 3, 30, 82; SMT 79, 80; LOW 30, 95). By car, take the Old Dalkeith Road (A68) south to Dalkeith. Reaching the T-junction at the top of the hill towards the town centre, turn left (away from A68). The park entrance gate and parking area is at the end of this road.

WALK DIRECTIONS

Pass through the entrance gate and turn right just past a church, up a grassy embankment on to a long, straight path through trees (Dark Wood Path). Where the path swings left and meets other paths, turn right to descend to the River South Esk then head downstream to a footbridge. Cross over and continue downstream. Soon the path passes through two tunnels, then emerges into a small amphitheatre. Follow the arrow on the far side up some steps and along another path above the river to a road bridge.

Cross over and follow the road past a conservatory and round some farm buildings (now a café, shop and toilets). Then turn right on to a footpath next to an open area on the right. At the end of this path, just before an adventure playground, turn right (opposite direction to arrow) and follow a road over the River North Esk. Shortly thereafter, turn left on to the Riverside Walk. Follow the river round to the right, then climb up to a dirt road.

Take the grassy track opposite (North Woods Walk), beside a sheep grazing paddock on the left. At the end turn right, cross a dirt road and continue directly ahead. Just beyond a small stone bridge over a burn, turn left on to a track. Follow this along a straight section, then round to the left to meet a dirt road. Turn right towards the large, ornate King's Gate. Just before the gate, turn left then left again at an arrow marker. At the next arrow marker, at a T-junction, go right. On reaching a dirt road with a stone wall ahead, turn left and follow the road past a sheep-grazing paddock to the sign 'North Woods Walk' which was passed earlier. Go diagonally right on to a rather overgrown path, through trees, back to the stone bridge across the river.

Cross the bridge once more and turn left, descending to the river. Pass beneath the bridge and head upstream to a footbridge (closed). Here, turn left and ascend some wooden steps. At the top, go right to return to the church and park entrance.

60. THE MUSSELBURGH WALK

ORDNANCE SURVEY MAP NO	LANDRANGER 66
	PATHFINDER 407 & 420
DISTANCE FROM EDINBURGH	17 KM (10½ ML)
WALKING DISTANCE/	13 KM (8 ML)/
WHITECRAIG START	9 KM (5½ ML)
AMOUNT OF CLIMBING	NEGLIGIBLE
ESTIMATED TIME	4 HR / 2¾ HR

DESCRIPTION An easy walk through varied terrain. It begins by passing through the remnants of mine dumps, then clings to the picturesque River Esk and finally hugs the coast of the Firth of Forth – sometimes close enough to get wet! The river and mudflats near Musselburgh are renowned for their plentiful and varied bird life. For a shorter walk, begin in Whitecraig.

START Thornybank, just outside Dalkeith. NT 342 676
FINISH Prestonpans, East Lothian. NT 389 745
BUS LINK SMT 242

HOW TO GET THERE By car, take the A1 east as far as the Wallyford turn-off, then follow the signs to Prestonpans. Park in one of the town's car parks and take the bus (SMT 242) from Preston Road (near the railway station) to Thornybank. Alternatively, take the train (ScotRail) to Prestonpans then the bus as above.

WALK DIRECTIONS
Close to the Thornybank roundabout, on the B6414, are a cluster of houses and a large furniture factory. Go along the track between the houses and the factory to a disused asphalt road and turn right. After a few paces, at a bridge, descend steeply to the left on to a footpath through trees to the start of an asphalt pathway. Follow this until you reach

WALK 60: THE MUSSELBURGH WALK

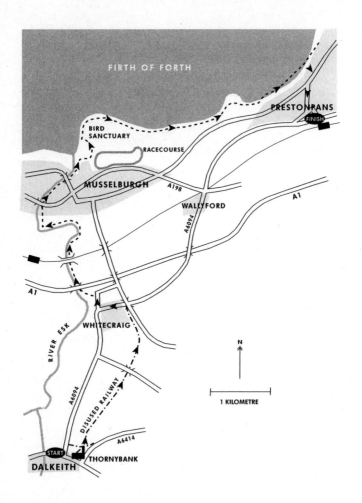

a road just before the village of Whitecraig. Turn left and walk through the village. On the far side, at a bend in the road to the left, turn right on to a minor road. After a short distance, where the road bends right, go straight ahead on to a footpath that leads down through trees and beneath two bridges before reaching the River Esk. Follow the river downstream all the way into the centre of Musselburgh.

Stay close to the river as it winds its way through the centre of Musselburgh and on to the sea. At the mouth of the river, walk around the ATC and Army cadets' huts, then along a gravel track following the sea wall. Follow this track past a bird sanctuary on the right, then some huge heaps of gravel, and on beside the sea to Prestonpans.

Having reached the outskirts of Prestonpans, walk either along the road into town or (if the tide is not too high) along the causeway between the houses and the sea. Keep going until an electricity generating station comes into view. Then cut right up one of the alleys to reach the centre of town.

WALK 61: VOGRIE COUNTRY PARK

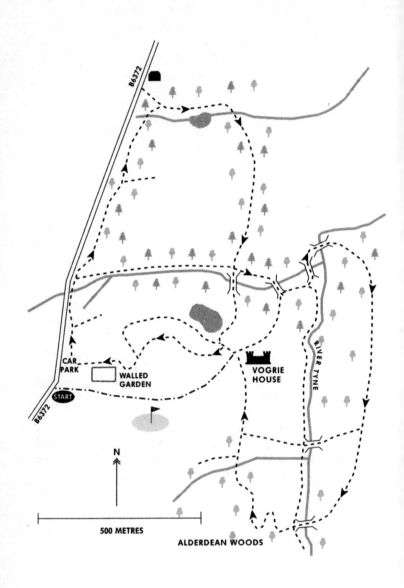

B6372

CAR
PARK

WALLED
GARDEN

START

B6372

VOGRIE
HOUSE

RIVER TYNE

N

500 METRES

ALDERDEAN WOODS

61. VOGRIE COUNTRY PARK

ORDNANCE SURVEY MAP NO	LANDRANGER 66
	PATHFINDER 420
DISTANCE FROM EDINBURGH	18½ KM (11½ ML)
WALKING DISTANCE	4 KM (2½ ML)
AMOUNT OF CLIMBING	110 M (360FT)
ESTIMATED TIME	1½ HR

DESCRIPTION This beautiful woodland and riverside walk lies entirely within Midlothian Council's Vogrie Country Park. There are many well-maintained paths within the park and numerous possible routes. The route described is one of the longest and encompasses most of the park. However, there are many possibilities for taking short-cuts. The park also has several toilets, refreshments, permanent exhibitions, picnic sites, play areas, crazy golf, a model railway and much more. There is a parking charge of £1 per vehicle.

START AND FINISH Vogrie Country Park. NT 375 631

HOW TO GET THERE By car, take the Dalkeith Road to Dalkeith, then the A68. Just beyond the residential area of Dalkeith, pass the right-hand turn-off to Mayfield and take the next right. Pass through the villages of Whitehill and Edgehead. At the next crossroads turn right. The entrance to Vogrie is a mile further along on the left. By bus, take LOW 30 to Edgehead and walk from there.

WALK DIRECTIONS
From the edge of the car park, close to the playground, follow the path and signpost for North Woods into the trees. At a fork, go left and down to reach the park perimeter fence. Continue along the main path. On reaching a small burn, do not turn to the right but stay close

to the edge of the park. Follow the path as it swings right near a white house visible through the trees, then into a strip of trees through which open areas can be seen to both left and right. Follow this path past a small pond then around to the right. Eventually you will reach a signpost and junction with an asphalt track going off directly ahead. Turn left here, following a burn downhill. Cross a footbridge to the far side of the burn and continue following it downhill. At the bottom, turn left, back over the burn again, then right to reach a bridge across the River Tyne.

Cross over and follow a steeply ascending path to the top of a ridge and the edge of the woodland. Continue along the ridge through the woodland then across rough grassland. Pass the first footpath descending to the right and take the next path downhill to a bridge across the River Tyne. Cross over and walk along a raised wooden walkway, past a disappearing stream, then up a steep, zigzag path into Alderdean Woods. At the top descend a little to cross a burn, then keep straight ahead to Vogrie House. Here there are refreshments, toilets, exhibitions and other amenities.

From the main entrance to Vogrie House, cross the lawn to the pond. Follow the Rhododendron Walk through trees and rhododendron bushes. Pass a huge tricycle, the Peace Gardens and a walled garden as you head back to the car park.

62. PENCAITLAND RAILWAY WALK

ORDNANCE SURVEY MAP NO	LANDRANGER 66
	PATHFINDER 407, 420 & 401
DISTANCE FROM EDINBURGH	25 KM (15 ML)
WALKING DISTANCE/	15½ KM (9½ ML)/
ORMISTON START/	12 KM (7½ ML)/
CROSSGATEHALL FINISH/	8½ KM (5½ ML)/
WHITECRAIG FINISH	11½ KM (7 ML)
AMOUNT OF CLIMBING	90 M (295 FT)
ESTIMATED TIME (COMPLETE ROUTE)	4¾ HR

DESCRIPTION This is a long but straightforward and fairly level walk through agricultural land, then through the grass-covered remnants of old coal mines and finally along the bank of the River Esk to Musselburgh. The route may be shortened by starting at Ormiston (bus SMT 113 from Musselburgh) or finishing at Crossgatehall (bus SMT C3 to Musselburgh) or Whitecraig (bus SMT C3 to Musselburgh).

START Wester Pencaitland, East Lothian. NT 441 689
FINISH Musselburgh. NT 342 727
BUS LINK SMT 113

HOW TO GET THERE By car, take the A1 east out of Edinburgh to the City Bypass, then continue directly ahead along Milton Road to Musselburgh. Park in one of the town's many car parks, then take the bus (SMT 113) to Wester Pencaitland. By bus, take service SMT 113 from Edinburgh all the way to Wester Pencaitland.

WALK DIRECTIONS
Walk west along the main road to the edge of the village then turn left down a lane beside a malting factory. At the end of the lane, turn right on to the Pencaitland Railway Walkway. For the next 8½ km to Crossgatehall, just

WALK 62: PENCAITLAND RAILWAY WALK

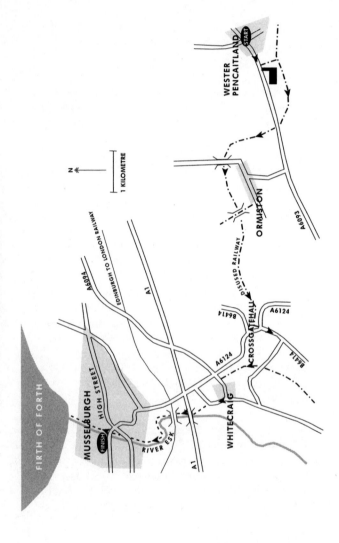

follow the main track and enjoy the scenery, birds and wild flowers. Take care crossing the busy A6093.

At Crossgatehall, pass through the walkway car park to a road, then go right to reach some traffic lights. Here take the road to the left (not the road over the bridge). Pass an old slag heap on the right, then turn right on to a country lane for a further kilometre to a bridge over the old railway track. Descend to the left to rejoin the railway track and follow it beneath the road bridge and on to Whitecraig.

When the track ends at a road, turn left and pass through the village of Whitecraig. Continue along the road until it swings left. Here turn right on to a minor road. After a short distance, where the road bends right, go straight ahead on to a footpath down through trees and beneath two bridges to reach the River Esk. Follow the river downstream all the way into the centre of Musselburgh.

WALK 63: THE PENCAITLAND WALK

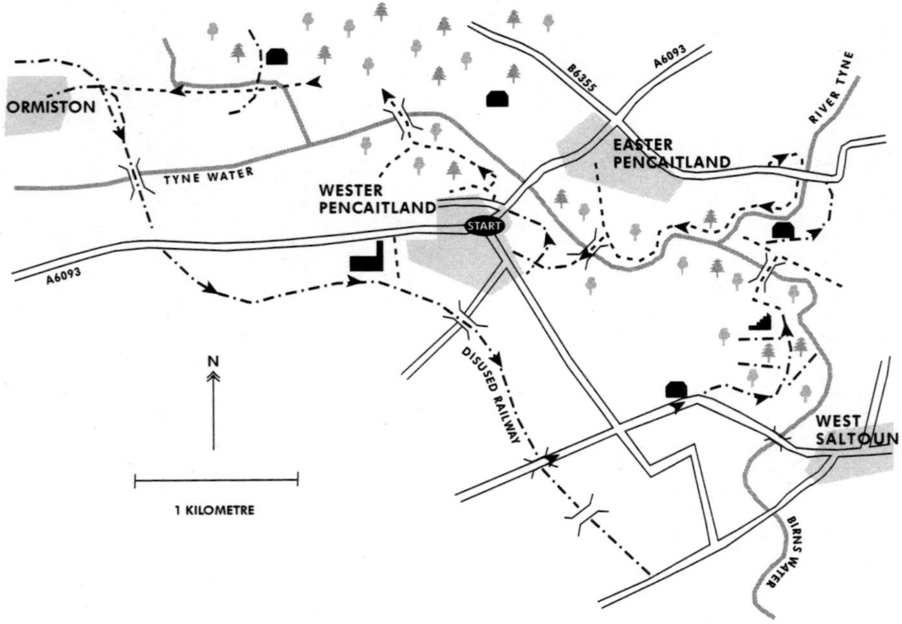

1 KILOMETRE

N

RIVER TYNE

A6093

B6355

EASTER
PENCAITLAND

WESTER
PENCAITLAND

START

DISUSED RAILWAY

WEST
SALTOUN

BIRNS WATER

TYNE WATER

ORMISTON

A6093

63. THE PENCAITLAND WALK

ORDNANCE SURVEY MAP NO	LANDRANGER 66
	PATHFINDER 421
DISTANCE FROM EDINBURGH	25 KM (15 ML)
WALKING DISTANCE	13 KM (8 ML)
AMOUNT OF CLIMBING	150 M (492 FT)
ESTIMATED TIME	4¼ HR

DESCRIPTION An easy and very interesting ramble through farmland and woodlands and along a river bank. Almost all of the route follows designated walkways and right-of-ways.

START AND FINISH Wester Pencaitland, East Lothian. NT 441 689

HOW TO GET THERE By car, take the A1 east to Tranent then the B6355 to Easter Pencaitland. Turn right at the crossroads, pass through Easter Pencaitland and continue over a bridge into Wester Pencaitland. Park on one of the side streets. By bus from Edinburgh, use service SMT 113 to Wester Pencaitland.

WALK DIRECTIONS
Walk towards the bridge with traffic lights that separates Wester Pencaitland and Easter Pencaitland. Just before the bridge, turn left on to a minor residential road. After a few paces, go right, cross a small bridge over a burn then right again into woodlands. Follow the main path through the woodland, passing a mansion house on the far side of the river. At a fork, go right to descend to the river. Cross a footbridge and pass through a kissing gate into a grazing paddock. Cross to the trees on the far side of the paddock and turn left. There is no path here but it is a right-of-way. Stay in a fairly straight line, crossing stiles and later walking alongside a small burn for a while, until the asphalt track of the Pencaitland Railway Walk is reached.

Turn left and follow the Railway Walk. Carefully cross the busy A6093 road, then rejoin the old railway. Soon, you will pass over a bridge with a view of the houses of Pencaitland to the left. Where the railway track passes beneath the next road bridge, leave the track and walk along the road to the left. Go over a crossroads and on to a bend to the right. Here, go straight ahead, past a stone gatepost bearing a 'no entry' sign – it is a right-of-way for pedestrians – on to a track through woodlands.

Follow this track round to the right towards a river. At a fork, go left (not down to the river) then, a few paces further along, where the main track swings left, go straight ahead on to a lesser track back into woodlands. Swing round to the left, past an old tower, then descend to a bridge over a river. Cross over and turn left then immediately right, climbing a little and passing a house on the left. Keep going until you emerge on to a road close to a long stone bridge across the river.

Cross the bridge then leave the road and follow the right-hand parapet back to the river. Proceed beneath the bridge and follow the river upstream. Pass a confluence of two rivers, then a sewage works, then enter some woodlands. Stay beside the river until you reach the base of a flight of steps. Here turn left over a footbridge across the river, then follow an asphalt footpath round to the right. At a crossroads, turn right (away from the nursing home) and follow the track back into Wester Pencaitland.

64. FROM HADDINGTON TO THE SEA

ORDNANCE SURVEY MAP NO	LANDRANGER 66
	PATHFINDER 408
DISTANCE FROM EDINBURGH	30 KM (18½ ML)
WALKING DISTANCE/	12 KM (7½ ML)/
LONGNIDDRY FINISH	8½ KM (5½ ML)
AMOUNT OF CLIMBING	50 M (164 FT)
ESTIMATED TIME	3¾ HR / 2¾ HR

DESCRIPTION A delightful walk along a disused railway track, then a right-of-way through woods and over fields, from the centre of agricultural East Lothian to the sea. Unfortunately there is a 2 km road section, but it is a country lane and carries little traffic. For a shorter walk, stay on the disused railway track to Longniddry and from there catch a bus (SMT 128) back to Haddington.

START Town Hall, Haddington, East Lothian. NT 515 739
FINISH Aberlady, East Lothian. NT 465 800
BUS LINK SMT 128

HOW TO GET THERE By car, take the A1 east to Haddington and park in one of the town's car parks or on a side street. By bus, take CCC 251, 253 or 256 or one of SMT's express services.

WALK DIRECTIONS
Head west along Court Street, past a library and council buildings, then over a crossroads into Station Road. Keep going, past a field on the left, almost to the outskirts of Haddington. At a blue sign for the Haddington to Longniddry Railway Walk, turn right into Alderston Road. Cross a bridge over an old railway track and descend left to join the railway path. Follow this track beneath the new A1

WALK 64: FROM HADDINGTON TO THE SEA

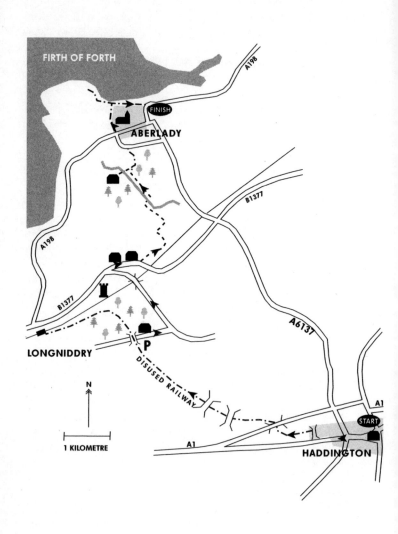

FIRTH OF FORTH

A198

FINISH

ABERLADY

B1377

A198

B1377

A6137

LONGNIDDRY

DISUSED RAILWAY

P

N

A1

START

A1

HADDINGTON

1 KILOMETRE

road, then out into open countryside. Eventually you will reach a bridge over a minor road. There is a walkway notice-board and nearby picnic site and car park just before the bridge. Unless proceeding to Longniddry, leave the railway track here.

Walk through the car park to a road and turn right. At a T-junction turn left. Follow this country lane over a railway to a main road and turn right. Just after passing a row of cottages, but before the road crosses the railway, turn left on to a track. Follow this track alongside the railway for a short distance then left along the edge of a field. At the next field, turn right then left into woodlands.

At the far end of the woods, go along the right-hand edge of a field to a small bridge over a burn. Cross and follow the burn through more woodlands, then along the edge of another field to reach a track just as it passes through a locked gate on the left. Go right along the track, around the edge of the woods, to a minor road. Carry on along the road to meet a main road on the edge of Aberlady. Take the footpath directly opposite, around a cemetery and down to the sea. Turn right to reach the centre of Aberlady and the bus back to Haddington.

WALK 65: HADDINGTON & THE RIVER TYNE

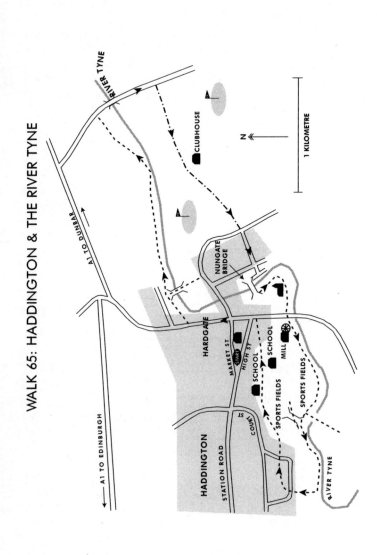

65. HADDINGTON & THE RIVER TYNE

ORDNANCE SURVEY MAP NO	LANDRANGER 66
	PATHFINDER 408
DISTANCE FROM EDINBURGH	30 KM (18½ ML)
WALKING DISTANCE	7 KM (4½ ML)
AMOUNT OF CLIMBING	40 M (130 FT)
ESTIMATED TIME	2¼ HR

DESCRIPTION A pleasant ramble, through a mixture of town and country, following the course of the River Tyne. Easy going throughout. Lots of birds to see on the river; and some extraordinary medieval architecture.

START AND FINISH Town Hall, Haddington. NT 515 739

HOW TO GET THERE By car, take the A1 east to Haddington and park in one of the town's car parks or on a side street. By bus from Edinburgh, take CCC 251, 253 or 256 or one of SMT's express services.

WALK DIRECTIONS
Walk along Market Street (to the left of the Town Hall) to the traffic lights and turn left into Hardgate. Just beyond a small park beside the river, turn right and follow the river past some houses and out into open countryside. Stay on the footpath beside the river as far as a road bridge over the river. Cross over and walk along the road for a short distance to an old stone entrance gate on the right. Pass through and take the path directly ahead. (Do not take the track round to the right). Follow this right-of-way through rhododendron bushes then along a track across a golf course, passing the clubhouse about Halfway, to another huge entrance gate. Pass through, cross the road outside and walk along the residential road directly opposite. Stay in a straight line as you go over a crossroads and down a

lane, to reach the River Tyne. To the right is the impressive, triple-arched, sixteenth-century Nungate Bridge.

Cross Nungate Bridge and walk upstream, passing the cathedral-like church of St Mary's. Swing round to the right, cross a road and pass an old mill. Just beyond a footbridge over the river, cross a millrace and turn left to continue beside the river; now on a dirt path. Eventually a fence obstructs further passage beside the river. Here turn away from the river into a housing estate. Cross a residential road and take the footpath opposite, round to the right and between houses.

Keep to a more-or-less straight line across another residential road, then along another path for a short distance to some sports grounds. Head diagonally left across the playing fields to a large school. Join an asphalt path and continue past another school and more playing fields until you eventually reach a road. Go right for a few paces to a main road (Sidegate) then left to return to the centre of Haddington.

66. ABERLADY BAY

ORDNANCE SURVEY MAP NO	LANDRANGER 66
	PATHFINDER 396 & 408
DISTANCE FROM EDINBURGH	34 KM (21 ML)
WALKING DISTANCE	10 KM (6 ML)
AMOUNT OF CLIMBING	50 M (164 FT)
ESTIMATED TIME	3 HR

DESCRIPTION A bracing coastal walk mainly along the edge of golf courses but sometimes over rocks and sandy beaches. Stunning views out to sea with several opportunities for a sheltered picnic or swim. Aberlady Bay is renowned for its bird life; the route actually passes through a bird sanctuary. The walk ends at the Green Craigs Restaurant where walkers will receive a very warm welcome whether they drop in just for tea, a drink, home-made soup or a full meal.

START Gullane, East Lothian. NT 481 827
FINISH Entrance to Green Craigs Restaurant, just east of Aberlady, East Lothian. NT 451 791
BUS LINK SMT 124

HOW TO GET THERE By car, take the A1 east out of Edinburgh then the A198 (signposted 'North Berwick') through Longniddry and Aberlady to Gullane. By bus, the same service that links each end of the walk (SMT 124) extends to the centre of Edinburgh.

WALK DIRECTIONS
Head towards the west end of Gullane and turn into the last road on the right (Sandy Loan). At the end of the road, turn left. Walk through Gullane Bents car park and on to a track, then path, over dunes following the coastline to the prominent, rocky Gullane Point. Note that there are several

WALK 66: ABERLADY BAY

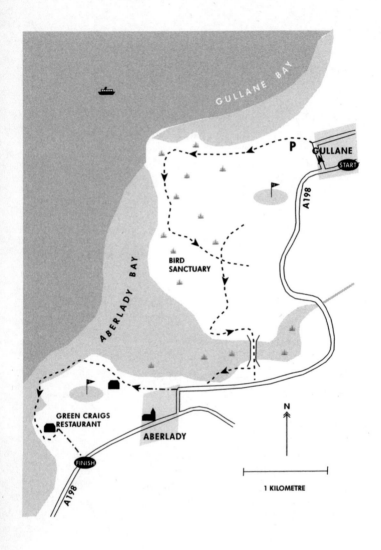

paths along this stretch, any of which may be used – or walk along the beach and over the rocks.

Beyond Gullane Point there is a vast stretch of beautiful, sandy beach. Either walk over the beach or take the undulating path over the dunes. At a prominent line of wooden stakes that stretches out to sea, turn inland. (The continuation of the coast from here is part of a bird sanctuary into which access is prohibited.) Follow the grassy path inland to the edge of a golf course and a junction of paths. Turn right and follow the permitted route (signposted) through the bird sanctuary. Pass a pond on the right, continue through stunted coastal trees and finally cross a long wooden bridge to a car park and main road.

From here to Aberlady, use either the path over the marshes or the path beside the road. At Aberlady stay on the foreshore past some houses, then along a track to the entrance of a golf course. From here use the grassy path around the perimeter of the golf course, staying close to the rocks. Beyond the rocks, walk over the sand as far as Green Craigs Restaurant. Follow the stone wall past the restaurant. Cross the lawn and pass through an archway into the restaurant car park. Then walk along the restaurant access road to a main road, from where a bus may be caught back to Gullane.

WALK 67: GULLANE DUNES

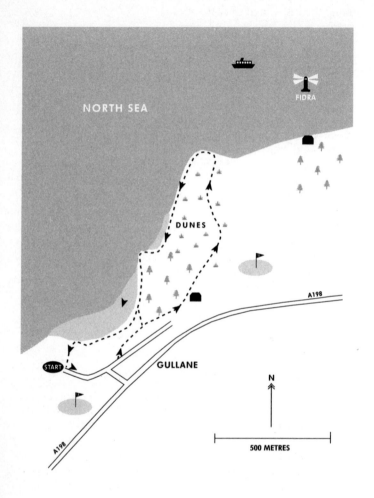

67. GULLANE DUNES

ORDNANCE SURVEY MAP NO	LANDRANGER 66
	PATHFINDER 396
DISTANCE FROM EDINBURGH	33 KM (20 ML)
WALKING DISTANCE	9 KM (5 ML)
AMOUNT OF CLIMBING	NEGLIGIBLE
ESTIMATED TIME	2¾ HR

DESCRIPTION A meandering coastal route over grass-covered dunes, rocks and sandy beaches. There is a vast variety of bird, animal and plants species that flourish only in this special habitat. A bird identification book would be very advantageous on this walk.

START AND FINISH Gullane Bents car park, Gullane, East Lothian. NT 477 832

HOW TO GET THERE Frequent bus service from Edinburgh (SMT 124). By car, take the A1 heading east then the A198 towards North Berwick. Pass through Longniddry and Aberlady. On entering Gullane, take the second road on the left. At the end of the road, turn left to the car park.

WALK DIRECTIONS
Walk back along the car park access road to the houses. Then take a grassy track on the left (signpost, 'overflow car park') across rough grassland. At this second car park, continue on the grassy track – now a bridleway – to a fork. Here go right, away from the sea and moving from the bridleway on to a footpath. Stay on the path as it first winds its way between sea buckthorn bushes, then passes alongside a conifer tree plantation on the left. On reaching a large shed with a golf course on the right, continue straight ahead along a grassy vehicle track. Soon the conifer plantation falls away to the left. The path now meanders

across rough grassland, then over grass-covered sand dunes, until it finally reaches the sea at a small sandy bay with a rocky island just offshore. Far to the right a large house on the edge of the shore should be visible; and out to sea, to the northwest, lies the island of Fidra with its prominent lighthouse.

The return route follows the shore for the entire distance. Either walk over the rocks and sandy bays, or take the slightly easier path along the top of the beach. Eventually the path crosses Black Rocks, a small rocky promontory with pine trees to the left. Beyond lies the great sandy expanse of Gullane Bay.

Walk around the bay (or across if the tide is out). At its far end, close to a navigation post, turn inland up a path through the dunes to return to the car park.

68. DIRLETON COASTAL WALK

ORDNANCE SURVEY MAP NO	LANDRANGER 66
	PATHFINDER 396
DISTANCE FROM EDINBURGH	35 KM (22 ML)
WALKING DISTANCE	11 KM (7 ML)
AMOUNT OF CLIMBING	NEGLIGIBLE
ESTIMATED TIME	3¼ HR

DESCRIPTION This is an easy yet interesting ramble through agricultural land, coniferous forest, sand dunes and finally along a rocky and sandy shoreline. There are good paths and tracks throughout. The walk begins and ends at Dirleton Castle, which is well worth a visit (Historic Scotland, small admission charge).

START AND FINISH Dirleton Castle, Dirleton, East Lothian. NT 514 839

HOW TO GET THERE By car, take the A1 then the A198 (towards North Berwick), through Longniddry, Aberlady and Gullane, to Dirleton and park in the car park close to the castle. There is also a frequent bus service (SMT 124) from Edinburgh.

WALK DIRECTIONS
Walk across a green opposite the castle, then along a road to a church, then along a track to the right of the church. Where the track turns right towards a farm, go straight ahead on a lesser track between fields to some woods. Follow this track beside the woods for a few paces. At an old wooden stile, turn left and pass the short distance through the woods. Go left, following another track, beside the woods then between fields to another woodland.

Just inside these woods, cross a tarmac track and continue on another track directly ahead. After 900 m, this

WALK 68: DIRLETON COASTAL WALK

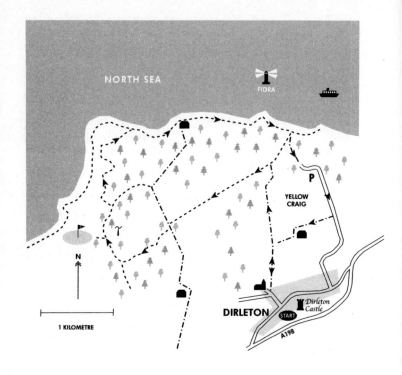

NORTH SEA

FIDRA

P

YELLOW
CRAIG

N

1 KILOMETRE

DIRLETON

START

Dirleton
Castle

A198

track swings round to the right and another track joins from the left. From here, the edge of the forest can occasionally be glimpsed through the trees to the left. Stay on the track, past a radio mast on the right, then some gas pipes within a fenced enclosure also on the right. Just beyond the latter, turn left on to another track out of the forest. After a few paces, bear left on a footpath that crosses rough grassland, close to a golf course, then swings right past some bushes on the right to a stile. Climb over and climb the sand dune ahead. On the other side is a track. Follow this as it meanders across the dunes for about a kilometre to the corner of a conifer plantation close to the sea.

Descend on to the sand and walk along the beach to some rocks. Climb back up on to the dunes. Follow the path over the dunes around a headland, past a mast and two houses; then down on to a beach to cross a small bay; then back up on to the dunes again. All along this stretch, Fidra Island and its prominent lighthouse will be visible just offshore. Shortly after passing the island, turn inland and follow a well-used track to a car park. From here, walk along the access road, round a bend, then turn right on to a farm track. Pass a derelict building on the right before walking through a farm. Continue on the farm track back to Dirleton Church and on to the castle.

WALK 69: PRESTON MILL & HAILES CASTLE

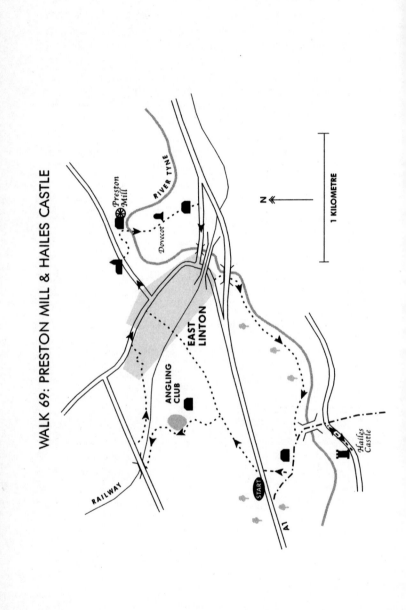

69. PRESTON MILL & HAILES CASTLE

ORDNANCE SURVEY MAP NO	LANDRANGER 67
	PATHFINDER 408
DISTANCE FROM EDINBURGH	37 KM (23 ML)
WALKING DISTANCE	10 KM (6 ML)
AMOUNT OF CLIMBING	130 M (430 FT)
ESTIMATED TIME	3¼ HR

DESCRIPTION A pleasant ramble through agricultural land and along beside a river. The route passes close to Preston Mill, Phantassie Dovecot and Hailes Castle – all of which are well worth a visit.

START AND FINISH Lay-by on the A1, 2 km west of East Linton. Toilets and café. NT 574 766

HOW TO GET THERE Frequent bus service from Edinburgh (SMT 106, X6; CCC 251, 253 or 256) but you will have to walk back from East Linton. By car, take the A1 east. The parking area is situated on the left on the brow of a hill, 7 km (4½ ml) beyond Haddington.

WALK DIRECTIONS
Head east along the A1 road for 400 m then turn left on to a track across field (signpost, 'Right of Way'). At the next signpost leave the right-of-way and continue straight ahead (northnorthwest) along the edge of a field. Go over a stile and along a track between bushes to a collection of small lochs and an anglers' clubhouse. Walk along a causeway to the left of Monastery Loch, then along a track beside a railway to a road. Follow the road over the railway and past some cottages. Turn right on to a footpath that passes alongside the railway then emerges on to a residential road in a housing estate.

Go right along the road and take the second left. At the

end of this close, continue ahead on a short footpath to another road and turn right to reach a main road. Go right along the main road towards East Linton. At a road junction with a blue signpost for Preston Mill, turn left and walk along as far as a church. Take the footpath opposite the church, past an old well, to a weir on the River Tyne. Cross a nearby bridge over a millrace and approach Preston Mill (National Trust for Scotland, admission charge).

From the mill head south across a small field, then cross a footbridge over the river and walk along a track to Phantassie Dovecot. Continue along the track, through Phantassie Farm, to a main road. Here turn right and follow the road over the river, into East Linton. Pass the Bridgend Hotel, then go under a railway bridge and turn left down a lane. At the bottom, cross some grass to a footpath signpost and follow the path beside the river beneath a road bridge. After 2 km you will reach a footbridge. Cross it and follow the path up to Hailes Castle (Historic Scotland, admission by donation into collection box).

Return to the bridge over the river, cross over, then climb a track up to Overhailes Farm. Walk around the left of a large barn. Pass a farmhouse on the right, then turn right on to a track. After a few paces, climb a grassy bank to the left up to an old wooden gate. Climb over and cross the main road ahead to reach the starting point.

70. TRAPRAIN LAW

ORDNANCE SURVEY MAP NO	LANDRANGER 67
	PATHFINDER 408
DISTANCE FROM EDINBURGH	37 KM (23 ML)
WALKING DISTANCE	8 KM (5 ML)
AMOUNT OF CLIMBING	270 M (890 FT)
ESTIMATED TIME	3 HR

DESCRIPTION Traprain Law is a large, volcanic outcrop in the heart of the rolling agricultural lands of East Lothian. The steep climb to the summit is rewarded by stupendous views across East Lothian, from the Lammermuir Hills to the sea. Also *en route* is Hailes Castle, a Historic Scotland monument open to the public. Note that a short section of the descent is over rocks and very steep, but passable with care. Good walking boots are recommended.

START AND FINISH Lay-by on the A1, 2 km west of East Linton. Toilets and café. NT 574 766

HOW TO GET THERE Frequent bus service from Edinburgh (SMT 106, X6; CCC 251, 253 or 256) but you will have to walk back from East Linton. By car, take the A1 east. The parking area is situated on the left on the brow of a hill, 7 km (4½ ml) beyond Haddington.

WALK DIRECTIONS
Cross the main road and climb over an old wooden gate. Descend right down a grassy bank, then go right along a track to farm access road. Go left along this road, past a large barn, then downhill to a footbridge over the River Tyne. Cross over and follow a path then a road to Hailes Castle. At the castle parking area, move on to a signposted footpath. Follow this up between fields until a gate is reached with a track going straight ahead. Here turn left on

WALK 70: TRAPRAIN LAW

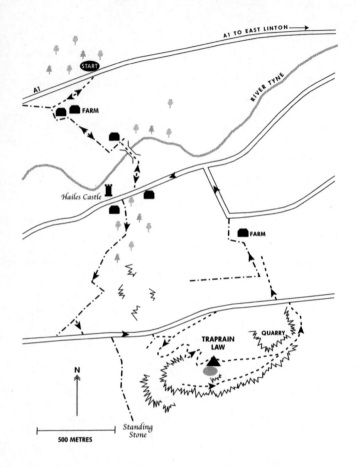

A1 TO EAST LINTON →

RIVER TYNE

START

A1

FARM

Hailes Castle

FARM

TRAPRAIN LAW

QUARRY

N

Standing
Stone

500 METRES

to a grassy track for a short distance to a minor road. Go left along the road. Do not take the footpath to the standing stone, but continue to Traprain Law. At the base of the Law, climb over a stile on the right. Go left on a path for a few paces then turn uphill to join a more substantial path heading right (west). Follow the marker posts, as the path swings round to the left then zigzags up to the summit of Traprain Law (221 m / 725 ft, triangulation point, stell).

From the summit walk across to the small tarn, and round the back of the nearby small rocky outcrop. Here go left on a path that leads to the rocky, eastern end of the summit ridge. A wire fence marking the top of a quarry will now be visible. Follow this carefully down a short but very steep and rocky descent. At the bottom, go left over a stile and follow the path between a fence and a dry-stone wall down to the road. Cross diagonally left and take a track heading towards a farm.

Halfway to the farm, move a few paces to the left on to a more substantial track, still heading towards the farm. Follow this track round to the left of the farm and on to another minor road. Follow this downhill to a T-junction and go left, still on a road, to reach the path to the river crossing used earlier. From here retrace your steps to the starting place.

WALK 71: NORTH BERWICK LAW

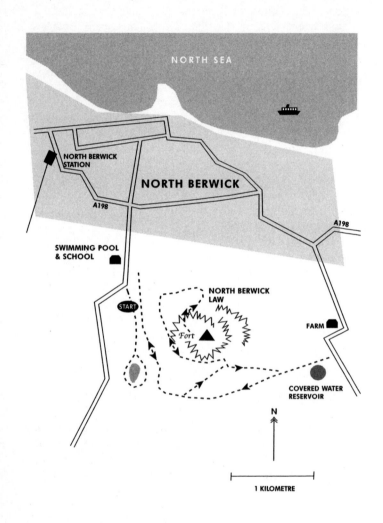

NORTH SEA

NORTH BERWICK
STATION

NORTH BERWICK

A198

A198

SWIMMING POOL
& SCHOOL

START

NORTH BERWICK
LAW

Fort

FARM

COVERED WATER
RESERVOIR

N

1 KILOMETRE

71. NORTH BERWICK LAW

ORDNANCE SURVEY MAP NO	LANDRANGER 66
	PATHFINDER 396
DISTANCE FROM EDINBURGH	40 KM (25 ML)
WALKING DISTANCE	3½ KM (2 ML)
AMOUNT OF CLIMBING	147 M (482 FT)
ESTIMATED TIME	1¼ HR

DESCRIPTION A short walk but a steep climb up one of East Lothian's most famous landmarks. The energetic ascent of this extinct volcano is rewarded by panoramic views over North Berwick and the Bass Rock, the whole of East Lothian and across the Firth of Forth to the Isle of May and the distant hills of Fife. On the summit are the remains of look-out posts, dating from as far back as the Napoleonic wars, and the jaw bones of a whale that beached itself in 1936. Although quite a short walk, this really is a route not to be missed.

START AND FINISH North Berwick Law car park. NT 553 843

HOW TO GET THERE By car, take the A1 east until close to Tranent, then the A198 to North Berwick. On entering the town, turn right at a signpost for Dunbar, pass the railway station, then turn right again at a signpost for Haddington. Pass a swimming pool and a school then, at a bend, go straight ahead along a track to a car park. Alternatively, take a bus (SMT 124) or train (ScotRail) to North Berwick Station and walk the mile to the car park.

WALK DIRECTIONS
Step through a gap in a stone wall at the rear of the car park and turn right on to a track. Follow this around a bend to the left, then move left on to a footpath ascending a steep

grassy bank. This path ascends steeply at first before easing a little as it traverses the south side of the law to a bench beneath some crags. Here the path doubles back on itself and begins the steep ascent back round to the west side, then up some crags to the summit (187 m / 614 ft, triangulation point, viewfinder, remains of look-outs, whale bones).

Descend from the summit on the same route as that used for the ascent, at least as far as the bottom of the crags. Note that there are other paths off the summit descending the crags of the west face – but their use is not recommended as they are very thin and slippery and, should a slip occur, there is nothing to halt one's fall for several hundred metres. From the bottom of the crags go left, down the grassy tail of the law, until another path is encountered close to some beech trees. Go right here, doubling back on yourself, around the southern base of the hill. This path soon becomes a track and leads all the way back to the car park.

OPTIONAL EXTRA As an optional extra little walk, follow a path alongside the car park side of the stone wall into a copse of trees. Here the path circles a small pond, then returns to the car park.

72. LAMMER LAW IN THE LAMMERMUIR HILLS

ORDNANCE SURVEY MAP NO	LANDRANGER 66
	PATHFINDER 421
DISTANCE FROM EDINBURGH	42 KM (24 ML)
WALKING DISTANCE	10 KM (6 ML)
AMOUNT OF CLIMBING	350 M (1,148 FT)
ESTIMATED TIME	3¾ HR

DESCRIPTION A lonely moorland walk, accompanied only by the sound of wind, lapwings and curlews, to the highest point in the Lammermuir Hills. The top of Lammer Law provides a stunning panoramic view of seemingly endless slopes, low hills and empty moorland. Good walking boots are required, plus a compass to navigate from Lammer Law to Widow's Knowe.

START AND FINISH Tollishill Farm by Carfraemill. NT 518 579

HOW TO GET THERE By car, take the A68 southeast out of Edinburgh, through Dalkeith and over Soutra Hill, as far as the roundabout at Carfraemill. Turn on to the A697, then immediately left again at the Carfraemill Hotel on to a minor road. At a fork go right. After 2 ml, near a cattle enclosure, go right around a hairpin bend. Tollishill Farm is at the end of this asphalt road. Park on the side of the road without causing any obstruction. Public transport is not available for this walk.

WALK DIRECTIONS

Pass through a gate and walk northeast along a gravel track. After 1 km go straight ahead, past a track to the right and another to the left, then pass beneath electricity transmission cables. From here the track makes a long, gradual ascent to pass close by the twin tops of Crib Law. It then descends and crosses a broad watershed before rising

WALK 72: LAMMER LAW IN
THE LAMMERMUIR HILLS

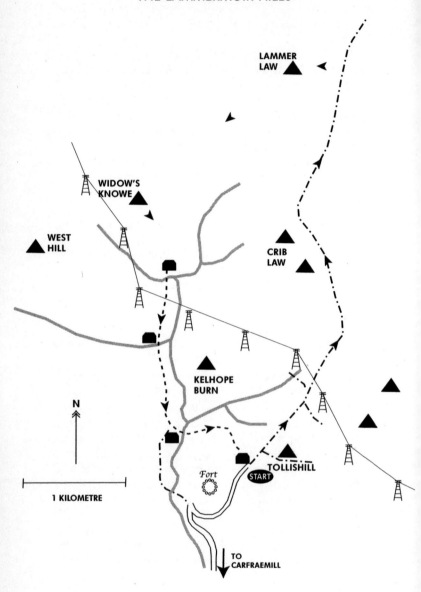

LAMMER
LAW

WIDOW'S
KNOWE

WEST
HILL

CRIB
LAW

KELHOPE
BURN

N

TOLLISHILL

START

Fort

1 KILOMETRE

TO
CARFRAEMILL

up the eastern shoulder of Lammer Law. At the highest point on this shoulder, turn left and cut up through the heather to the summit of Lammer Law (527 m / 1,728 ft, triangulation pillar, cairn).

Leave the summit down the gently sloping shoulder that heads southwest to a lower hill, Widow's Knowe. From the top of Widow's Knowe, turn southeast and descend to the point where the two tributaries of Kelhope Burn come together.

Ford the stream, then follow a path downstream to some farm buildings and the start of a track. Here turn left, off the main track, and follow a path over Tollishill and back to the start.

WALK 73: LAUDER TO EDGARHOPE LAW

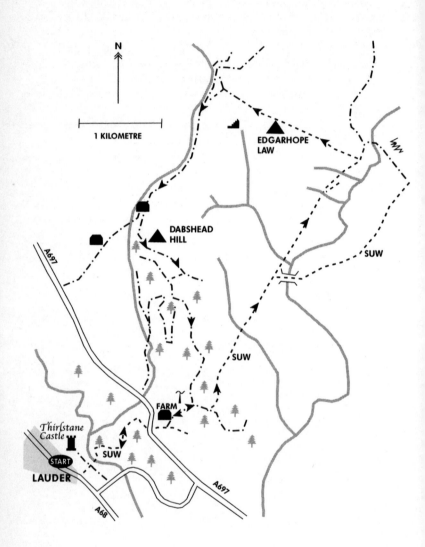

73. LAUDER TO EDGARHOPE LAW

ORDNANCE SURVEY MAP NO	LANDRANGER 73
	PATHFINDER 449
DISTANCE FROM EDINBURGH	43 KM (27 ML)
WALKING DISTANCE/	21 KM (13 ML)/
SHORT VERSION	11 KM (7 ML)
AMOUNT OF CLIMBING	560 M (1,837 FT)/
	250 M (820 FT)
ESTIMATED TIME	6–7 HR / 3 HR

DESCRIPTION A fairly long but rewarding walk into a remote moorland area in the Lammermuir Hills. There is a feeling of isolation during this walk. For many hours neither buildings nor roads can be seen, and one's only company are the many grouse, pheasants and sheep.

START AND FINISH Lauder. NT 530 475

HOW TO GET THERE By car, take the A68 through Dalkeith and over Soutra Hill to Lauder. Park near the Community Hall in the town, or on a side street. By bus, use service LOW 29 or 30.

WALK DIRECTIONS
Walk south along the A68, past a police station, then next left down a track to a bridge over a small river. Cross over and follow signs for the Southern Upland Way (SUW) to the left, round grazing land, then up through woodlands to a main road. Cross over, walk up a track to a farm, turn left and continue uphill, past a transmitter mast, into woodlands. At a T-junction turn right. On leaving the woodland, turn left over a stile then follow the upper edge of the forest for a while. Next, bear off over grazing land following SUW marker posts.

Continue along the SUW, over a burn then up over a

ridge and down, until a second burn with a wooden footbridge and adjacent red plaque can be seen ahead. At a gate through a stone wall, before the descent to this bridge, leave the SUW and continue straight ahead on a grassy track. Go through a second gate and across a smaller burn, then along a track through heather, traversing the hill to the left of the larger burn. Eventually you will reach a wooden gate roughly level with the end of the woodland and a small quarry on the far side of the valley. Do not pass through this gate, but turn left on to a thin path through heather that gently ascends to the highest point on the ridge (Edgarhope Law, 367 m / 1,204 ft, two small cairns).

Just beyond the second cairn, join a gravel track. Follow it over another lower ridge then steeply downhill. At a fork, go left to reach a valley bottom with a burn and a more substantial track. Follow this track down through the valley until some stables are reached. Just beyond the stables, pass above a large house with a tennis court and swimming pool, then fork left and climb steadily around Dabshead Hill. Towards the summit the track passes alongside Edgarhope Wood – look out for splendid views across Lauder to the distant hills.

Where the track bears away to the left, continue straight ahead alongside the wood, down into a gully. At the bottom, turn right over an old gate and enter the woodland. Walk along a short grassy path to a second gate, then go left along a moss-covered track. At a fork go left and continue through the forest, until the SUW is once more encountered. Turn right and follow the outward route back to Lauder.

SHORT VERSION Follow the SUW as far as the T-junction in Edgarhope Wood. Turn left and follow the track through the wood then along a zigzag descent and out to a main road. Carefully, walk along the road to rejoin the SUW back to Lauder.

74. JOHN MUIR COUNTRY PARK

ORDNANCE SURVEY MAP NO	LANDRANGER 67
	PATHFINDER 396
DISTANCE FROM EDINBURGH	44 KM (27 ML)
WALKING DISTANCE	9 KM (5½ ML)
AMOUNT OF CLIMBING	NEGLIGIBLE
ESTIMATED TIME	2¾ HR

DESCRIPTION A seashore and river estuary walk within the northern section of the John Muir Country Park. There are stunning views out to sea and the park is renowned for its sea birds. No special clothing is required, although a towel and swimming costume may be desirable.

START AND FINISH car park on Tyninghame House Estate between North Berwick and Dunbar. NT 626 809

HOW TO GET THERE By car, take the A1 east towards Dunbar. A little beyond East Linton, turn left on to the A198 towards North Berwick. Pass through the village of Tyninghame, then turn next right on to a minor road. The car park is at the end of this road, beside a farm. Public transport is not practical for this walk.

WALK DIRECTIONS
At the end of the car park turn right off the main track, around a wooden gate, on to a straight, tree-lined track beside a field. Where this track bears right, turn left on to a grassy track towards the sea marsh and then into some woods. Immediately on entering the woods, turn right on to a path along the edge of the woods to the marsh. Continue beside the marsh for a few paces to a grassy sandbank stretching out to sea between the marsh and the sea. Follow this natural causeway out to a tree-covered promontory of land (Sandy Hirst). Then return to the mainland and

WALK 74: JOHN MUIR COUNTRY PARK

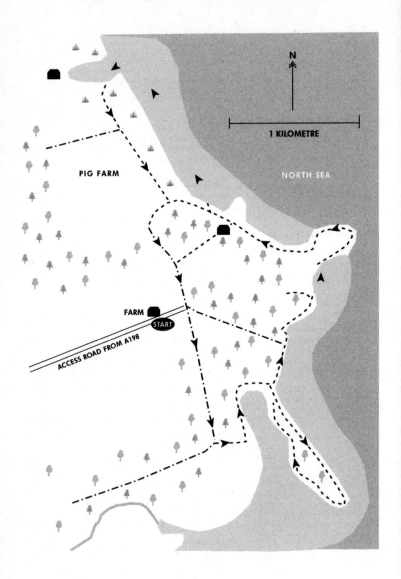

N

1 KILOMETRE

PIG FARM

NORTH SEA

FARM

START

ACCESS ROAD FROM A198

continue along the top of the beach to a park notice-board and nearby track heading inland.

Do not take the inland track, but continue along the top of the beach. After a few paces, step left over a wire fence on to an undulating footpath, parallel to the beach, just within a woodland. Where this path turns inland, descend to the right on to sand. Proceed along the beach for a further 50 m to some steps up a grassy bank. Climb these, then follow a path across a grassy headland to a seat carved out of red rock.

From the seat continue along the path to a large, rocky outcrop. Pass either behind or in front of this, then walk the length of the beach to a river inlet. Turn into the inlet for 100 m to another park notice-board. Here turn left on to a path through dunes, then on to a track heading back between the dunes and a pig farm. On reaching a stone wall, follow the track round to the right, then left into a woodland. At a junction of tracks go directly ahead to return to the car park.

WALK 75: PRESSMENNAN WOOD

75. PRESSMENNAN WOOD

ORDNANCE SURVEY MAP NO	LANDRANGER 67
	PATHFINDER 409
DISTANCE FROM EDINBURGH	45 KM (29 ML)
WALKING DISTANCE	5½ KM (3½ ML)
AMOUNT OF CLIMBING	120 M (400 FT)
ESTIMATED TIME	1¾ HR

DESCRIPTION Pressmennan Wood has been preserved by local people and the Woodland Trust because of its outstanding natural beauty and importance to wildlife. There is a loch that runs the length of the woodland which was specifically built at the end of the nineteenth century to attract birds and wildlife. Nowadays, thanks to the Woodland Trust, one can often see roe deer and other animals; and several interesting wooden sculptures have been installed.

START AND FINISH Pressmennan Wood, near Stenton, East Lothian. NT 620 725

HOW TO GET THERE By car, take the A1 east. At East Linton, follow the A1 over a railway then turn right towards Stenton. Continue along this minor road to a T-junction with the B6370 and turn left. On entering Stenton, take the first road to the right. Keep going until you pass through a farm. Turn left along a rough track to reach a car park at the entrance to Pressmennan Wood.

WALK DIRECTIONS
From the car park take the right-hand (upper) track into the woodland and climb steadily for a little more than a kilometre to a high point. Continue on the track downhill for a further 600 m – passing on the way a downward-pointing yellow arrow on a tree and a burn. At the end of

the track the route continues ahead on a path. Follow this path around to the right, then left along the upper edge of the wood. This section can be quite wet. Soon the path descends steeply down a fire break until it meets another forestry track just above a dam wall.

Go right along this track, parallel with the stream flowing out of the reservoir. After 400 m, at the end of the woods, stay on the track as it doubles back and returns to the dam wall on the far side of the burn. Cross the dam wall and climb a short path back on to the forestry track (look for the wooden carving of a fox between the dam wall and the track). Follow this track to the right for 800 m to a fallen tree cleverly carved into a seat. Turn right here on to a footpath beside another interesting wooden seat and descend to the water's edge.

Follow the path through the woods, roughly parallel with the loch, until it finally emerges on to a dirt road. Here, immediately turn left on to another path back into the woods. This is only a short path and soon emerges on to a road close to the car park.

76. EAST LINTON TO DUNBAR

ORDNANCE SURVEY MAP NO	LANDRANGER 67
	PATHFINDER 408 & 409
DISTANCE FROM EDINBURGH	50 KM (31 ML)
WALKING DISTANCE	14 KM (8½ ML)
AMOUNT OF CLIMBING	NEGLIGIBLE
ESTIMATED TIME	4¼ HR

DESCRIPTION This long walk passes through a range of terrain: from rural village and agricultural land, along a river bank and through woodland, to estuary, coastal and, finally, urban. Highlights include the scenic village of East Linton, Preston Mill, the aquatic bird life of the John Muir Country Park and the historic town of Dunbar with its cliffs, harbour, castle and battery. The route along the River Tyne is a right-of-way throughout its length, but the short section beyond the ford is little used and may be overgrown. The rest of the route is through the John Muir Country Park and along public paths.

START East Linton, East Lothian. NT 592 772
FINISH Dunbar. NT 681 793
BUS LINK SMT 106

HOW TO GET THERE From Edinburgh there is a frequent train (GNER) and bus (SMT 106; CCC 251, 253 or 256) service. By car, take the A1 east to Dunbar and park beside the swimming pool near the harbour. Walk to the bus shelter in the High Street and take a bus (SMT 106) to East Linton.

WALK DIRECTIONS
Head north along Bridge Street. Turn left at the junction with a blue sign for Preston Mill. At a church, turn right on to a footpath and descend past an old well to a weir on the

WALK 76: EAST LINTON TO DUNBAR

River Tyne. Cross a nearby millrace then follow it to Preston Mill (National Trust for Scotland, admission charge).

From the mill, cross a small field to the river and follow the far bank downstream. Cross again to the opposite bank at the next bridge and continue downstream to a weir. Here the route leaves the river for a short distance, following a small burn to a cottage, then returns to the river at a ford and footbridge. Cross over and continue downstream, through long grass then along the edge of a field, to a road bridge. Pass beneath the bridge. Clamber up on to the road and follow it south. After 300 m, turn left on to a farm track and enter the John Muir Country Park. Continue along the track without deviation for 1½ km to an embankment and the estuary marshes.

Swing right with the track, then immediately turn left on to a footpath along the edge of the marshes and across a tributary to a fire point at the edge of a coniferous woodland. For a short-cut, go straight ahead; otherwise turn left and follow a path around the headland and into Belhaven Bay. At the end of the woodland, pass a car park, toilet and barbeque site (on the left). If the tide is out, turn left here and cross the marshes, then a sand bank and footbridge (on the sand) to reach a cluster of wooden chalets at Belhaven. If this route is submerged, walk around the bay to Belhaven. From here follow a footpath around a golf course, then along the cliff tops to a swimming pool and harbour.

WALK 77: WHITEADDER WATER

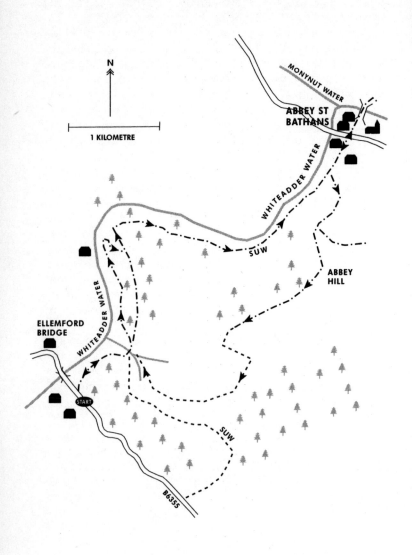

77. WHITEADDER WATER

ORDNANCE SURVEY MAP NO	LANDRANGER 67
	PATHFINDER 422
DISTANCE FROM EDINBURGH	56 KM (35 ML)
WALKING DISTANCE	11 KM (7 ML)
AMOUNT OF CLIMBING	200 M (660 FT)
ESTIMATED TIME	3¾ HR

DESCRIPTION An easy walk through a pine forest beside Whiteadder Water to Abbey St Bathans, returning via a higher route across grazing land. Most of the route follows forest tracks which are mainly dry but muddy in places. The final section is on a path over grazing land which can be muddy.

START AND FINISH Ellemford Bridge near Duns. NT 730 599

HOW TO GET THERE By car, take the A1 east. Turn off at Tranent and follow the B6355 for 25 very scenic miles to Ellemford Bridge. Park just over the bridge on the left-hand side of the road.

WALK DIRECTIONS
Climb over a metal gate and follow a dirt track through a forest. Where the track swings left over a burn and forks, go left down into the darkness of the forest beside a burn. At the bottom of the hill, take a right-hand fork and continue along the track (now rather muddy) through woods above a river. You will soon see a house on the far side of the river. Shortly afterwards the path swings right and climbs steeply to join another forest track. Go left. This is now the Southern Upland Way (SUW). Follow the track as it leaves the forest and passes through a number of gates before its final gradual descent into Abbey St Bathans.

Cross a road and continue on a track directly ahead. At a

footbridge that carries the SUW across Whiteadder Water, turn back and return up the track back through the village, across the road and uphill to a fork with a gate across each track. Take the left-hand track, leaving the SUW, uphill then along the edge of a pine-tree wood. At a fork, go right through a gate and then away from the woods. Shortly after the gate there is a splendid view of the Whiteadder Valley. The track taken through the forest earlier can clearly be seen. Continue along the track. From here the next gate passes through an *electric* fence, so take care. Stay on the track past a copse of pine trees and on to a second copse. Here the path ends at a wooden gate.

Climb over the gate and walk directly ahead along a narrow path beside a fence (*electrified*, so be careful) across grazing land. At a corner, follow the fence left to another pine forest, then along the edge of the forest. Soon the top of a gully is reached. Descend to the bottom and a wooden fence. Climb over and rejoin the forest track used earlier. Turn left and follow the track back to the start.

78. PEASE DEAN & PENMANSHIEL WOOD

ORDNANCE SURVEY MAP NO	LANDRANGER 67
	PATHFINDER 409 & 422
DISTANCE FROM EDINBURGH	61 KM (38 ML)
WALKING DISTANCE	6 KM (4 ML)
AMOUNT OF CLIMBING	250 M (820 FT)
ESTIMATED TIME	2¼ HR

DESCRIPTION A fascinating ramble through Pease Dean Nature Reserve, followed by a walk through a conifer plantation returning to Pease Bay via part of the Southern Upland Way (SUW). The nature reserve contains a variety of trees and wildlife and many paths, all undulating with many wooden steps and bridges. There are superb panoramic views of the coastline on the return through Penmanshiel Wood. Pease Bay has one of the cleanest beaches in Britain and provides an ideal spot for a picnic or swim after the walk. This walk may be extended by starting in Cockburnspath and following the SUW past Cove and along the cliffs to Pease Bay.

START AND FINISH Pease Bay near Cockburnspath. NT 795 706

HOW TO GET THERE By car, take the A1 towards Berwick. At the roundabout just beyond Torness Power Station, turn left on to a minor road to Pease Bay. Cross the ford beside the caravan park and park in the public car park to the right. Alternatively, use bus service CCC 251, 253 or 256 to Cockburnspath and walk along the SUW to Pease Bay.

WALK DIRECTIONS
Cross the footbridge beside the ford and turn left on to the SUW footpath into Pease Dean Nature Reserve. Where the SUW turns left and crosses a burn, continue uphill on the right of the burn. Follow this undulating path round to the

WALK 78: PEASE DEAN & PENMANSHIEL WOOD

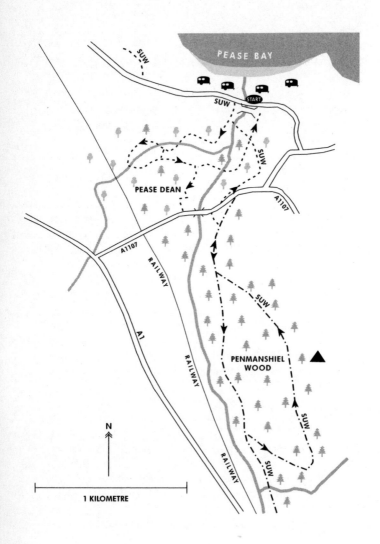

right, crossing the stream twice, then across the burn again and back along the far side of the burn. The path climbs through the woodland and meets another path coming up from Pease Bay. Turn right here and continue uphill until the path emerges on to a road close to a high bridge.

Cross the road bridge and turn right to rejoin the SUW footpath. After a few steps, join a grassy track through a conifer plantation. At a fork, take the lower track (leaving the SUW). Follow this track until a second fork is reached. Go left here and so rejoin the SUW. Follow this track round to the left, then uphill. At the top of the long, gradual incline there are superb views over the surrounding countryside.

Continue ahead to descend back to the road bridge crossed earlier. Go right along the road for a few paces, then left on to the SUW footpath. This leads back down the glen to a junction of paths beside a notice-board. Do not cross the burn to the left, but go straight ahead, through a gate and small caravan park, to the car park.

WALK 79: FAST CASTLE

NORTH SEA

Fast Castle

TELEGRAPH HILL

DERELICT COTTAGES

DOWLAW FARM

P

P

START

FARM ACCESS ROAD

N

500 METRES

79. FAST CASTLE

ORDNANCE SURVEY MAP NO	LANDRANGER 67
	PATHFINDER 423
DISTANCE FROM EDINBURGH	68 KM (42 ML)
WALKING DISTANCE (THERE AND BACK)	3 KM (2 ML)
AMOUNT OF CLIMBING	180 M (590 FT)
ESTIMATED TIME	1¼ HR

DESCRIPTION A relatively long journey for a short walk, but definitely worth it. The drive along the coast is spectacular in itself; the walk is even more so. The grassy path leads over the tops of some very dramatic cliffs, then descends steeply to a massive rock stack on which are the remains of Fast Castle. There is little left of the castle but its location is most spectacular. There are deep drops on all sides with gulls and other sea birds soaring around. To reach the stack it is necessary to cross a narrow bridge (with chains for support) over a particularly deep chasm. This is not a walk for a windy day, vertigo sufferers or anxious parents.

START AND FINISH Dowlow Farm, near Cockburnspath. NT 855 703

HOW TO GET THERE By car, take the A1 past Dunbar. A little beyond Cockburnspath, turn left on to the A1107 towards Coldingham. After 3 ml, turn left on to a minor road to Dowlaw Farm. Park at the end of this road.

WALK DIRECTIONS
Turn left just before Dowlaw Farm on to a track leading to a row of derelict cottages. Just beyond the cottages, pass through a gate and turn right. From here, follow a grassy path around Telegraph Hill, then across cliff tops and down to a rocky stack on which are the ruins of Fast Castle.

The return is a reversal of the outward route, as there are no viable alternatives.

WALK 80: ST ABB'S HEAD

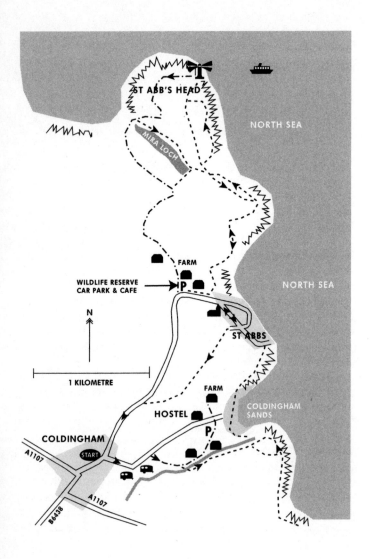

NORTH SEA

ST ABB'S HEAD

MIRA LOCH

NORTH SEA

FARM

WILDLIFE RESERVE
CAR PARK & CAFE

P

N

1 KILOMETRE

ST ABBS

FARM

HOSTEL

P

COLDINGHAM
SANDS

COLDINGHAM

START

A1107

A1107

B6438

80. ST ABB'S HEAD

ORDNANCE SURVEY MAP NO	LANDRANGER 67
	PATHFINDER 423
DISTANCE FROM EDINBURGH	79 KM (49 ML)
WALKING DISTANCE	12 KM (7½ ML)
AMOUNT OF CLIMBING	330 M (1,080 FT)
ESTIMATED TIME	4¼ HR

DESCRIPTION A long drive but well worth it. A stunning coastal walk along rugged cliffs, with many dramatic views down to the sea. St Abbs is a very picturesque village and St Abb's Head is a wildlife reserve renowned for its bird life. Binoculars and a bird identification book would be very useful.

START AND FINISH Coldingham. NT 904 661

HOW TO GET THERE By car, drive along the A1 for 41 ml beyond the City Bypass. Turn left on to the B6438 to Coldingham and park in the village. There is a parking area on the road to St Abbs just beyond the turn-off to Coldingham Sands. By bus, CCC 253 is an hourly service from Edinburgh to Coldingham, St Abbs and Eyemouth.

WALK DIRECTIONS
Walk through Coldingham on the road towards St Abbs, but turn right at the sign for Coldingham Sands. Turn right again just beyond a caravan park on to a dirt track. At a left-hand bend, go right on to a thin path down to a burn. (If this turn-off is missed, continue along the track past a youth hostel, then turn right on to a farm track to rejoin the footpath). Step across the burn and follow the path alongside the burn. After a short distance the path widens then meets a farm track. Go up the track for a few paces towards a gate into a field, then bear left back on to the footpath.

As you leave the trees bear right (uphill) beside a fence to a gate, then left, still beside a fence, then downhill to meet a coastal path. Go left along the coastal path, over Coldingham Sands and along the cliff tops, to the outskirts of St Abbs. Here follow a signpost along a residential road heading towards a church. At a main road, turn left. Pass the church and turn right on to a footpath to St Abb's Head. Once over the first hill, you can either stick to the main path or take one of the more interesting alternative paths to the right. Either way, keep going as far as the lighthouse.

Walk around the lighthouse buildings, then along an asphalt track down to Mira Loch, and turn left on to a path beside the loch. At the dam wall, go left and rejoin the outward path to St Abbs. Take the same residential road through St Abbs but, Halfway along, turn right into Creel Road. At the end of this road join a footpath across fields back to Coldingham.

ALTERNATIVE ROUTE Park in the wildlife reserve car park, take the bus (CCC 253) to Eyemouth. There join the coastal path along the cliffs to St Abbs.

WESTERN REGION

WALK 81: THE HEART OF THE PENTLAND HILLS

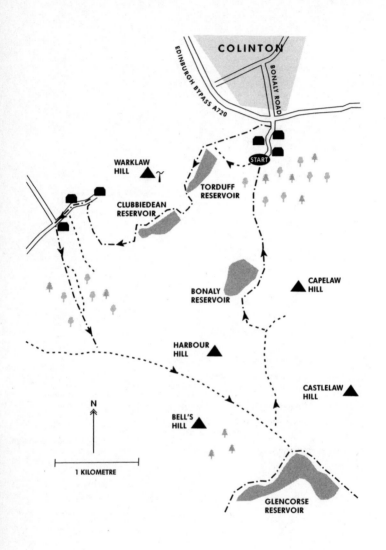

81. THE HEART OF THE PENTLAND HILLS

ORDNANCE SURVEY MAP NO	LANDRANGER 66
	PATHFINDER 419 & 420
DISTANCE FROM EDINBURGH	10½ KM (6½ ML)
WALKING DISTANCE	11½ KM (7 ML)
AMOUNT OF CLIMBING	300 M (980 FT)
ESTIMATED TIME	4½ HR

DESCRIPTION A splendid hill walk deep into the heart of the Pentland Hills. There is nothing too strenuous or steep and there are reasonable paths throughout – although some are rough and some are muddy. Stout walking boots are recommended.

START AND FINISH Car park at the end of Bonaly Road, a little south of Colinton, Edinburgh. NT 211 673

HOW TO GET THERE By car, drive to Colinton. At the fork and traffic lights in the centre of the village, take the upper road (Woodhall Road) then second left into Bonaly Road. Follow this over the City Bypass then straight ahead along a narrow lane to a car park at the end of the road.

WALK DIRECTIONS
Pass through a gate and turn right on to the path towards Torduff Reservoir. Follow this over a small, rocky hill then across the dam wall of Torduff Reservoir. Turn left on to an asphalt track. Pass the reservoir, then cross a bridge beside a small waterfall and continue on to Clubbiedean Reservoir. When the tarmac ends just beyond Clubbiedean Reservoir, continue on a gravel track along a ridge through grazing land. Along this stretch there are great views across the River Forth to the Ochil Hills. Proceed round to the right and downhill to the farm of Easter Kinleith.

Double back on a minor road following the signpost for

Harlaw. Pass the entrance to Poet's Glen and keep going along the road to a junction with a white house on the left. Turn left here, through a gate, on to a gradually ascending gravel track. Near the top of the incline one can either continue on the track or take the more interesting parallel path through the trees on the left. At the end of the woodland, climb over a stile and continue ahead over rough grassland for a short distance to a signpost and another footpath. Turn left towards Glencorse. Follow the path through the pass between Harbour Hill and Bell's Hill, then down towards Glencorse Reservoir. A little above the reservoir, at a signpost near the beginning of a small copse of conifer trees, turn left on to the path to Bonaly.

Climb over another pass then, at a signpost near some trees, turn left to continue the descent to a gravel track. Near here is Bonaly Reservoir, but it can only be seen by taking a short detour to the left. To continue, take the gravel track leading downhill across open hillside, then through a woodland, to return to the Bonaly car park.

82. THE POET'S GLEN

ORDNANCE SURVEY MAP NO	LANDRANGER 66
	PATHFINDER 419 & 420
DISTANCE FROM EDINBURGH	10½ KM (6½ ML)
WALKING DISTANCE	5 KM (3 ML)
AMOUNT OF CLIMBING	135 M (443 FT)
ESTIMATED TIME	1¾ HR

DESCRIPTION An easy walk that traverses one of the lower Pentland Hills and then descends the narrow, wooded Poet's Glen to the Water of Leith. The return route runs alongside the river for a while, then crosses agricultural land. From the higher ground there are excellent views of Arthur's Seat, Edinburgh Castle, Corstorphine Hill and the Firth of Forth.

START AND FINISH The end of Torphin Road, just beyond Colinton, Edinburgh. NT 203 679

HOW TO GET THERE By car, drive to Colinton. At the fork and traffic lights in the centre of the village, take the upper road (Woodhall Road) then, at a sign for Torphin Golf Course, turn right into Torphin Road. Pass the golf course and park at the end of the road beside a disued quarry. By bus, take LRT 10 to its terminus close to Torphin Golf Course and walk the short remaining distance.

WALK DIRECTIONS
Head off past the quarry on the signposted right-of-way footpath and follow it over the side of Torphin Hill to Easter Kinleith Farm. Just beyond the farm, at a signpost, turn right into woods and Poet's Glen. Follow the main path down through the glen, passing a pond then crossing a wooden bridge. On reaching a road at the bottom, turn right and follow the road around to the left. At the next

WALK 82: THE POET'S GLEN

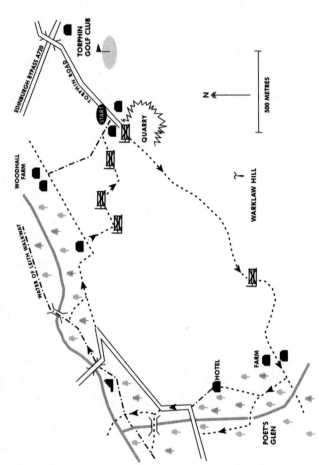

EDINBURGH BYPASS A720

TORPHIN GOLF CLUB

TORPHIN ROAD

START

QUARRY

WOODHALL FARM

WATER OF LEITH WALKWAY

WARKLAW HILL

HOTEL

FARM

POET'S GLEN

N

500 METRES

bend, at a signpost, 'Water of Leith', turn left on to a footpath through more woods. Pass (but do not cross) a footbridge over a burn. Continue downhill on the main footpath until it meets the Water of Leith Walkway. Turn right.

Follow the Water of Leith Walkway past an old mill (currently being demolished) and beneath a road bridge. Just before the walkway crosses the river, turn right and climb a steep path through trees to another footpath. Follow this to the left. On reaching Woodhall Estate, follow the path round to the right then to the left.

Shortly after this, turn right on to a grassy track gently rising between fields. At the top, pass through a gate and follow the edge of the field to the left. Pass through the next gate, then turn right and ascend beside a hedgerow along the edge of sheep-grazing land. Bear left around the top of the paddock. At the next corner, turn right on to a track back to the starting point.

WALK 83: THE FORTH BRIDGES

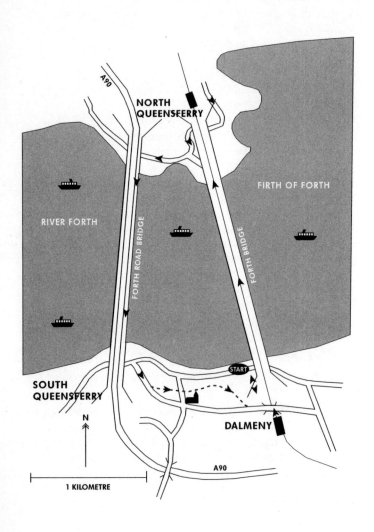

NORTH
QUEENSFERRY

A90

FIRTH OF FORTH

RIVER FORTH

FORTH ROAD BRIDGE

FORTH BRIDGE

START

SOUTH
QUEENSFERRY

DALMENY

N

A90

1 KILOMETRE

83. THE FORTH BRIDGES

ORDNANCE SURVEY MAP NO	LANDRANGER 65
	PATHFINDER 406 & 394
DISTANCE FROM EDINBURGH	15 KM (9 ML)
WALKING DISTANCE	6 KM (4 ML)
AMOUNT OF CLIMBING	NEGLIGIBLE
ESTIMATED TIME	1¾ HR

DESCRIPTION A fascinating walk with a touch of adventure for children; a train ride across the famous Forth Bridge; and a walk across the road bridge, which can be felt to move when a heavy lorry passes or if there is a strong wind. This walk provides a unique seagull's view of the Forth, its islands and shipping plus a non-tourist route through South Queensferry. Note that crossing the bridge in winter can be extremely cold if there is a brisk wind and that very strong winds may make passage on foot impossible.

START AND FINISH Hawes Pier, South Queensferry. NT 137 784

HOW TO GET THERE Frequent bus service from Edinburgh to Dalmeny Station (MB 47) or train (ScotRail) direct to North Queensferry. By car, take the A90 (Queensferry Road) then the B9245 to South Queensferry and park in the car park on the right just beyond the rail bridge.

WALK DIRECTIONS
Ascend the steps behind the Hawes Inn, then follow a footpath beside the railway to Dalmeny Station. Take a north-bound train to the next station, North Queensferry (30-minute service, 2-hourly on Sundays).

From North Queensferry Station, follow a twisting road downhill towards the Forth. Continue on the road round to the right until it passes beneath the Forth Road Bridge. Climb the stairs on to the bridge and use either walkway to cross to South Queensferry. The walkway on the right (west) side of the bridge provides views of Rosyth Naval Docks and the upper reaches of the Forth, while from the left walkway one can see the Forth Bridge, Inchgarvie forts and the Firth of Forth.

Just before the toll booths (no fee for pedestrians), descend some steps to the base of the bridge support and turn right into Stewart Terrace. After 50 m, go down a short footpath on the left, then turn right along Morison Gardens. At a T-junction, cross a main road and take the paved footpath (Back Brae) beside the kirk. Follow Back Brae round to the right, past a bowling club and small park, then turn left through a gap in a wall and descend steps into a woodland.

Follow a path through the woods, across a small bridge over a burn, and finally emerge on to an asphalt road close to a bus stop. Go left along this road to Dalmeny Station, then follow the signposted path beside the railway down to the Hawes Pier.

84. THE UNION CANAL FROM RATHO

ORDNANCE SURVEY MAP NO	LANDRANGER 65
	PATHFINDER 406 & 419
DISTANCE FROM EDINBURGH	17 KM (10½ ML)
WALKING DISTANCE/	13½ KM (8½ ML)/
SHORT ROUTE	8 KM (5 ML)
AMOUNT OF CLIMBING	120 M (395 FT)/
	70 M (230 FT)
ESTIMATED TIME	4 HR / 2½ HR

DESCRIPTION An interesting route along a canal and a river valley. There are good paths throughout, but some can be muddy. Note that there is a section along a road, although it carries very little traffic. Highlights of this route include the Canal Centre at Ratho with the option of boat rides (including a meal while cruising, if desired); Lin's Aqueduct (a huge stone structure with water cascading down it); and part of Almondell Country Park. The route may be shortened by omitting the Almond Valley section, or by arranging to travel along the canal by boat. Refreshments are available at the halfway point.

START AND FINISH Car park close to the Bridge Inn and canal, Ratho. NT 139 710

HOW TO GET THERE Frequent bus service from Edinburgh (SMT 37). By car, take the A8 west out of Edinburgh to the Newbridge roundabout. From the roundabout, take the second exit (B7030) and immediately turn left again. Follow this road to Ratho and park in the public car park just before the bridge over the canal.

WALK DIRECTIONS
Follow the road beside the car park away from the canal for a few paces to a junction. Here turn left up a lane. This soon

WALK 84: THE UNION CANAL FROM RATHO

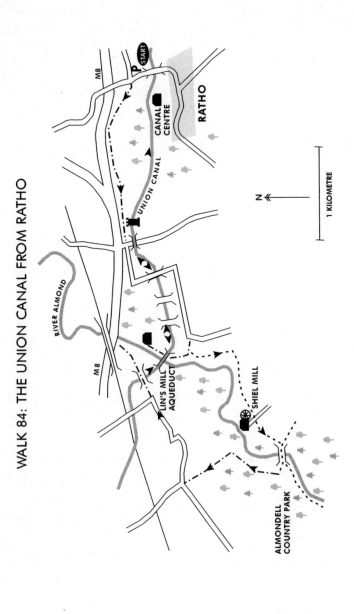

reaches a swing barrier then continues as a track, passing some buildings on the left, then running between a motorway on the right and an enormous quarry on the left. Follow the track over the top of the hill and down to where it meets the canal (close to a 'castle'). Move on to the canal towpath. Pass over a small aqueduct, then beneath three bridges and on to another, much bigger, aqueduct (Lin's Mill Aqueduct).

At the start of the aqueduct, turn right, down some steps and on to an access road to pass beneath the aqueduct. Follow the road to the top of a hill where a footpath signpost indicates the next section of the route along the River Almond Valley, to Almondell Country Park. For most of the way, this path runs beside a millrace (now used as a feeder for the Union Canal) and so keeps closely to the valley contours. Eventually you reach Shiel Mill (now a private residence and stable). Cross the access road and continue along the footpath to a large, metal footbridge that spans the River Almond. Cross the river. (A little way to the left is the park visitor centre and a small café.)

From the bridge walk directly ahead, away from the river, then bear right on to an asphalt track that leads to the park's northern entrance. From here, walk along the road to a crossroads then turn right. Stay on this minor road, round a double bend, to a farm on a corner of the road. Go straight ahead on a farm track that leads to a bridge over the Union Canal. Cross the bridge, then follow the towpath all the way back to Ratho.

WALK 85: ALMONDELL & CALDERWOOD COUNTRY PARK I

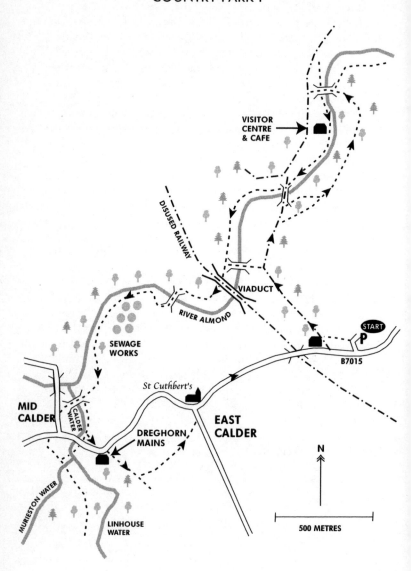

VISITOR CENTRE & CAFE

DISUSED RAILWAY

VIADUCT

RIVER ALMOND

START
P

B7015

SEWAGE WORKS

St Cuthbert's

MID CALDER

CALDER WATER

DREGHORN MAINS

EAST CALDER

MURIESTON WATER

LINHOUSE WATER

N

500 METRES

85. ALMONDELL & CALDERWOOD COUNTRY PARK I

ORDNANCE SURVEY MAP NO	LANDRANGER 65
	PATHFINDER 419
DISTANCE FROM EDINBURGH	19 KM (12 ML)
WALKING DISTANCE	6½ KM (4 ML)
AMOUNT OF CLIMBING	60 M (200 FT)
ESTIMATED TIME	2 HR

DESCRIPTION This is an easy circular walk along good paths, almost entirely within the very scenic Almondell Country Park. The terrain includes mixed woodland and a river valley. Refreshments may be obtained *en route* from the café at the park's visitor centre.

START AND FINISH East Calder, West Lothian. NT 092 682

HOW TO GET THERE Frequent bus service from Edinburgh (SMT D26, D27). By car, take the A71 southwest out of Edinburgh. Just beyond the village of Wilkieston, turn right on to the B7015 (signposted 'Camps and East Calder'). Just before East Calder, turn right into the country park's car park.

WALK DIRECTIONS
Follow the arrow on the ground close to the car park entrance through the woods for a short distance, then turn right on to an asphalt track. Shortly after passing around a curve to the right, bear right on to a red shale path behind some rhododendrons. (If the path is missed and a large stone bridge across the river is reached, turn right immediately before the bridge on to a footpath up through the woodlands to rejoin the route.) Follow the path along the upper edge of the woodlands, high above the River Almond, until it finally descends to an impressive metal footbridge across the river.

Cross over and follow the riverside path upstream. Pass the visitor centre and café on the right, a large stone bridge over the river (Naysmith Bridge) and a footbridge, then go through a wooden archway beneath a high, stone viaduct. Continue upstream, crossing the river to the far bank at the next bridge and entering a wooded area. From here the path passes a sewage works then gradually climbs until it reaches some open ground and an old wooden stile on the left. Do not cross the stile, but descend the steps directly ahead to a stream (Calder Water, a tributary of the River Almond). Do not cross the bridge here, but turn left and follow the path upstream to a fork just before a main road. Go left to reach the road, cross and turn left.

After a few paces, at the entrance to Dreghorn Mains, turn right on to the path that runs between rough grassland and woodland to a residential area. Turn left, passing the backs of the houses, then step across a wire fence to the right on to a parallel path. This leads to a road near some traffic lights. Turn right at the lights and walk past a ruined church (St Cuthbert's) then through the village of East Calder. Return to the car park.

86. THE UNION CANAL, WEST LOTHIAN

ORDNANCE SURVEY MAP NO	LANDRANGER 65
	PATHFINDER 406
DISTANCE FROM EDINBURGH	20 KM (12½ ML)
WALKING DISTANCE	9 KM (5 ML)
AMOUNT OF CLIMBING	40 M (131 FT)
ESTIMATED TIME	2¾ HR

DESCRIPTION This route leads along a particularly scenic stretch of the Union Canal and through dense woodland. There are many ducks and swans along the canal, and hawks can often be seen the woodlands. There are several possibilities to shorten this walk.

START AND FINISH Winchburgh, West Lothian. NT 089 750

HOW TO GET THERE By car, head west out of Edinburgh on the A8. At Newbridge roundabout, take the A89 towards Broxburn. Just beyond a railway viaduct turn right and proceed to Winchburgh. Park on one of the side streets there. By bus from Edinburgh use MB 38, 455 or 456.

WALK DIRECTIONS

From the junction in the centre of Winchburgh, head west along the B9080 for a few paces to a bridge over the Union Canal. Descend some steps on the north side of the road to the towpath and follow the canal away from Winchburgh into the countryside. Pass beneath the first bridge encountered and continue on the towpath around a bend to the next bridge. Cross the canal here and turn right on to a muddy track through a narrow strip of woodland running parallel to the canal.

Where the field on the left gives way to woodland, turn left off the main track on to a path along the edge of the woods. After 185 paces (almost to the end of the woodland)

WALK 86: THE UNION CANAL, WEST LOTHIAN

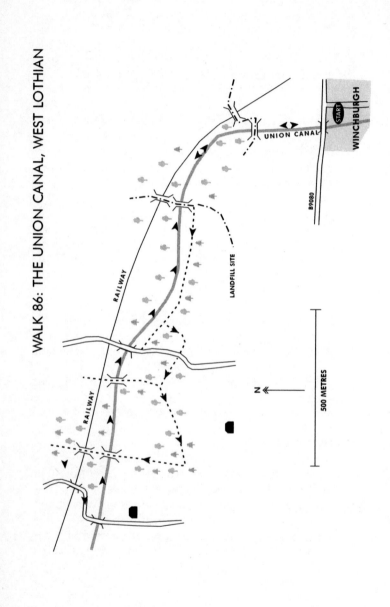

turn right on to a slightly overgrown track. This leads past a beehive and on through the woods to an asphalt road. Cross over and take the track opposite, into more woods. Keep going until a fork is reached and take the left branch to continue through a strip of woodland between fields.

At the end of the field on the right, the woodland expands a little and the track ends. Turn right here along a thinner strip of woodland. At first there is only a very thin path but it soon joins a track serving a field on the right. Keep going until the Union Canal is reached once more.

Cross the bridge over the canal and continue directly ahead, through woodland, then over another bridge over a railway. Turn left and walk through the trees, following the railway, for a short distance to a road. Follow the road over the railway and around a bend to return to the Union Canal. From here, follow the canal towpath all the way back to Winchburgh.

WALK 87: ABERCORN TO BLACKNESS CASTLE

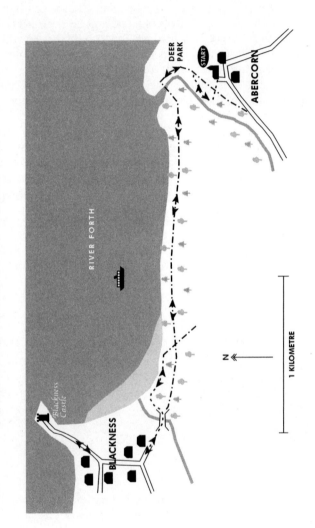

RIVER FORTH

DEER PARK

START

ABERCORN

Blackness Castle

BLACKNESS

N

1 KILOMETRE

87. ABERCORN TO BLACKNESS CASTLE

ORDNANCE SURVEY MAP NO	LANDRANGER 65
	PATHFINDER 406 & 394
DISTANCE FROM EDINBURGH	21 KM (13 ML)
WALKING DISTANCE	8 KM (5 ML)
AMOUNT OF CLIMBING	120 M (394 FT)
ESTIMATED TIME	3 HR

DESCRIPTION A woodland walk beside the River Forth to Blackness Castle. Unfortunately, it is necessary to return by the same route used on the outward leg; but it is such a pleasant walk that you are bound to enjoy it in both directions. Of particular interest is Abercorn Museum (just inside Abercorn Churchyard) and Blackness Castle (Historic Scotland, small admission charge).

START AND FINISH Abercorn Church, West Lothian. NT 081 790

HOW TO GET THERE By car, head west out of Edinburgh on the A90. Just before the Forth Road Bridge, turn left on to the A904. Pass through Newton, then turn right on to a minor road to Abercorn. The church is off the road to the right. There is a parking area beside the church (not available on Sunday mornings). There is no public transport.

WALK DIRECTIONS
Climb over some stone steps to the left of the churchyard entrance and follow a path through trees, across a grassy track, then steeply down through more trees. At the bottom the path swings round to the right then joins a track. Go left along the track beside a burn to a bridge (Nethermill Bridge). There is a deer park to the right of the bridge.

Cross the bridge and follow the signposted track around

to the right. This track runs through the woods parallel to, and about 10 m from, the seashore. At the time of writing, there were a number of fallen trees across the track, but all were easily negotiable. After 1½ km the track is crossed by another that runs to a gate in the wall on the right. From here Blackness Castle can clearly be seen across the bay. Go through this gate, then continue in the same direction on a footpath along the top of the beach.

On reaching a small stream, head inland for a few paces to the trees where there is a small bridge across a burn. Cross over and walk through the small park ahead to a metal gate. Pass through and continue on a minor road, past houses, to a T-junction. Go downhill to another T-junction in the centre of the village of Blackness.

Go right, past a boat club, and along the foreshore to Blackness Castle (Historic Scotland, small admission charge). The return is a reversal of the outward route.

88. ALMONDELL & CALDERWOOD COUNTRY PARK II

ORDNANCE SURVEY MAP NO	LANDRANGER 65
	PATHFINDER 419
DISTANCE FROM EDINBURGH	21 KM (13 ML)
WALKING DISTANCE	5 KM (3 ML)
AMOUNT OF CLIMBING	125 M (400 FT)
ESTIMATED TIME	1¾ HR

DESCRIPTION A meandering stroll over the tree-covered hills that lie between two tributaries of the River Almond. The entire route falls within the southern sector of the Almondell and Calderwood Country Park. Note that the paths can be muddy and very wet, but the worst parts can usually be avoided by means of short detours.

START AND FINISH Mid Calder, West Lothian. NT 077 677

HOW TO GET THERE Frequent bus service from Edinburgh (SMT D26, D27). By car, take the A71 southwest out of Edinburgh. Just beyond the village of Wilkieston, turn right on to the B7015 (signpost, 'Camps') through East Calder to Mid Calder. On entering the village of Mid Calder, cross the bridge over the river and immediately turn right on to the B8046 (signpost, 'Pumpherston'). Park in the car park 100 m along this road on the right.

WALK DIRECTIONS
Leave the car park via a footpath beside some bottle recycling bins and descend to a burn (Calder Water). Cross a footbridge here and turn right (upstream). At a fork just before a main road, go right and descend some steps to pass beneath the road. After a few paces, cross a footbridge over the stream then turn left and cross another footbridge over a second stream (Murieston Water). Follow the footpath

WALK 88: ALMONDELL & CALDERWOOD
COUNTRY PARK II

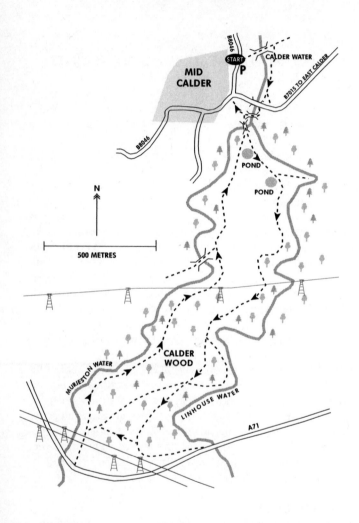

START
P
B8046
MID CALDER
CALDER WATER
B7015 TO EAST CALDER
B8046
POND
POND
N
500 METRES
CALDER WOOD
MURIESTON WATER
LINHOUSE WATER
A71

directly ahead, up a small rise and round to the left, then past the first of two ponds. Stay on the path across rough grassland to a second pond. The left path of a fork here takes one through a few trees to a view down to the river.

To continue on the main route, take the right-hand fork at the pond. Follow the path across more rough grassland with woodlands to the left, then beneath an electricity transmission line and into Calder Wood. Stay on the main path through the woods as it follows the top of the ridge above Linhouse Water. Do not take any of the paths going off to the right. On reaching an open area the path crosses a particularly wet section. This may be avoided by taking the rather longer path to the left. It is then back into the trees until the path emerges from the woodland near a stone wall, with pasture land and two electricity lines beyond.

Turn right here for a short distance to a T-junction within the woodland. Go left and descend steeply to Murieston Water. Follow the path upstream, then up to the right and along the top of a ridge. On reaching a path that descends back down towards the water, continue straight ahead on the top of the ridge, through woods, then across rough grassland to a small hill. Climb over the top and descend to join the path used earlier close to the footbridge over Murieston Water. Cross only the first bridge, then climb to the left to emerge on to the road in Mid Calder. Cross over and take the road opposite back down to the car park.

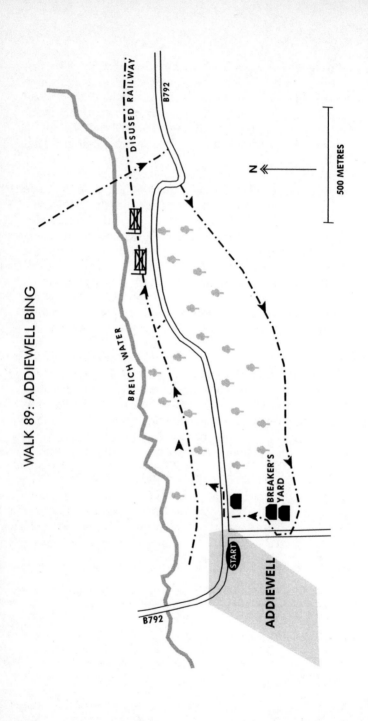

WALK 89: ADDIEWELL BING

N

500 METRES

DISUSED RAILWAY

B792

BREICH WATER

B792

START

BREAKER'S YARD

ADDIEWELL

89. ADDIEWELL BING

ORDNANCE SURVEY MAP NO	LANDRANGER 65
	PATHFINDER 419
DISTANCE FROM EDINBURGH	29 KM (18 ML)
WALKING DISTANCE	5 KM (3 ML)
AMOUNT OF CLIMBING	50 M (160 FT)
ESTIMATED TIME	1¾ HR

DESCRIPTION This old slag heap from the mines is now totally unrecognisable. It has been converted into a nature reserve with many trees, wild flowers and an abundance of birds. The route passes through dense conifer and mixed woodlands, and over a long stretch of open grassland. Paths are of grass and can be wet after heavy rain. There are good views in all directions but the most prominent feature is the Five Sisters, five large slag heaps now covered with grass.

START AND FINISH Addiewell, West Lothian. NS 994 627

HOW TO GET THERE Frequent bus and train service from Edinburgh (SMT 276; ScotRail). By car, take the A71 (towards Kilmarnock) through southern Livingston to West Calder. Turn right on to the B792 towards Bathgate. Addiewell is a further 2 ml along this road. Park in one of the side streets.

WALK DIRECTIONS
Walk east out of Addiewell along the B792 until 200 m beyond the last building. Enter Addiewell Bing Nature Reserve through a gate on the left. Climb to the top of the hill ahead, then follow a path through the woods. To the left are frequent glimpses of Breich Water in the valley below and the Five Sisters may be seen in the distance. At the point where the trees change from conifer to deciduous, it is possible to make an optional detour to the left down to

the water's edge. However it is necessary to return to this point to continue the route.

Follow the slowly descending path along the ridge. Take neither the path on the right towards the road, nor the later stile on to the road. A little beyond the stile there is another over the boundary fence of the nature reserve. Climb over this and continue ahead on a narrow path, along an old railway embankment. On reaching a breach in the embankment (where the railway once crossed a track coming up from the river) descend on to the track and follow it away from the water.

At a main road, go right as far as a bend. Here climb a stile on the far side of the road and take a path through a small area of woodland to emerge on to open grassland. Follow the path directly ahead across grassland for 1½ km. On the far side, go along a gravel track through scrub land and past a car-breaker's yard. When close to a road, pass the entrance to the breaker's yard and continue along the footpath to return to the starting point.

90. LINLITHGOW LOCH

ORDNANCE SURVEY MAP NO	LANDRANGER 65
	PATHFINDER 406
DISTANCE FROM EDINBURGH	29 KM (18 ML)
WALKING DISTANCE	5 KM (3 ML)
AMOUNT OF CLIMBING	NEGLIGIBLE
ESTIMATED TIME	1½ HR

DESCRIPTION A pleasant stroll around a loch with the impressive Linlithgow Palace as an ever-present background. May easily be combined with a visit to the Palace (Historic Scotland, small admission charge).

START AND FINISH Linlithgow, West Lothian. NT 002 772

HOW TO GET THERE Frequent bus and train service from Edinburgh (MB 38; ScotRail). By car, head west out of Edinburgh then take the M9 to Junction 3 and turn left for Linlithgow. There is a car park (admission charge) close to the palace; if you are also visiting the palace, park at the palace entrance.

WALK DIRECTIONS
Walk to the palace entrance and go around the left (west) side of the building. Then descend to the edge of the loch. Turn left and follow the path around the loch. On the north side of the loch the path passes between the loch and a motorway, but the latter is hidden from view and hearing by an embankment.

When you reach a road beyond the east end of the loch, turn back and right through a kissing gate. Cross sheep-grazing land to another road. Go right along road for 100 m, then turn right down an alley to re-enter the grounds of Linlithgow Palace and return to the start.

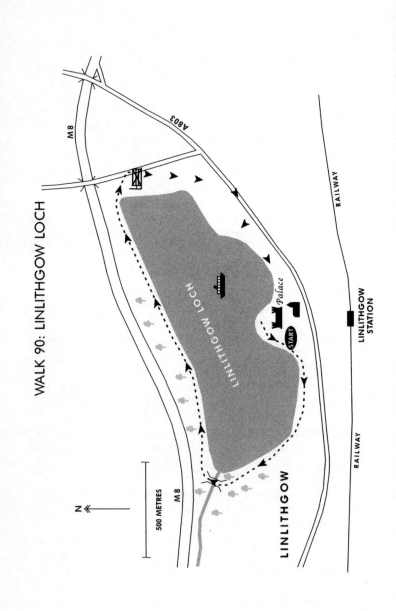

WALK 90: LINLITHGOW LOCH

N

500 METRES

M 8

M 8

A803

LINLITHGOW LOCH

Palace

START

LINLITHGOW

RAILWAY

RAILWAY

LINLITHGOW STATION

RAILWAY

91. ANTONINE WALL & KINNEIL WOOD

ORDNANCE SURVEY MAP NO	LANDRANGER 65
	PATHFINDER 393 & 405
DISTANCE FROM EDINBURGH	32 KM (20 ML)
WALKING DISTANCE	3 KM (2 ML)
AMOUNT OF CLIMBING	NEGLIGIBLE
ESTIMATED TIME	1 HR

DESCRIPTION An undulating walk through a coniferous forest. The final section follows the route of the Roman Antonine Wall: there are remnants of the second-century wall, a Roman fort, a church – and the workshop where James Watt performed his early experiments on the steam engine. There is also an interesting museum. Many paths and tracks lead through the forest. The described route is just one of many possible variations.

START AND FINISH Kinneil House, Bo'ness. NS 983 805

HOW TO GET THERE By car, take the M9 towards Stirling and turn right at Junction 3 on to the A904. Do not turn right at a signpost for the Bo'ness & Kinneil Railway, but carry on straight ahead into Bo'ness. At a crossroads go straight across. Then, just round a right-hand bend, turn left into Provost Road and immediately right to Kinneil House. Drive along the access road to the main house and turn left, passing a children's play area and entering a woodland where there are several parking places. By bus, take MB 42 from Edinburgh to Bo'ness and walk to the west end of Bo'ness.

WALK DIRECTIONS
Follow the road that ascends from Kinneil House, through the woods, to an estate entrance and a main road. Turn right just before the entrance on to a footpath through the trees.

WALK 91: ANTONINE WALL & KINNEIL WOOD

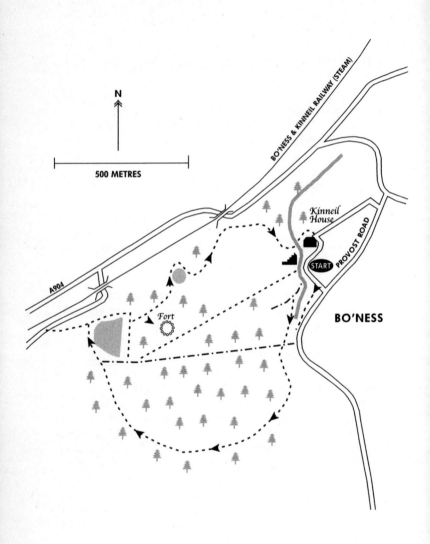

Descend to the right to cross a burn via a small bridge, then ascend to the left to join a more prominent track. After a few paces, bear left on to a footpath that soon reaches the boundary of the estate and then follows a stone wall to another estate entrance. Cross a track here. Follow the signposted pony trail opposite around the southern and eastern edges of the forest, until a pond is reached.

Pass to the left of the pond. At a T-junction of paths by a corner of the pond, turn right to stay beside the pond. At the next corner, leave the pond by descending a few steps into open grassland. Walk across to the rise in the centre of the field. Here you will find the remains of a Roman fort and part of the Antonine Wall.

Head across to the northeast corner of the field. Take a footpath around another, smaller pond then along the edge of another field to the remains of a church. From here follow another path round to the left of Kinneil House, then pass a museum and the front of Kinneil House to return to the starting place.

WALK 92: BATHGATE TO BLACKRIDGE

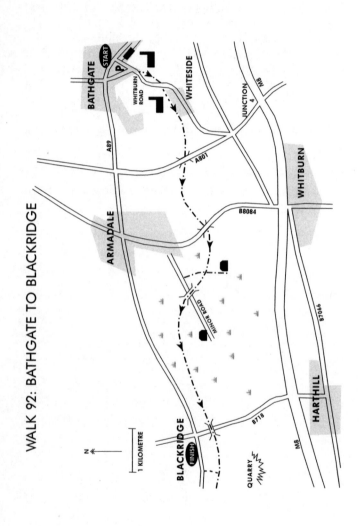

BATHGATE
START
WHITBURN ROAD
WHITESIDE
JUNCTION 4
M8
A89
A801
ARMADALE
B8084
WHITBURN
MINOR ROAD
B7066
HARTHILL
BLACKRIDGE
FINISH
B718
M8
QUARRY

N ←
1 KILOMETRE

92. BATHGATE TO BLACKRIDGE

ORDNANCE SURVEY MAP NO	LANDRANGER 65
	PATHFINDER 418
DISTANCE FROM EDINBURGH	32 KM (20 ML)
WALKING DISTANCE	10 KM (6½ ML)
AMOUNT OF CLIMBING	100 M (330 FT)
ESTIMATED TIME	3¼ HR

DESCRIPTION An easy walk from the centre of Bathgate, past factories then up on to open moorland and heath. The route follows a disused railway track. This has been converted to an asphalt cycletrack and walkway by Sustrans, the organisation devoted to producing traffic-free routes for cyclists and walkers. This particular section is part of the proposed Route 75, from Gourock to Edinburgh. Along the route are several interesting statues and, from the higher sections, many moorland birds and open vistas may be seen.

A longer walk may be achieved by continuing along the track beyond Blackridge, past Hillend Reservoir, to either Caldercruix (an extra 7½ km) or Airdrie (an extra 12½ km). However, the return bus trip will require a change of buses in Blackridge.

START Railway Station, Bathgate. NS 975 685
FINISH Blackridge, West Lothian. NS 890 671
BUS LINK SMT 16

HOW TO GET THERE By car, take the M8 motorway to Junction 3A and park in one of the many Bathgate car parks. There is a free car park near the start of the walk in Whitburn Road, but it is sometimes used as a market. By public transport, travel to Bathgate either by train (ScotRail) or bus (SMT 16).

WALK DIRECTIONS

Turn left out of the station, then left again into Whitburn Road. The signposted Route 75 goes off to the left shortly after a mini-roundabout. Follow the track behind some houses, then beneath a road bridge. Shortly thereafter, close to some more houses, go directly ahead on a gravel path between the houses and a factory. Then rejoin the tarmac track.

Follow the gradually ascending track through grazing land; then on to pass to the south of Armadale; then up on to moorland. The next cluster of buildings to be seen across to the right is Blackridge. Cross over a road bridge here and keep going past the houses until you are level with a quarry over to the left. Here, turn right and follow a path up to the main road in Blackridge. The bus stop is to the right, on the far side of the road.

93. BO'NESS & KINNEIL

ORDNANCE SURVEY MAP NO	LANDRANGER 65
	PATHFINDER 393 & 394
DISTANCE FROM EDINBURGH	32 KM (20 ML)
WALKING DISTANCE	7 KM (4 ML)
AMOUNT OF CLIMBING	NEGLIGIBLE
ESTIMATED TIME	2¼ HR

DESCRIPTION A pleasant walk through a nature reserve beside the upper reaches of the Firth of Forth. There are lots of sea birds, several picnic sites and, during the summer, occasional views of steam trains puffing past. This walk can easily be combined with a ride on a steam train and a visit to a clay mine and railway museum (seasonal). Café and toilets available at Bo'ness Station.

START AND FINISH Bo'ness Station, Bo'ness. NT 004 817

HOW TO GET THERE By car, take the M9 towards Stirling, turning right at Junction 3 on to the A904. Follow signs for Bo'ness, then for the Bo'ness & Kinneil Railway. Park in the car park beside the railway station. By bus, take MB 42 from Edinburgh to Bo'ness Station.

WALK DIRECTIONS
Cross the railway via the footbridge and head west along a footpath between the railway and the old quay, then beside the water's edge to an island. Cross the causeway. Walk across (or around the edge of) the island, to a second causeway. Cross back to the mainland and turn right, taking a path beside the water around a promontory and into an inlet. At a landfill site, turn back towards Bo'ness. Climb over a tree-covered hill then follow the railway back to the footbridge.

Turn left, away from the footbridge, then left again to walk around the quay. At the end of the quay, bear right.

WALK 93: BO'NESS & KINNEIL

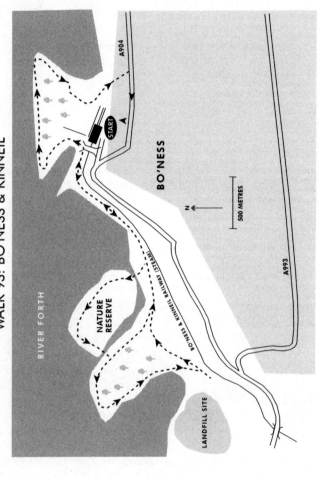

RIVER FORTH

NATURE
RESERVE

LANDFILL SITE

BO'NESS & KINNEIL RAILWAY (STEAM)

BO'NESS

START

A904

A993

N

500 METRES

Follow a path between the Forth and some trees to a point of land, from which the Forth bridges are clearly seen. From here head inland, passing the back of the railway sidings, to a road. Go right along the road for a short distance, then turn right on to a track that will return you to the station car park.

Path beside the steam railway, Bo'ness

WALK 94: BEECRAIGS COUNTRY PARK

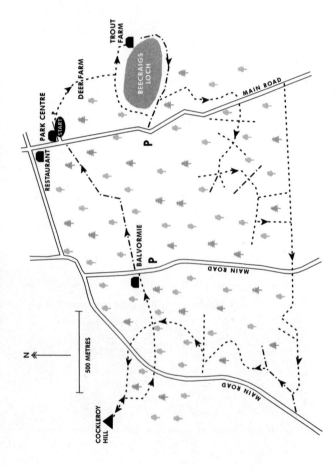

N

500 METRES

RESTAURANT

PARK CENTRE

START

DEER FARM

TROUT FARM

BEECRAIGS LOCH

MAIN ROAD

BALVORMIE

P

P

MAIN ROAD

MAIN ROAD

COCKLEROY HILL

94. BEECRAIGS COUNTRY PARK

ORDNANCE SURVEY MAP NO	LANDRANGER 65
	PATHFINDER 405 & 406
DISTANCE FROM EDINBURGH	33 KM (20 ML)
WALKING DISTANCE	8 KM (5 ML)
AMOUNT OF CLIMBING	230 M (754 FT)
ESTIMATED TIME	3 HR

DESCRIPTION A superb woodland walk through a well-managed country park. There is plenty to see: a deer farm, a trout farm, a loch, picnic sites, breathtaking views from Cockleroy and many different kinds of trees, birds and woodland plants. The park is criss-crossed with paths and tracks, so it is easy to find alternative routes. There are also many way-marked routes (leaflets from the park centre). Please also take a bag and collect any litter you might find.

START AND FINISH Park Centre, Beecraigs Country Park, West Lothian. NT 007 749

HOW TO GET THERE By car, take the M9 motorway to Junction 3. Pass through the centre of Linlithgow then turn left, following the brown signs for Beecraigs Country Park. In summer it is possible to take the train to Linlithgow, then bus MB 484.

WALK DIRECTIONS
Take the walkway through the deer farm to Beecraigs Loch. Then turn left, via the trout farm, and along the far side of the loch. Where a burn passes beneath the road, turn left on to a path through woodlands to a main road. Cross carefully and take the path marked by a red arrow directly opposite. Follow this over three bridges, up a bank, diagonally over another path, then alongside a burn. Later, the path crosses another path and finally ends at a stone wall with a forestry

road beyond. Turn left at the nearby footpath signpost. After a few paces, continue directly ahead – ignoring the 'red route' that goes off to the right – over a small bridge and along a grassy track. Cross a forestry road on to a red-shale forest road directly ahead. Follow this around to the right, then take the first forest ride to the left (at the point where the shale road ends).

At the end of the ride, turn right and follow the edge of the forest, carefully crossing a main road. Carry on until a forestry road is encountered. Go right on the road to a bend; then left on to a path, over open ground then back into the forest and down a muddy firebreak. At the bottom, cross a wet area with fallen trees and go round to the right on a grassy track. After 150 m, turn left on to a wooden walkway, then a forestry road to a T-junction with another road. Go straight ahead on to another wooden walkway, up a bank, then diagonally left across another path and back into the woods. After a few paces, turn left on to a more substantial path and immediately right. Follow this path, the 'light-blue route', over a busy main road and along a dirt track. At the end, climb over a stile on the right then climb up on to Cockleroy Hill (278 m / 912 ft, triangulation pillar, view-finder, fort, superb view).

Return to the stile – but instead of taking the track down to the road, go straight ahead on a path into the woods. At a junction of paths go straight ahead, following the sign for a viewpoint. Follow the path around to the left. Go over a bank, back across the main road, over a stile and through the forest to Balvormie (car park, toilets, picnic site). From here, follow the signposted track back to the park centre.

95. FORTH COAST – BO'NESS TO QUEENSFERRY

ORDNANCE SURVEY MAP NO	LANDRANGER 65
	PATHFINDER 394 & 406
DISTANCE FROM EDINBURGH	33 KM (20 ML)
WALKING DISTANCE	12 KM (7½ ML)
AMOUNT OF CLIMBING	80 M (260 FT)
ESTIMATED TIME	3¾ HR

DESCRIPTION A walk through woodlands along the edge of the River Forth, passing close to Blackness Castle. This is a fairly long route. However the bus route linking each end also passes through Blackness, so the walk may easily be spit into two sections: Bo'ness to Blackness and Blackness to Queensferry. Note that passage between Nethermill Bridge and Society may be difficult at high tide.

START Carriden Church near Bo'ness. NT 019 813
FINISH South Queensferry. NT 125 784
BUS LINK MB 47

HOW TO GET THERE By car, take the A90 then the B924 to South Queensferry. Just beyond the Forth Road Bridge, at a sign for Hopetoun House, turn right and park on the side of the street. Walk back to the main road and take a bus (MB 47) to Carriden Church, Bo'ness. Alternatively, take the same bus from Edinburgh direct to Carriden.

WALK DIRECTIONS
Walk along the dirt track beside Carriden Church to an industrial area, then take a path signposted as a right-of-way to Blackness. Follow this path down to the sea and along the coast beside a woodland. After a short distance, move on to another path in the same direction but within the woods. Follow this for a kilometre until it ends at a metal gate leading into grazing pasture. There is a small ruin here

WALK 95: FORTH COAST – BO'NESS TO QUEENSFERRY

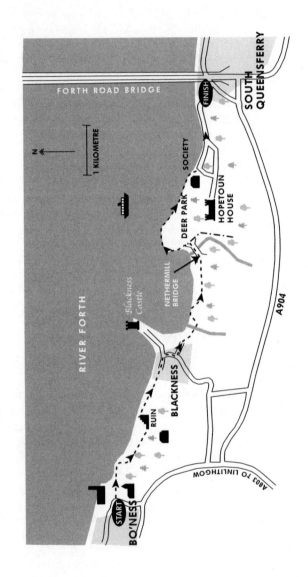

and, high up to the right, a large house may be seen. Walk through the ruin to the beach. Go right for a few paces, then up on to a path just above the beach. Be careful here, as there are a number of small but deep holes in the path. Follow this gradually improving path along the top of the shore to Blackness.

Here one can make a short detour and visit the intriguing and formidable Blackness Castle (small admission charge). To continue the route, turn uphill at the Blackness Inn, then left at the war memorial on to a minor road past a few houses. At the end of this road, pass through a metal gate. Cross a small park, then a footbridge over a burn, and follow another path along the top of the beach to an old gate in a stone wall on the right. Enter the woods here. Continue on a track along the coast but now just within the woodland. At the end of this straight track, swing left and cross a bridge (Nethermill Bridge) over a burn. Ahead is a high stone wall with a deer park beyond.

Immediately turn left down to the beach. Then walk along the foreshore, over the rocks beside the deer park, then past a woodland, until some houses (Society) and a road are eventually reached. Follow the road, along the coast, back to South Queensferry.

WALK 96: EAST WHITBURN WOODLANDS

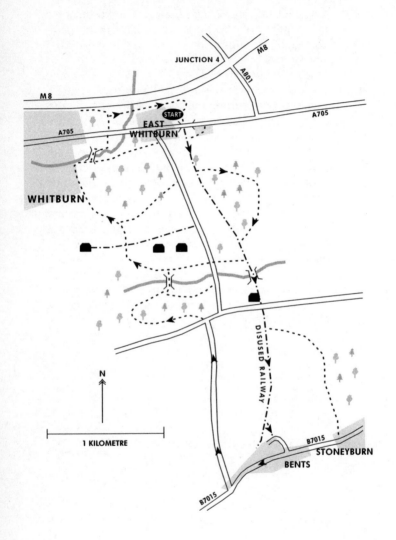

96. EAST WHITBURN WOODLANDS

ORDNANCE SURVEY MAP NO	LANDRANGER 65
	PATHFINDER 418
DISTANCE FROM EDINBURGH	35 KM (22 ML)
WALKING DISTANCE	10 KM (6 ML)
AMOUNT OF CLIMBING	110 M (360 FT)
ESTIMATED TIME	3¼ HR

DESCRIPTION The area of farmland and disused mining bings to the south of the village of East Whitburn, West Lothian, has been transformed by the Woodland Trust and other landowners who have planted much of the area with trees. At the time of writing, the trees were very young. But as they mature, so wild animals, birds, insects and plants will be attracted to the area, bringing ever increasing enjoyment to this very pleasant ramble. Note:

1. Some of the paths may be quite muddy or pass through long grass which may be wet.
2. The old railway section before Bents is covered with gorse which may make the path rather narrow.
3. There is a short section along a quiet, narrow country lane.
4. The final short section involves leaping across a small burn. This may be impossible after heavy rain. However, this section may be avoided by walking along the road to East Whitburn.

START AND FINISH East Whitburn old railway station, West Lothian. NS 963 653

HOW TO GET THERE By car, take the M8 motorway to Junction 4 and turn left. In a short distance, at a T-junction, turn right. On entering East Whitburn, cross an old railway bridge and pass a pedestrian crossing with lights, then turn right into a residential area. Turn immediately right again.

Then at a left-hand bend, turn right to reach the remains of a railway station. By bus, take SMT D27 to East Whitburn.

WALK DIRECTIONS

Climb down on to the old railway track; follow it beneath a road bridge and on into a woodland. Turn left on to a path that meanders over the old bings before rejoining the old railway track. Continue along the disused railway track. At a minor road, cross over and continue along the course of the old railway until some houses are reached (Bents).

Turn left, away from the railway, into the housing estate and on to a residential road. Walk left to a main road and turn right. Take the next road to the right, a narrow country lane towards East Whitburn. After a kilometre, at a T-junction, pass through a gate directly ahead on to a path into more woodlands. Bear left, up over a ridge, then down out of the wooded area and over a footbridge across a burn. Climb the opposite bank to join another path. Turn left. Follow this path as it swings round to the right and crosses a gravel track back into another woodland. On reaching a gravel path with an adjacent carved seat, turn left. This path skirts the edge of some houses then follows a burn to a footbridge. Cross over and follow the path until it reaches a main road (A705) a little west of East Whitburn.

Pass through a gate opposite into more woodlands and follow the path until you come close to a motorway. Bear right on to a grass path to a small burn. Jump or wade across. Then pass between the houses of East Whitburn and the motorway. Continue straight ahead along a track to an old railway bridge. Pass underneath and turn right along the edge of a field, to return to the start.

97. POLKEMMET COUNTRY PARK

ORDNANCE SURVEY MAP NO	LANDRANGER 65
	PATHFINDER 418
DISTANCE FROM EDINBURGH	38 KM (24 ML)
WALKING DISTANCE	5 KM (3 ML)
AMOUNT OF CLIMBING	60 M (197 FT)
ESTIMATED TIME	2 HR

DESCRIPTION An easy and delightful ramble beside a river and through the woodlands of Polkemmet Country Park. In addition to the walks, the park has facilities for golf and bowling, an imaginative children's play area, toilets, shop, restaurant and bar. 'The Horn' is a tall, metal statue reputed to have cost £145,000. It is one of several statues along the M8 motorway.

START AND FINISH Central car park in Polkemmet Country Park, West Lothian. NS 925 649

HOW TO GET THERE By car, take the M8 motorway to Junction 4, turn right and follow the brown signs for Polkemmet Country Park. By bus, take SMT D27 from Edinburgh, through Livingston and Whitburn, to the park entrance.

WALK DIRECTIONS
From the car park, head back along the road towards the park entrance until the river is crossed. Turn right on to a footpath beside the river. Stay on this path, following the green arrows, past a footbridge across the river then through some trees to a junction of paths. Turn right. The path now runs parallel to a stone wall with a main road on the far side. Cross a small bridge over a burn and continue directly ahead, still close to the road. Just before the point where the path joins the road, double back on to another path that

WALK 97: POLKEMMET COUNTRY PARK

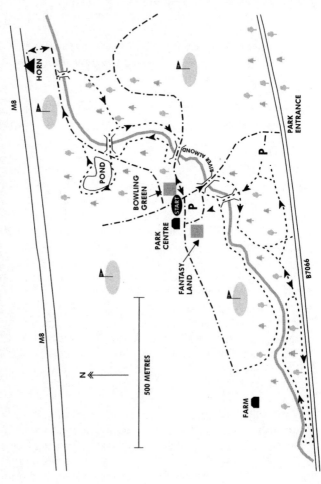

N

500 METRES

M8

M8

HORN

POND

BOWLING GREEN

START

PARK CENTRE

FANTASY LAND

P

RIVER ALMOND

P

PARK ENTRANCE

B7066

FARM

follows the river bank. Continue on this path back to the small bridge. Turn left to take the path used earlier back to the junction of paths. This time keep right to pass through woodlands close to the main road. Just before reaching a car park, turn left, descend to the river, cross the path used earlier and then a footbridge over the river. Ascend across grass to an asphalt road. Follow this to the left, past the children's Fantasy Land, to the park centre and central car park.

From here head east on a park road, past the car park and a bowling green. Proceed down towards a stone bridge over the river. At the top of the slope before the bridge, turn left into woodlands and follow the 'blue' route alongside the river. At the next footbridge, turn left to circumnavigate a pond. Then continue beside the river, now on a track, past another footbridge and around the edge of a golf course, to the huge statue of a horn.

Turn around and return to the first footbridge across the river. Cross over and follow the path through woodlands until it returns to the river and meets another path. Turn left and stay beside the river until you reach the stone bridge seen earlier. Cross over and follow the track back to the main car park.

WALK 98: RIVER AVON & THE UNION CANAL

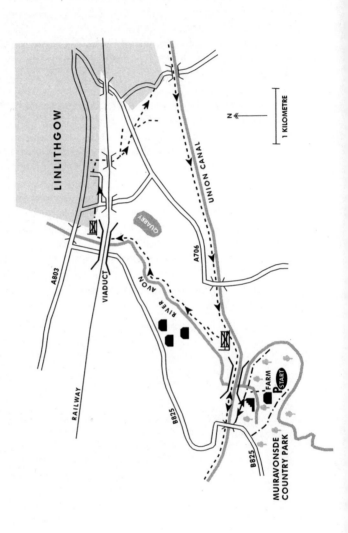

98. RIVER AVON & THE UNION CANAL

ORDNANCE SURVEY MAP NO	LANDRANGER 65
	PATHFINDER 405
DISTANCE FROM EDINBURGH	38 KM (24 ML)
WALKING DISTANCE	10 KM (6 ML)
AMOUNT OF CLIMBING	60 M (200 FT)
ESTIMATED TIME	3 HR

DESCRIPTION A rural walk along a meandering river valley returning via the Union Canal. Includes crossing the longest aqueduct in Scotland and passing beneath a high railway viaduct. A visit to Newlands Farm, close to the parking place, will fascinate young and old alike.

START AND FINISH Muiravonside Country Park. NS 963 753

HOW TO GET THERE By car, take the M9 to Junction 4 then the A801 towards Blackburn. After 2 ml, at a roundabout, turn left to pass through Loan village, then turn right into Muiravonside Country Park. Park close to Newlands Farm.

WALK DIRECTIONS
Walk through the farm and into the woods at the back. (If parked in the overspill car park, take the path through trees along the top of the valley to the farm). Descend steps and cross a bridge over a small burn, then pass an old lime-kiln and climb up to join a track. Go left along the track until it emerges on to a road close to a road bridge over the Union Canal. Cross the bridge and take the canal towpath heading east. Follow the canal over an aqueduct and round a bend to the left. Descend a few steps on the left and follow a path to the right through trees for a short distance, to a stile leading into a field. Cross, turn left and follow the edge of the field until it is possible to re-enter the trees on left. Now follow the

way-marked path along the river for 2 km to a railway viaduct.

Pass beneath the viaduct and immediately pass through a gate on the right. Walk along a lane to a road. Go right along the road, then next left into a residential road just before a railway bridge. Near the end of this road, take the passageway adjacent to house no. 60 to reach a footpath. Go right along the path, passing beneath a railway, then straight ahead (not across the sports fields) to a main road. Cross over and follow the lower of two footpaths between a housing estate and a stream to a road.

Walk along the road, still beside the stream, until the road passes beneath the Union Canal. Here, climb up the zigzag path to the left to join the canal towpath. Head west. After 3 km, cross the aqueduct encountered earlier, then retrace your footsteps back to the start.

99. CALLENDAR PARK, FALKIRK

ORDNANCE SURVEY MAP NO	LANDRANGER 65
	PATHFINDER 405
DISTANCE FROM EDINBURGH	40 KM (25 ML)
WALKING DISTANCE	12½ KM (8 ML)
AMOUNT OF CLIMBING	140 M (460 FT)
ESTIMATED TIME	4 HR

DESCRIPTION This is a delightful walk through the grounds of Callendar House (now a public park), Callendar Wood and along a section of the Union Canal including a stretch through a long, dark tunnel. Please note that some of the paths through the woodland are quite muddy, so take appropriate footwear, and do remember to take a torch and raincoat for the tunnel. While you are in the area, Callendar House and the adjacent stables tea-rooms are well worth visiting.

START AND FINISH Car park at the entrance to Callendar Park, Falkirk. NS 894 795

HOW TO GET THERE By car, take the M9 motorway to Junction 5. Follow the signs to Falkirk then the brown signs to Callendar Park. Alternatively, take a bus (MB 38) to Falkirk town centre, or a train (ScotRail) to Falkirk High Station, and start and finish the route from this point.

WALK DIRECTIONS
Follow the track into the park as far as a kiosk. Go diagonally right on a grey, gravel path across the lawns behind Callendar House, then into Callendar Wood. Keep climbing in a straight line through the woods. Cross the first track encountered and continue to a second track at the top of the hill. Turn right and follow this track through Callendar Wood. Eventually you will reach a junction of

WALK 99: CALLENDAR PARK, FALKIRK

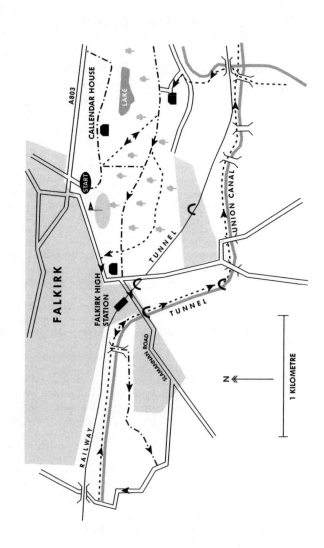

paths, just before a black wooden gate through the estate boundary wall with an adjacent cottage (South Lodge). Turn right here on to a short path through the trees to a road. Do not exit the woodland through the South Lodge gate.

Go left along the road for a few paces to a T-junction. Turn left again, then right into Slamannan Road. Follow this road for 400 m to the point where it crosses the Union Canal. Turn right, descend to the canal and follow the towpath to the first bridge. Cross the canal here and follow a track on the far side through parkland. At the end of the track walk across the grass ahead and a little uphill to the corner of the park. From here follow a minor road past fields, round to the right then downhill to the start of the Union Canal.

From here, walk along the towpath. At the point where you joined the canal earlier continue alongside the canal through a long, dark tunnel, then through the countryside, until the canal and a railway line come together. At the next canal bridge (broken), turn left away from the canal and follow a small burn beneath the railway. Carry on downhill to a road. Go right along the road for a few paces, then left up a farm access road. Just before the farm, turn right and re-enter Callendar Wood. Here follow a track directly ahead (not to the right), downhill to a junction of tracks. Then follow the path used earlier down through the woods and across the park, back to the car park.

WALK 100: THE FALLS OF CLYDE

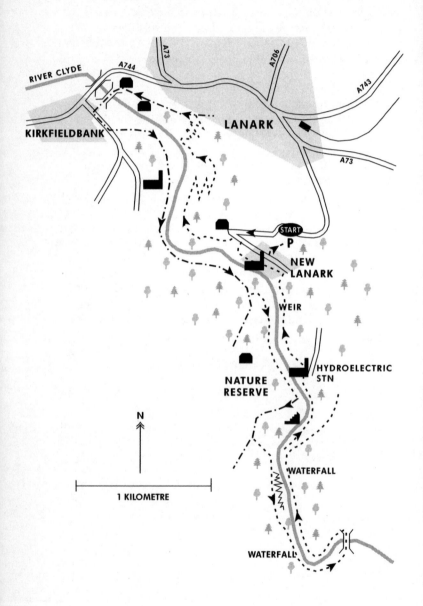

RIVER CLYDE

A744

A73

A706

A743

LANARK

KIRKFIELDBANK

A73

START
P

NEW
LANARK

WEIR

HYDROELECTRIC
STN

NATURE
RESERVE

N

WATERFALL

1 KILOMETRE

WATERFALL

100. THE FALLS OF CLYDE

ORDNANCE SURVEY MAP NO	LANDRANGER 71
	PATHFINDER 446
DISTANCE FROM EDINBURGH	55 KM (34 ML)
WALKING DISTANCE	11 KM (7 ML)
AMOUNT OF CLIMBING	360 M (1,180 FT)
ESTIMATED TIME	4 HR (BUT ALLOW LONGER TO APPRECIATE EVERYTHING THIS WALK HAS TO OFFER)

DESCRIPTION A phenomenal walk – probably the most picturesque in this book – along an incredibly dramatic section of the River Clyde. The western bank of the river is a nature reserve which is very scenic in itself, but the highlights of the route are the spectacular waterfalls of Corra and Bonnington (the 'Falls of Clyde'). Although these falls can be seen from both sides of the river, the best views by far are from the nature reserve. If you really want to see the falls in their full glory with spray reaching high above the gorge, and to appreciate fully the power of the river, you should choose a day following several days of heavy rain. Finally, but not least, the restored mills at New Lanark – a World Heritage Site – provide the walker with a wonderful finish to the walk (plus the opportunity to make use of the restaurant, toilets, shops and other facilities).

START AND FINISH Main car park above the restored mills at New Lanark. NS 882 427

HOW TO GET THERE By car, take the A70 to Lanark and follow the brown tourist signs to New Lanark. Alternatively, take a train from Edinburgh to Lanark (change at Bellshill), or bus (WS 100) to Biggar then a second bus (Wilson 191) to Lanark, and walk down to New Lanark.

WALK DIRECTIONS

Walk back to the roundabout and down the road towards New Lanark. Just beyond a hairpin bend, turn right on to the Clyde Walkway. Follow the path down through some woodlands above the River Clyde, then up a zigzag path to an asphalt track. Turn left. At the end of the track, continue on a footpath directly ahead, following the walkway signpost, across open ground then through a farmhouse to a bridge over the river. Turn left and follow a minor road uphill alongside a stone wall. Just beyond a gate in the wall, turn left through a gap in the wall. Join a pine needle-covered track through more woodlands following the course of the river. Later there are occasional glimpses through the trees of the New Lanark mills.

After 2 km, at a junction with a yellow-topped post, go left. This footpath continues through the woodland above the River Clyde. Soon a weir will be seen (and definitely heard) and, on the far bank, the large white hydroelectric generating station. On reaching a small ruined castle, go round to the right then follow a path to the left to regain the river. Do not take any of the paths or tracks to the right. However there are several short detours to the left, each of which gives a different – and stupendous – view of Corra Linn and, later, Bonnington Linn.

Just beyond the final and most dramatic waterfall, the path swings round to the left. Shortly thereafter it crosses a bridge over the river. On the far side, turn left and follow another riverside path downstream. At a viewpoint above Corra Linn, descend to the left on to an intermittently wooden-floored path through trees, heading towards the electricity generating station seen earlier from the far side of the river. Continue along the path beside the river to New Lanark mills. Then, after exploring this remarkable heritage site, climb the footpath back to the main car park.

AUTHOR'S NOTES & COMMENTS

ACCESS AND WALKERS' RESPONSIBILITIES
In Scotland, there is generally a good relationship between those who work on the land and those who walk through the countryside for pleasure. But always remember that the livelihood of local people often depends upon the land over which you are walking. Recreational walkers have a responsibility to ensure that their passage does nothing to disturb the land or anything on it. Always follow the Country Code. Do not stray from paths or trample across cultivated fields or heather. Avoid grouse moors during the nesting season (mid-June until August) and when a shoot is in progress. (The shooting season is from 12 August until 10 December.) Maintain the peace and tranquillity of the countryside and do not frighten grazing animals. In particular, if crossing grazing land with a dog, ensure that your pet is on a leash and well behaved. During the lambing season it is better to leave Rover at home or choose an alternative walk.

LITTER
Never drop any litter. Crisp packets, sweet wrappers, plastic bags, aluminium foil, bottles and cans do not decompose. Not only are they unsightly, they may damage agricultural machinery or, worse still, injure or kill a farm animal or a wild animal or bird. The attraction of some of the more popular walks has been totally spoilt by the irresponsible actions of a few. When one walks in such places, it is easy to understand why some landowners become antagonistic towards outsiders and why access to some popular areas is being denied. If an item can be carried into the countryside, it can be carried out again. Better still, take a carrier bag and plastic glove and help remove other people's litter. This will improve the environment for everyone and greatly engender the goodwill of landowners.

WEATHER

The weather in Scotland is highly variable and can change from one hour to the next. A day that begins dull and wet may later revert to brilliant sunshine, or vice versa. A hilltop on a windy summer day can be bitterly cold, while a sheltered sunny valley in February may feel quite balmy. Haar, a common occurrence in the southeast, can make conditions very cold and damp, but there will often be warm sunshine just a few miles away or an hour or two later. The main recommendation is to hope for the best but prepare for the worst.

Be particularly cautious of the weather when undertaking one of the hill walks, because conditions on the tops are often very different from those at lower levels. If there is a breeze in the valley, there is sure to be a far stronger wind on the hill and the wind chill effect can be very dramatic if you are not adequately protected. Climbing into cloud will cause a dramatic fall in temperature and make navigation extremely difficult. Unless you are fully competent in navigation over rocky terrain using only map and compass, avoid cloud or hill mist if you possibly can. Of course, the weather is not always worse on the hills. Sometimes it is possible to climb above a bank of cloud or mist filling a valley, then emerge into brilliant sunshine above a sea of cloud and feel as if you are on the top of the world.

Coastal walks are also likely to be cooler and fresher than inland areas. This may be an incentive for selecting such a route on a hot summer day or a reason for wrapping up well during a bracing winter ramble.

Also be wary of the sun. Recent thinning of the atmospheric ozone layer has increased the risk of sunburn, heat stroke and skin cancer. On a sunny day, protect all exposed skin with a good quality sun screen cream and wear a sun hat. If you are out all day in snow, a peaked cap and sunglasses will considerably reduce the glare to your eyes.

Do not be deterred by the weather. The worst that Nature can offer may be tolerated and even enjoyed if you are adequately protected. Persistent, wind-blown rain may be miserable, but the smells of the forest after a heavy downpour are most rewarding and the best time for a hill or moorland walk is in the early morning in winter, when the frost crunches under foot and the air is crisp and clear.

Before you go, check the local weather report. A good source of information is the outdoor activities forecast broadcast daily on BBC Radio Scotland at 6.55 p.m. Recorded local reports are available by telephone from the Meteorological Office on 0898 500422 or the *Scotsman* Weather Call Service on 0891 787 953 (both premium rate); or from the Internet at www.met-office.gov.uk/scotland or www.bbc.co.uk/weather.

COMPANIONS

While a walk in the countryside on one's own can be very enjoyable – solitude is, after all, one of the attractions of open spaces – most walkers find companions an added pleasure. Conversation when on a track or having a bite of food, or even snatches of talk when striding along a path, can be most satisfying. Companions on a walk can also be an added safeguard should a mishap occur. If a walker becomes unable to continue, some members of the party can stay with him while help is sought by another (or preferably two others).

Ideally, groups should consist of no more than five or six. Larger parties require additional planning and preparation; a leader to set the pace and make route decisions; a large parking area; and an established and previously reconnoitred route. Also, large groups are frowned upon by some landowners so, if intending to lead such a group, you should first seek approval of the owners of the land over which you wish to walk.

CLOTHING

The type and amount of clothing used depends upon the walk, the season and the weather forecast. In summer, the shorter walks close to town can easily be completed with everyday leisure wear. No special clothing is required. Slacks, a T-shirt, a pair of trainers and perhaps a woolly jumper and anorak are all you need. Longer routes, hill walks and winter walking will require a little more preparation.

FOOTWEAR A stout pair of walking shoes is adequate for low-level routes, but boots that will protect the ankles are essential for hill walks. Footwear should be tough, flexible, comfortable and waterproof. You will need a good, thick sole to cover rough ground and a good grip for wet, slippery rocks. They must also keep the feet dry. When you are choosing footwear, imagine wearing them all day and using them to walk through puddles and wet grass, or having all the rain hitting overtrousers and draining over the boots. Once you have completed a few walks you will wish to do more, so high-quality footwear will be a good investment.

SOCKS Wear two pairs of thick, woollen socks, the inner pair extending up to the knee, with a shorter outer pair folded down over the boots to prevent the intrusion of small stones. Wearing two pairs of socks reduces the friction between boots and skin. Some walkers wear the cut-off foot section of a pair of old stockings between the socks to enhance this effect. Woollen socks are preferred for their warmth and comfort. They also repel rain and the water from wet grass.

BREECHES, TROUSERS, SKIRT Breeches, shorts, skirt or kilt are preferable to long trousers, as the latter will soon become sodden and uncomfortable when you are walking through wet grass. Whatever is worn, it should not be tight fitting and should be capable of either repelling water or drying quickly when wet. For this reason, jeans and shell suits are unsuitable. Jeans are particularly dangerous for hill walking in winter. When wet, they stay wet for a long time and cause rapid cooling of the thighs, which can lead to hypothermia.

SHIRT OR BLOUSE A lightweight shirt or blouse of absorbent material, preferably cotton, with open neck and fold-over collar is desirable. The collar is to protect the neck from the sun. It also makes carrying a map case round the neck far more comfortable.

PULLOVER A wool jumper or fibre-pile jacket, either worn or carried, is essential both for warmth and for absorbing perspiration at all times of the year.

ANORAK This garment is essential to retain body heat, to stop cold winds penetrating and to keep out the rain or snow. Some people prefer two garments: a lightweight outer jacket that is both wind-proof and waterproof; and an inner fleece jacket for warmth that can be worn separately. For winter use, the jacket should be capable of being closed by zip fasteners and Velcro strips, should have good size pockets with zips and flaps, and have a hood that can be drawn closed by means of a cord and toggle.

OVERTROUSERS These are not essential but will keep the legs dry in heavy rain. It is now possible to buy lightweight overtrousers that roll up to a size that will fit in an anorak pocket. The type with side zips can be put on without first removing one's boots.

GAITERS These are not really necessary unless you anticipate doing a lot of hill climbing in harsh conditions. There are two types, knee-length and ankle gaiters. The former will keep the lower legs warm and dry in the heaviest rain and when walking through deep snow. The latter are useful for keeping rain and snow out of one's boots, and burrs and twigs from attaching to one's socks.

GLOVES A small, cheap item but they will greatly improve one's comfort during a walk on a cold and windy winter's day.

HEADWEAR The body loses sixty per cent of its heat through the head. In cold or windy conditions, a woolly hat can be a real blessing. One that can be pulled down over the ears can be a great asset. In summer, do not forget to take a sun hat, especially if you are thinning on top, and perhaps a scarf to protect the neck.

BUFFALO CLOTHING This is a relatively new type of clothing which reverses all previous principles. With traditional clothing, insulation is enhanced by increasing the number of layers worn so as to trap pockets of air. Buffalo clothing consists of a single layer that has an outer windproof skin and thermopile on the inside. It is worn directly against the skin. Nothing is worn either beneath or on top. It is highly effective in keeping out the wind, retaining one's warmth and 'wicking away' perspiration.

SPARE CLOTHING It is a good idea to leave a towel and spare shoes and clothing in your vehicle, to change into on completion of the walk. If not soaking from rain, you will probably be wet from perspiration. A rub-down and fresh clothing make the journey home far more comfortable.

KIT – WHAT TO CARRY
Travel light. Carry only what you need and spread the load among members of the party, but don't omit any of the essentials. What you actually carry depends upon the weather forecast, the type of walk and its length. Here are a few things that you should consider carrying.

RUCKSACK This is by far the best way to carry such articles as an anorak, spare jumper, snacks and refreshments. A small daypack is perfectly adequate. Choose one with side and top pockets, so that small items may be reached without you having to remove the rucksack. A wide waistband will spread the weight between shoulders and hips so that you will be hardly aware of carrying the pack. If one is not already fitted, use a loop of Velcro to link the straps across the chest to prevent the shoulder straps slipping down. Clothes in the rucksack should be enclosed within in a heavy-duty plastic bag, in case it rains heavily and the rucksack leaks.

MAP An Ordnance Survey map is essential for hill walks and highly desirable for all other walks. The 1:50,000 Landranger series is the most appropriate. The 1:100,000 Pathfinder maps provide even greater details for those wishing an in-depth knowledge of the area through which they are walking – but each map covers only a fraction of the area of a Landranger map and the cost of sufficient maps to cover several walking routes is quite substantial. The number of the map(s) relevant to a particular walk will be found near the start of each route description in this book.

MAP CASE Before leaving home, fold your map to display the area to be covered and insert it into a transparent, waterproof map case. Cases specially designed for this purpose, together with a cord with which to suspend the case from the neck (if desired), cost very little and are available at most outdoor-activities shops.

COMPASS Useful for hill walks and many of the lower-level routes. A good choice is the Silva-type which has bearings on a revolving bevel and is mounted on an oblong perspex plate with an arrow for direction. If unfamiliar with its use, you should practise navigating with map and compass before leaving home.

FIRST AID KIT This can be purchased but it is far cheaper to make up your own. Use a good quality, waterproof plastic box and fill it with a selection of the following: plasters (assorted sizes), small roll of adhesive tape, small pair of scissors, triangular bandage, cotton bandages, crêpe bandage, sterile gauze pads, antiseptic wipes (individually wrapped), spray-on dressing (for superficial lacerations), cold pack (chemical type, for sprains and bruises), antihistamine cream (for insect stings or nettle rash). Of course you will have to know how to use these things so, if not already trained, read the St John's/Red Cross first aid book before you go. Better still, take a first aid course.

MOBILE TELEPHONE One of the joys of walking through the countryside is the peace, tranquillity and isolation, so you'll not want the office phoning every few minutes. However a mobile telephone can be a lifesaver if you are in trouble in a remote area. Beware, though, that coverage in Scotland is still patchy, especially in rural areas far from towns and major trunk routes. Also, reception will be poor in valleys surrounded by hills.

EXTRA WOOLLEN JUMPER In case it turns out colder than expected.

TORCH Useful for those few walks that require passage through tunnels; and in case a walk takes longer than anticipated and the walking party is overtaken by nightfall. If caught out after dark, try to walk by whatever light may be available. If you use a torch, your eyes won't adjust to the darkness – you will only see whatever falls within the beam of light, and be unable to see anything of your surroundings. Also, a flickering light in the hills at night may be interpreted as a distress call. After a few minutes of darkness your eyes will become adjusted and the light from the moon, or reflected from low clouds, will be sufficient. Try to restrict the use of a torch to tricky sections of terrain, map reading and road walking (to warn drivers of your presence).

FOOD AND DRINK Some walkers like to carry a good packed lunch when out all day, while others eat little. It is advisable always to carry some sustenance. Mars bars, Snickers or the like, chocolate slabs, peanuts, raisins and fruit all make ideal snacks and provide a rapid source of energy. A plastic box is a useful way of carrying such items. A vacuum flask (the unbreakable kind) full of hot water, plus tea bags or packs of instant coffee carried separately, add a touch of luxury. The best way to carry soft drinks is in foil packets as they take up little room and, when empty, take up even less space. Never leave any food wrappers behind. Take a supermarket carrier bag to collect your refuse and carry it to a litter bin – or take it home. On a hill walk into a remote area, carry extra snacks just in case you are forced to remain on the hill for longer than planned.

GROUND SEAT During breaks you may wish to sit down. You can, of course, sit upon a waterproof garment, or you may wish to purchase a small, padded square specifically designed for this purpose.

CARRIER BAG AND DISPOSABLE GLOVES As mentioned elsewhere, litter in the countryside is a real problem. Use a carrier bag to collect one's own litter and that of less responsible walkers. Let's leave the countryside the way we would wish to find it.

APPENDIX 1 PUBLIC TRANSPORT OPERATORS

Public transport to the start of each walk is described where this is practical but, in rural areas, the frequency of services and the areas covered are often very limited. If travelling by public transport, you are strongly recommended to contact the service operator beforehand, to check that the service is still operational and to establish times.

PUBLIC TRANSPORT OPERATORS

ABBREVIATION	COMPANY	ENQUIRY TEL. NO.
ScotRail	ScotRail, Caledonian Chambers, 87 Union Street, Glasgow G1 3TA	0345 48 49 50
GNER	Great North Eastern Railway, Waverley Station, Edinburgh EH1 1BU	0345 48 49 50
SMT	SMT, St Andrew Square, Edinburgh EH1 3DS	0131 663 9233
LRT	Lothian Region Transport plc, 1–4 Shrub Place, Edinburgh EH7 4PA	0131 555 6363 (24 hrs)
MB	Midland Bluebird, Carmuirs House, 300 Stirling Road, Larbert FK5 3NJ	01324 613777
FS	Fife Scottish Omnibuses Ltd, Esplanade, Kirkcaldy KY1 1SP	01592 261461
WS	{ Western Buses Ltd, Sandgate, Ayr KA7 1DD	01563 22551
	MacEwan's Coach Services, Johnfield, Amisfield, Dumfries DG1 3LS	01387 710537

CCC	Cross Country Connections, 68 Church St, Berwick-upon-Tweed TD15 1DU	01289 308719
LOW	Lowland Omnibuses Ltd, 14–16 Eskbank Road, Dalkeith EH22 1HH	0131 663 1945 0131 663 9233 (0600–2400 hrs)
Wilson	Wilson's Coaches, Medwyn Garage, Peebles Road, Carnwath ML11 8HU	01555 840 249
CityLink	Scottish CityLink Coaches Ltd, St Andrew Square Bus Station, Clyde Street, Edinburgh EH1 3DU	0990 50 50 50

TRAVEL INFORMATION LINES (OPERATED BY LOCAL COUNCILS)

Edinburgh	0800 23 23 23	0131 225 3858
Dumfries & Galloway	0345 090510	
Falkirk	01324 504724	
West Lothian	01506 775288	
Fife	01592 416060	
East Lothian	0800 23 23 23	
Midlothian	0800 23 23 23	

APPENDIX 2 USEFUL ORGANISATIONS

HISTORIC SCOTLAND

Owns and maintains many castles, buildings and monuments throughout Scotland, all of which are open to the public. Many of the routes in this book pass close to Historic Scotland properties, visits to which may well enhance your day out. For a very reasonable annual fee, members of the public may become Friends of Historic Scotland and in so doing support Historic Scotland in its preservation work, gain free entry to all Historic Scotland properties, receive a quarterly magazine, be invited to special events and receive a substantial discount at property shops.

Friends of Historic Scotland, Longmore House, Salisbury Place, Edinburgh EH9 1SH
Tel. 0131 668 8600

SCOTTISH RIGHTS OF WAY SOCIETY

A right-of-way is a route through private property over which the public has right of passage. In these days of increasing demands upon the land, the Scottish Rights of Way Society does an immense amount of work to maintain and protect this vital national resource and deserves support from all walkers. The way to do this is to join the society and pay the very modest membership fee.

Scottish Rights of Way Society, 24 Annandale Street, Edinburgh EH7 4AN
Tel. 0131 558 1222

THE WOODLAND TRUST

Dedicated to the protection and conservation of ancient and native woodland throughout Great Britain. Through funds raised, it purchases woodlands under threat and purchases other land for planting. Several of the walks in this book pass through Woodland Trust property including Pressmennan Wood in East Lothian, Currie Wood in Midlothian and the recently planted Blaeberry Wood in West Lothian. Apart from the trees, the Trust builds and maintains paths through the woodlands, often installing seats and wooden sculptures so that everyone may enjoy the woods.

The Woodland Trust Scotland, Glenruthven Mill, Abbey Road, Auchterarder, Perthshire PH3 1DP
Tel. 01764 662554

SUSTRANS

Standing for 'sustainable transport', a charity which works on projects to encourage people to walk and cycle more. One of its projects is the creation of 8,000 miles of traffic-free cycleways and walkways throughout Britain by the year 2005. It is well on the way to achieving this goal. Several of the tracks are in Scotland, including Route 75 which will provide a traffic-free corridor from Edinburgh to the west coast. In this book Walk 92, Bathgate to Blackridge, includes part of a Sustrans track.

Sustrans, PO Box 21, Bristol BS99 2HA
Tel. 0117 929 0888
Website www.sustrans.org.uk

THE NATIONAL TRUST FOR SCOTLAND

The National Trust for Scotland mostly owns great houses, but also owns and manages a considerable amount of land. Among the National Trust properties is the beautiful Dollar Glen, through which Walk 31 passes.

The National Trust for Scotland, 28 Charlotte Square, Edinburgh EH2 4ET
Tel. 0131 243 9300